4.95

77 - 505r

Liking and Loving
An Invitation to Social Psychology

Date Due

Liking
and
Loving

An Invitation
to Social Psychology

Zick Rubin

Harvard University

HOLT, RINEHART AND WINSTON, INC.
New York   Chicago   San Francisco   Atlanta
Dallas   Montreal   Toronto   London   Sydney

Photographs by Fred Weiss.

In memory of my father,
Dr. Eli H. Rubin

Preface

All of us devote a substantial portion of our time to liking and loving, to discovering these sentiments, playing at them, worrying about them, suffering through them. But the possibility that liking and loving may constitute topics of scientific inquiry as well as leisure-time activities must seem, to many readers, rather remote. In this book I hope to make it seem less so. In the process, I will try to move toward two goals at once. The first is to explore liking and loving, as they have been approached in recent years by social scientists. The second is to provide an invitation to the discipline (or, as we will see, *inter*discipline) of social psychology, which has been responsible for most of the investigations we will examine. It is an "invitation" rather than an "introduction," for particular topics within social psychology are given heavy emphasis, while others are slighted. Rather than presenting the reader with a complete overview of the field, I will attempt to whet his appetite by presenting that portion of it which I find most fascinating. We will discover, nevertheless, that liking and loving—or "interpersonal attraction," as the social-psychological in-crowd sometimes calls them—are very central concerns of the student of social behavior.

In our quest for the principles of liking and loving, we will find ourselves dealing with a wide range of social-psychological topics, including affiliation, social exchange, person perception, sex roles, prejudice, group dynamics, and intergroup relations. I will also try to provide the reader with an inside look at the assortment of ways in which the social psychologist goes about his work, ranging from laboratory experiments to nationwide surveys. My hope is that the book will be of interest to several audiences: the student of social psychology; the student who wants to find out what social psychology is *before* he decides to become a student of it; and the general reader who is certain that he does not want to become a student of social psychology, but would still like to find out whether social scientists really have anything to say about liking and loving. The book should also be useful to students and professionals in other areas, most notably the sociology of marriage and the family.

I am very grateful to a number of people for reading and commenting on earlier versions of the manuscript. Theodore M. Newcomb, Elizabeth Douvan, and Carol Rubin each read the entire manuscript with great care and made many valuable suggestions for improving it. I owe special debts to Professor Newcomb for stimulating my interest in liking and loving as topics of scientific inquiry in the first place and for encouraging me to write this book. It turns out, however, that whereas I like both Professor Newcomb and Professor Douvan a great deal, I love them less than I do the third-named reader. This is not pure speculation on my part. It was confirmed by my scores on carefully constructed scales which I will go into in Chapter 10. I also want to thank Nancy M. Henley, Anne Peplau, Ira L. Reiss, and Harold Proshansky for their helpful comments on earlier versions of the manuscript. Finally, I am greatly indebted to Susan Willard, Claire Engers, and Richard Werther for their help in preparing the manuscript.

Z.R.

Cambridge, Massachusetts
January 1973

Contents

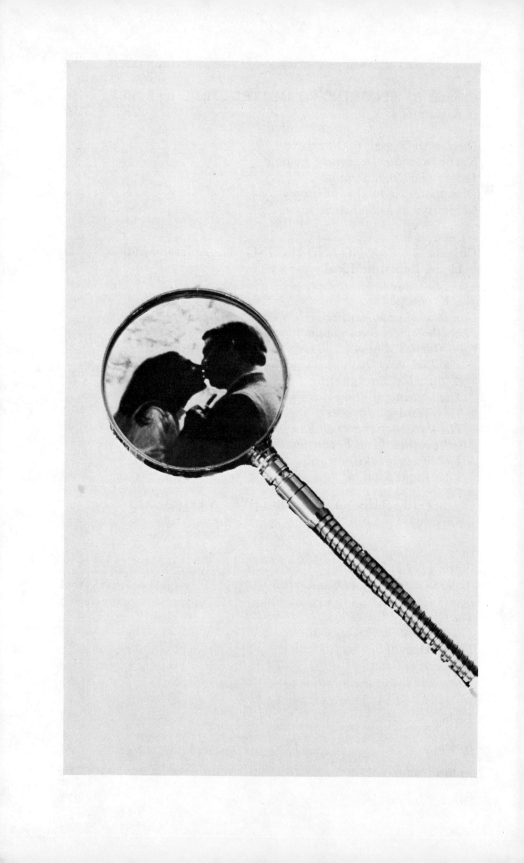

Chapter 1
LOVE AND SCIENCE
The Belated Arrival
of Social Psychology

All life is an experiment.
> —Justice Oliver Wendell Holmes, Jr.

The nature and causes of interpersonal passions and preferences have fascinated men and women throughout history. But it is only during the past fifteen or twenty years that the investigation of interpersonal attitudes and bonds has been systematically undertaken by social scientists. Until very recently we could safely state that we knew far more about the mutual attraction of material bodies than about the mutual attraction of people, or that we understood the mechanisms underlying chemical combinations considerably better than the mechanisms underlying human ones. These statements are still true, but not nearly so true as they used to be. There has been no single remarkable breakthrough, as that of a Newton or an Einstein, but rather a general, concerted, and widely heard calling to arms. Hundreds of investigations by scores of researchers have by steady accumulation already illuminated a great deal more about liking and loving in the years since World War II than had been unearthed over the course of many preceding centuries. The results are not all in. In fact, the search for the principles of interpersonal attraction is only now getting into full swing. It is a search that I personally find to be enormously exciting, and it is this search that I invite you to join.

A Latecomer to the Party

The party had been going on for some time, and the guests had long since begun to mill about the room. Some of them encountered

1

long-lost friends and proceeded to reminisce about old times. Others began conversations with people they had never met before, gradually progressing from tentative probes about places of origin and mutual acquaintances, to exchanges of opinion about matters of current interest, to deeper disclosures about their self-conceptions and views of life. Some of the pairs seemed to hit it off well, and they retired to private corners of the room to continue their mutual exploration. Others excused themselves abruptly and headed off in opposite directions. One young man looked across the crowded room and caught the eye of one young woman in an opposite corner. Although they had never seen each other before, their faces simultaneously lit up with the recognition that they had found each other at last. They worked their way through the crowd toward one another and wordlessly clasped hands.

A group of poets got to the party early in the evening and proceeded to write a series of sonnets about what they saw. "But love is blind," one long-haired, bearded poet declared to a woman standing near him, "and lovers cannot see the pretty follies that themselves commit."[1] The woman thought for a moment and replied, "I think true love is never blind/ But rather brings an added light,/ An inner vision quick to find/ The beauties hid from common sight." A group of poetry judges went into a quick huddle and then awarded the woman one point. Another of the poets spied the man and woman who were strangers to each other until they met from across the crowded room and promptly wrote a verse about it. He scurried off to the kitchen, where his partner, a talented composer, set the verse to music.

Shortly afterward a group of playwrights arrived at the party. They mingled with the crowd to catch snatches of dialogue, cupping their ears so they wouldn't miss a word. They were later able to put the snatches to good use in works that became known as *Romeo and Juliet*, *Death of a Salesman*, and the pilot episode of *Love, American Style*. An older woman accidentally bumped into an intense-looking novelist, knocking his martini to the floor. "I'm terribly sorry," the woman blurted. The novelist looked at her directly and solemnly responded, "Love means not ever having to say you're sorry."[2]

Several journalists also made their appearance and busily began to take notes on who was spending time with whom. The biggest scoop came when the wife of a South American ambassador was seen doing the marimba with a special assistant to the President. A philosopher had been at the party from the start. He spent most of the time debating the question of whether parties are good or evil. After prolonged consideration he came to the conclusion that parties are good if they are populated by good people and evil if they are populated by evil people. As soon as he had made this discovery, he shouted "Eureka!" and poured himself another drink. There was also a classical historian at the party who bumbled around the room and kept muttering to himself, "I saw better orgies than this when I was in junior high school."

The night wore on and the party began to wane. Some of the couples who had been conversing in private corners left the party together. Others found that there was nothing left to explore and awkardly took leave of one another. One woman threw a platter of liver paté into her escort's face and stalked out of the room. A man who had been standing by himself against the wall was attracted to a woman some distance away. He started to make his way toward her, then thought better of it and took several steps backward, then took a deep breath and headed forward again, then shook his head and went into retreat a second time. He vacillated in the middle of the room like a yo-yo for two and a half hours. A theologian who happened to catch the scene took out a little notebook and wrote down the words, "existential dilemma."

Finally, in the wee hours of the morning, the social psychologist arrived. Some of the guests had already gone home. Others had passed out on the floor. Before anyone else could leave, the social psychologist ran around the room giving out mimeographed questionnaires that asked each person to provide a brief personal history and to name the three people he liked most and the three he liked least at the party. He collected the questionnaires, ran to an empty bedroom to tabulate them, and drew up a chart that he called a "sociogram," indicating who liked and who disliked whom.[3] He discovered, among other things, that the man and woman who had wordlessly fallen in love from across the crowded room happened to be of the same race, religion, and political affiliation, and had in fact grown up on the same block in Philadelphia. He handed another questionnaire to the man who was vacillating in the center of the room and found that he scored extremely high on a measure of "fear of rejection"—and he wrote down in *his* little notebook the words, "approach–avoidance conflict."

In the course of history—just as at our party—poets, playwrights, philosophers, and theologians started to ask questions about liking and loving long before the social psychologist did—in fact, many centuries before social psychologists even existed. And the pressing question remains:

Why did the social psychologist get to the party so late?

Robert Zajonc has instructively placed the development of a scientific approach to social behavior in relation to the development of other sciences:

> Around 250 B.C. the Greek astronomer Eratosthenes calculated the circumference of the Earth by comparing the angles of the noon sun in Alexandria and in Aswan, which lies directly to the south on the tropic of Cancer, and where on the day of the summer solstice the angle of the noon sun is exactly 90°. His results—among the first scientific observations recorded in history—differ from the present estimates by about 180 miles, or less than 1 percent.
>
> The velocity of light was first measured in 1675 by the Danish astronomer Ole Römer, who compared the observed eclipses of Jupiter's moons with predictions based on precise theoretical calculations. His results also agree very closely with the present ones. . . .
>
> The first experimental observation in social psychology was performed in 1897 by Triplett. It dealt with the effects of competition on human performance. Triplett measured the average time required to execute 150 winds of a fishing reel. His subjects performed the task while working alone and while competing in pairs against each other. Performance was found to improve when carried out in competition.
>
> The first scientific measurement preceded the first social–psychological measurement by twenty-one centuries. Social psychology, then, is almost entirely the product of this century and of this generation. Social psychologists credited with the crucial developments in the field are still alive. . . . More than 90 percent of all social–psychological research has been conducted during the last twenty years, and most of it during the last ten.[4]

Zajonc notes that the social psychologist's late arrival could not have been due to the unavailability of any necessary equipment. Eratosthenes' measurement of the Earth's circumference depended on the previous development of geometry by Euclid, about half a century earlier, and Römer's calculation of the velocity of light would not have been possible before the construction of telescopes. But the knowledge and techniques necessary for Triplett's experiment have been available for at least four thousand years. All he needed were people who could be observed working alone or in groups, a task they would work on in both conditions, and a means of counting units of work on this task per unit of time. All of these prerequisites were surely present in Egypt at the time of the Pharaohs. The same holds true for the techniques of the social psychologist who finally arrived at our party. The asking of questions and the recording of answers, which are the most widely used techniques of the social psychologist, have been human skills for thousands of years, dating at least as far back as the censuses that were taken in Old Testament days.

The explanation for the social psychologist's belated arrival, then, is neither that his questions are new ones, nor that necessary technological advances first had to be made. Part of the explanation, rather, seems to be that, although we are only now beginning to answer the questions about liking and loving that have fascinated human beings for so long, people have often thought that they already knew the answers. Instead of being based on objective and systematic research, these earlier answers were founded on a mixture of tradition, folklore, and common sense. It is only recently that we have begun to recognize that it is possible to go beyond such "common-sense" explanations to a fuller understanding of the underlying mechanisms.

The Ovid–Horwicz Phenomenon

A case in point begins with Ovid's *Ars Amatoria* ("The Art of Love"), the first-century Roman handbook to romantic conquest whose closest modern parallels are perhaps Albert Ellis's *Sex and the Single Man* and Helen Gurley Brown's complementary *Sex and the Single Girl*. (Ovid himself was not at all biased about the matter, freely dispensing his advice to both sexes alike.) When addressing himself to the Roman male, Ovid good-humoredly considered all conceivable aspects of a man's hunt for a desirable—and, preferably, married—woman. His recommendations range from espionage (such as to seduce the woman's maid) to affectionate gestures (playing footsy under the table) to grooming hints (deodorize carefully) to facial expressions (adopt a look of suffering). One of Ovid's most intriguing tactical suggestions was that an excellent time to arouse passion in a woman was while watching gladiatorial combat. In modern America the recommendation might be translated into the idea of taking a date to a wrestling match or a particularly violent hockey game.

Ovid himself did not explain why he thought watching gladiators disembowel one another has the capacity to foster passionate love. His recommendation was derived from personal observation and experience—or perhaps what he would call "common sense"—rather than any underlying scientific principle. Some 1,900 years later, in the late nineteenth century, a German psychologist named Adolf Horwicz provided a more general explanation for Ovid's recommendation by suggesting that *any* strong emotional arousal can have the effect of heightening the experience of love:

> Love can only be excited by strong and vivid emotion, and it is almost immaterial whether these emotions are agreeable or disagreeable. The Cid wooed the proud heart of Donna Ximene, whose father he had slain, by shooting one after another of her pet pigeons.[5]

Thus Ovid's recommendation might be viewed as one specific application of Horwicz's general principle: By taking one's date to the arena, where strong emotions of repulsion or fear would undoubtedly be aroused, the arousal of love might be facilitated as well. But Horwicz's principle was still an intuitive one. It was not based on any empirical evidence about the psychological processes that mediate the linking of one sort of arousal to another.

Much more recently, in the early 1960s, social psychologist Stanley Schachter developed a two-component theory of emotion, which may help us to understand the Ovid–Horwicz phenomenon more fully.[6] Schachter's theory postulates that emotion is jointly determined by two factors. The first is the experience of intense physiological arousal, such as increased heart rate, flushing, and heightened respiration rate. The second is the *labeling* of this physiological arousal as being due to some specific cause. One possibility raised by the research of Schachter and subsequent investigators is that people may sometimes *mislabel* the arousal they experience. Thus the spectator of a gladiatorial bloodbath may erroneously interpret the arousal she experiences as having been caused by her passionate feelings toward her companion, rather than by the terrifying scene in the arena.

This possibility is plausible to the extent that the physical "symptoms" that people come to associate with love in a particular culture resemble the physiological effects likely to be produced by grisly situations. In the sixth century B.C. the poetess Sappho set forth a symptomatology of lovesickness that was used as a diagnostic aid by Greek physicians for centuries thereafter. It included heart palpitations, flushing, auditory disturbances, and muscle tremors, followed by faintness and pallor. These symptoms seem to be remarkably like those that might be experienced by a person who was exposed to a bloody scene in the arena. Quite similar symptoms are often linked with love in contemporary American culture. In 1934, the sociologist Joseph Folsom described the "cardiac-respiratory" variety of love, which he saw as common among young people, in the following terms: " 'In-loveness' implies catching of the breath, a deep sigh, a feeling about the heart, as if it had stopped, followed by palpitation or rapid breathing, a feeling akin to fear. . . ."[7] Or, as the Supremes put it in a song of the 1960s, "Love is like an itching in my heart." Thus, the possibility that people will mislabel fear or repulsion as love may be a real one in our society.

It would be premature to assert that the Schachterian explanation of the Ovid–Horwicz phenomenon is correct. In fact, further research is necessary to confirm the suggestion that such a phenomenon exists at all, beyond specific instances such as those described by Ovid and Horwicz. In addition, one would want to weigh the validity of other possible explanations of the same phenomenon, including Freud's suggestion that a close connection between aggression and love is established during the early stages of an individual's psychosexual development.[8] If both the Ovid–Horwicz hypothesis and the proposed "mislabeling" explanation for it are borne out by further research, however, we would have a considerably more precise understanding of one aspect of love than was heretofore available.

Robert Zajonc suggests that people did not begin to recognize the inadequacy of traditional or intuitive explanations like those provided by Ovid or Horwicz until the Industrial Revolution and the accompanying decline of the traditional society. In such a society, where norms and customs constrain people to behave in relatively uniform and predictable ways, tradition and folklore can provide reasonably satisfactory explanations of social behavior. For example, when marriages were arranged by parents and matchmakers rather than by the prospective bride and groom themselves, the matchmaker's truisms might indeed have provided acceptable explanations of attraction. In one instance the matchmaker might assert that the couple would get along well because the two seemed very much alike to her, and, as is well known, "birds of a feather flock together." In another case the success of the match was assured because the young man and woman seemed strikingly different from one another, and, as is well known, "opposites attract." Similarly, in societies in which friendships are regulated to a large degree by ties of kinship, one might "understand" the basis of such attraction by recognizing that "blood is thicker than water." In modern societies, the greater freedom and diversity of social behavior has made such common-sense explanations less adequate.

The Kitty Genovese Incident

Although insight and intuition may often tell us a great deal about the causes of social behavior even in modern society, they can also lead us astray. When we try to trace a particular event or experience back to the factors that gave rise to it, we often tend to overestimate the importance of certain causal factors, and to underestimate or ignore certain others. An example is the public reaction to a widely publicized instance of antisocial behavior about ten years ago. A young woman named Kitty Genovese was attacked by a male assailant as she returned at night to her home in Kew Gardens, Queens. Thirty-eight of her neighbors watched the scene from their respective apartment windows without doing anything to intervene—not even so much as to call the police—although it took her assailant over half an hour to murder her. Since that time many similar cases have been played up in the news, invariably in urban locations.

The most popular intuitive explanation offered for these events was that people who live in cities are "apathetic" or "indifferent." Some educated observers dressed up these labels in more elaborate terms. For example, one psychoanalyst attributed the Kew Gardens incident to "the effect of the megalopolis in which we live, which makes closeness very difficult and leads to the alienation of the individual from the group."[9] There may well be some truth to this explanation, but it is to be noted that it relies on a quite general characterization of the sort of people city-dwellers have come to be: "apathetic," "indifferent," "alienated." As such, the explanation is weakened by the fact that there are countless instances in which city-dwellers behave altruistically and even herocially. Even the thirty-eight witnesses of the Genovese murder did not seem to behave in an "indifferent" manner. They did not simply look at the scene once and then turn away and ignore it. Instead, they continued to stare out of their windows at what was going on—fascinated, distressed, and conflicted. People in cities—perhaps quite as much as people elsewhere, for the matter remains to be resolved—do feel compassion for their fellow human beings. But apparently this compassion sometimes leads to action and sometimes does not. A remaining task for the social psychologist is to go beyond the labeling of particular categories of people as "apathetic"—or, in other cases, as "intelligent," "ambitious," or "friendly"—to the characteristics of particular *situations* that determine to a large degree how people will actually behave.

In the case of "bystander apathy," for example, a recent

series of experiments by social psychologists Bibb Latané and John Darley has led to an account of the decision-making sequence that determines whether or not a bystander will take action.[10] The sequence is seen as having three major steps. First, one has to *notice* the emergency. Second, one has to *label it* appropriately as an emergency, rather than as a prank or as a situation that the victim would prefer to deal with by himself. Third, one has to *take personal responsibility* for acting—that is, one must decide to do something oneself rather than assume that someone else will do it. A major conclusion of Latané and Darley's research is that the more other bystanders are present in an emergency situation, the less likely it is that any given bystander will move toward taking action. In the Genovese case, each of the thirty-eight witnesses may have failed to report the emergency not because he lacked compassion but because he was aware that other people were also watching the scene and assumed that someone else had called the authorities.

This explanation does not change the unfortunate fact that in the densely populated urban environment people may be unlikely to act in emergency situations. But the causal attribution is shifted from one that blames urban residents for being apathetic by nature to one that considers their behavior in light of the structure of the situations in which it occurs. The latter sort of explanation is particularly valuable because it allows us to predict and to understand variations in helping behavior from one situation to another, within nonurban as well as urban locales. The Latané and Darley explanation is also a socially useful one because, by providing greater insight into why we may fail to intervene in emergencies, it can help us to overcome our reluctance to help others. In this instance, as in others to be explored in this book, a greater understanding of the forces that govern our social behavior can serve the invaluable purpose of helping us to liberate ourselves from blind obedience to them.

Going beyond the Obvious

Despite the social scientist's endeavor to go beyond "common-sense" explanations, an objection that is still regularly put forth against research in the social sciences is that it belabors the obvious. To help us gain some perspective on this issue, let me list a number of "obvious" findings from recent research on interpersonal attraction, together with brief interpretive comments:

1. People are more inclined to have social contact with a handicapped person if they feel that they share basic attitudes and opinions with this person than if they feel that they are in basic disagreement. (*The bond produced by the recognition of shared attitudes helps to overcome the aversion produced by the other's handicap.*)
2. Being induced to do a favor for a virtual stranger will usually result in decreased liking for that stranger. (*People don't enjoy being imposed upon.*)
3. Continually being exposed to another person in the absence of any positive or rewarding interaction will result in gradually decreased liking for the person. (*Familiarity breeds contempt.*)
4. When members of a dating couple sit opposite one another, the man spends considerably more time looking at the woman than vice-versa. (*A man is more concerned with his date's physical appearance than a woman is.*)
5. People are perceived as being more intelligent when they answer the initial problems in a series incorrectly and then improve their performance than when they answer the initial problems correctly and then become less accurate. (*The capacity to improve is the best proof of one's ability.*)
6. The cultural pattern of "romantic love" is more likely to be found in societies like contemporary America where newlyweds must set up a household of their own than in societies where they continue to live with one of the partners' families. (*Romantic love should arise in the former societies as an effective means of cementing marriages in the face of the relative absence of social support from other family members.*)

These examples might reinforce the contention that research on liking and loving belabors the obvious, were it not for the fact that *every one of these statements is the direct opposite of what was actually found.*[11] If the correct findings had been listed, together with the best available explanation for each, they would have seemed "obvious" as well. As sociologist Paul Lazarsfeld has concluded, "Obviously something is wrong with the entire concept of obviousness."[12] Lazarsfeld noted that it is hard to find a form of social behavior that has not been observed somewhere. As a result, whenever a study reports a prevailing regularity, people are likely to respond by thinking "of course that is the way things are."

The social psychologist tries not to give particular credence to what is "obviously true" nor to reject what is "obviously false" until he puts the matter to an empirical test. In doing so he attempts to go beyond such "obvious" generalizations as "birds of a feather flock together" or "opposites attract"—each of which is surely true in one instance or another—toward careful specification of the conditions under which each of these principles is likely to hold.

A Flight from Tenderness

The eminent psychologist Gordon Allport has suggested that the appearance of a scientific approach to social behavior in the twentieth century was finally precipitated by the unique combination of American ideals of pragmatism and the existence of social problems of great magnitude and urgency. Allport wrote:

> National emergencies and conditions of social disruption provide special incentive to invent new techniques, and to strike out boldly for solutions to practical social problems. Social psychology began to flourish soon after the First World War. This event, followed by the spread of Communism, by the great depression of the 1930's, by the rise of Hitler, the genocide of the Jews, race riots, the Second World War, and the atomic threat, stimulated all branches of social science. A special challenge fell to social psychology. The question was asked: How is it possible to preserve the values of freedom and individual rights under conditions of mounting social strain and regimentation? Can science help provide an answer? This challenging question led to a burst of creative effort that added much to our understanding of the phenomena of leadership, public opinion, rumor, propaganda, prejudice, attitude change, morale, communication, decision-making, race relations, and conflicts of value. While other nations have been confronted with the same world-wide emergency, it seems that in the United States the soil of western thought, fortified by practical meliorism, proved most fertile for the assertive growth of social psychology and related disciplines.[13]

It is noteworthy that Professor Allport did not include mention of liking or loving—or such near-synonyms as "interpersonal attraction," "affiliation," or "human relationships"—on his list of phenomena that were illuminated by the social psychologist's "burst of creative effort." This omission is justified, especially with respect to the period from 1920 to 1950 that he was writing about. For the fact is that if the average social psychologist was dreadfully late to the party, the social psychologist who applies his skills to the mysteries of liking and loving was even later. As Allport pointed out, "Psychologists, in their research and in their theory, devote far more attention to aggressive, hostile, prejudiced behavior than to the softer acts of sympathy and love, which are equally important ingredients of social life." He observed that there has been among social scientists a strange manifestation of what has been called a "flight from tenderness."

Other leading social scientists have made similar observations about the lack of systematic knowledge about liking and loving. In his presidential address to the American Psychological Association in 1956, social psychologist Theodore Newcomb declared,

> It has often seemed to me that we psychologists, who like to pride ourselves in recognizing that nothing takes place apart from its necessary and sufficient conditions, have come very close to treating the phenomena of interpersonal attraction as exceptions to the general rule. It is almost as if we, like our lay contemporaries, assumed that in this special area the psychological wind bloweth where it listeth, and that the matter is altogether too ineffable, and passeth even psychological understanding.[14]

In another presidential address to the same organization two years later, experimental psychologist Harry Harlow appraised the situation as follows:

> Love is a wonderous state, deep, tender, and reassuring. Because of its intimate and personal nature it is regarded by some as an improper topic for experimental research. But, whatever our personal feelings may be, our assigned mission as psychologists is to analyze all facets of human and animal behavior into their component variables. So far as love or affection is concerned, psychologists have failed in their mission. The little we know about love does not transcend simple observation and the little we write about it has been written better by poets and novelists.[15]

The reluctance of social scientists to explore liking and loving may be attributed at least in part to the assumptions of "ineffability" or "impropriety" identified by Newcomb and Harlow. Such attitudes are clearly at the root of some laymen's criticisms of those who do conduct scientific research on liking and loving. For example, a recent editorial in the Topeka *Daily Capital* reacted to my own initial investigation of romantic love as follows: "Especially as spring is approaching, when Tennyson said that a young man's fancy turns to thoughts of love, it is somewhat disconcerting to discover that a Harvard scientist has reduced the tender sentiment to scientific terms."[16] Somewhat more surprisingly, similar views continue to be expressed by social scientists themselves. "The scientist in even attempting to interject love into a laboratory situation," one psychologist recently declared at a professional convention, "is by the very nature of the proposition dehumanizing the state we call love."[17] This psychologist's aversion to investigating love did not, however, prevent him from pontificating about its nature in terms of the Freudian theory of "genital primacy." Thus, he did not seem to oppose theorizing or speculating about love, but only the attempt to check out these speculations systematically. Freud himself, who based his theories on clinical cases rather than on his own free associations, would not have taken such an antiempirical view.

In the past few years, the social scientist's "flight from tenderness" seems to have been brought back to earth. This is a fortunate development. For it is clear that if we are to understand human social behavior—and, ultimately, to contribute to the solution of practical problems of aggression and conflict, mistrust and loneliness—then we must learn more about the "positive" as well as the "negative" side of human relationships. In this book we will survey much of recent social–psychological research, including research on conflict and hostility. But I will attempt to redress the imbalance of previous decades by focusing most directly on what Allport called "the softer acts of sympathy and love." My intention is by no means to demean the value of poetic or philosophical approaches to liking and loving. As Peter Berger has written, "The botanist looking at a daffodil has no right to dispute the right of the poet to look at the same object in a different manner."[18] Each of the two makes a valuable contribution by approaching the daffodil in his own distinctive way. One can only hope that the poet will take as generous a view of the botanist.

The Weapons of the Hunt

Before we can join the social psychologist on his hunt for the principles of liking and loving, we must first familiarize ourselves with the weapons he takes along with him, the methods employed in his research. Let us consider in turn five varieties of methods— laboratory experiments, real-life experiments, surveys and interviews, naturalistic observation, and archival studies.

Laboratory Experiments

The social psychologist's laboratory is often a suite of soundproof rooms equipped with one-way mirrors, an intercom system, and an assortment of electrical gadgetry. Nothing so elaborate is required for many experiments, however, and the "laboratory" can also be an ordinary classroom or auditorium. In its more general sense it is any place where people come to participate in an experiment. These human guinea pigs, like their animal counterparts, are called *subjects*. One laboratory procedure that has been used extensively to explore the conditions under which similarity of attitudes produces attraction may be termed the "phantom-other paradigm."[19] At an initial session each subject is asked to complete a questionnaire that calls for his opinions on a variety of political and social issues. At a subsequent session a week or so later the subject is shown a questionnaire that has purportedly been filled out by another subject. He is asked to indicate how much he thinks he would like or dislike this other person, using numerical scales ranging from 1 ("dislike very much," "would not like to work with") to 7 ("like very much," "would very much like to work with"). In order to increase the precision of this procedure, the "other person's" questionnaire is in fact filled out by the experimenter during the intervening week in a pattern that indicates that the "other person" agrees or disagrees with the subject's own attitudes to a specified degree. In a typical experiment, one group of subjects is confronted with "other people" who agree with them two-thirds of the time, another group with "other people" who agree with them half the time, and a third group with "other people" who agree with them only one-third of the time.

A highly consistent result of a long series of such studies is that the more the phantom-other agrees with the subject, the more the subject indicates that he would like him. Of course this basic finding merely confirms what most of us knew all along—that we like people who share our own opinions more than those who do not. The real value of the experimental paradigm emerges, however, when it is used to *specify* the agreement principle. For example, what sorts of people are most influenced by attitudinal agreement and what sorts of people care less about it? With respect to what sorts of attitudes is agreement most important? What happens when the phantom-other's questionnaire is combined with other information about him? As we shall see in Chapter 7, the paradigm has also been used to uncover conditions under which disagreeing others are liked more than others who agree.

One of the strengths of the phantom-other paradigm is its

very artificiality. The researcher need not wait for any particular combination of people to occur in real life, for the procedure enables him to *create* an unlimited number of combinations in the well-controlled confines of the laboratory. At the same time, however, the artificiality of the procedure makes its applicability to real-life attraction rather uncertain. One way to increase realism without losing a great deal of precision and control is the dramatic laboratory experiment. In these studies the subject who arrives at the laboratory may be caught up in an unexpected stream of events that seem to have nothing to do with the "experiment" itself, but that in fact are its very substance. In one recent experiment with college women, for example, while the subject was waiting for the experimenter to arrive, a dashing male graduate student wandered into the room, casually began a conversation, and (in 32 of 37 cases) successfully executed his assigned mission of making a date with her.[20] In another—this time with male students—the subject was escorted to a canteen where he "accidentally" encountered an attractive female confederate of the experimenter—or, in other experimental conditions, the same young woman made up to look rather unattractive. The purpose of both studies, which we will revisit in Chapter 4, was to investigate the ways in which a person's self-esteem affects his or her romantic inclinations.

The dramatic laboratory experiment provides a combination of realism and experimental control that makes it an extremely valuable research tool. But it has its liabilities as well. One of the most troubling of these is its frequent reliance on deceptions in order to establish an involving plot. Only after the experiment is concluded does the experimenter reveal to the subject that the date will never take place, or, in other experiments, that he will really not receive electric shocks, that he really does not have homosexual inclinations, or that the "person" in the next room was really a tape recording. It is possible that participation in some laboratory dramas could have adverse psychological effects on subjects.[21]

Real-Life Experiments

Although dramatic laboratory experiments continue to be widely used, there is increasing appreciation of the care and discretion that they require. Meanwhile, investigators of liking and loving are making increasing use of the opportunity to conduct experiments that are less dramatic but even more realistic by taking real-life situations as their laboratory. A pioneering real-life experiment on the process of making friends was conducted by Theodore Newcomb in the 1950s.[22] Newcomb rented a rooming house at the University of Michigan and offered free room and board to incoming transfer students in return for their participation in his study. Over the course of a school term the students, all of whom were initially strangers, periodically filled out measures of their evolving feelings toward one another. In this way Newcomb was able to follow the course of the "acquaintance process" from its inception. Other investigators have set up "computer dances" as a means of investigating the bases of heterosexual attraction.[23] Within such a framework the researcher can match couples either randomly or according to specific criteria (for example, on the basis of personality test scores) and subsequently assess the relative success of the matches. Natural events may also provide the opportunity for real-life experiments. Anne Peplau and I conducted one such "natural experiment" during the 1971 national draft lottery.[24] Since all of our nineteen-year-old subjects were directly affected by the results of the random drawing, it provided an excellent opportunity for us to test hypotheses about the ways in which a person's fate affects other people's feelings toward him.

All of the methodological approaches described so far have been *experimental*. The experimenter randomly assigns subjects to specific conditions or situations and then observes the impact of these conditions on indexes of interpersonal attraction. In the social sciences, as in the natural sciences, the experimental method has a unique advantage over other methods of observation in that it enables the scientist to venture more boldly beyond statements of *correlation* (i.e., the occurrence of X is associated with the occurrence of Y) to statements of *causation* (i.e., a specific alteration in X tends to produce a specific alteration in Y). Simply observing that people who are friends tend to have similar attitudes would not tell us whether the agreement led to the attraction or the attraction led to the agreement—or whether it was some third factor such as a common social background that led to both. The experimental method gets around this impasse by showing that, when all other factors are held constant, variations in agreement produce specifiable variations in attraction. In many cases experimentation is impossible, however, and instead the researcher must obtain his information about people's feelings toward one another through the old and venerable method of asking them.

Surveys and Interviews

There is no sharp line to be drawn between the survey and the interview study. In both cases the technique is to ask people about their interpersonal sentiments and relationships. If the sample is large—and, in the ideal case, adequately representative of some larger population—it is more likely to be called a "survey." If the sample is smaller and the answers are given in greater detail, it is more likely to be called an "interview." In some survey or interview studies the researcher simply asks the respondent *who* he likes or loves, without giving any particular attention to the precise nature of his feeling or the history of the relationship. By the simple expedient of asking some 1,000 Detroit men for the names and basic demographic characteristics (such as age, occupation, religion, and national origin) of their three closest friends, a group of University of Michigan researchers was recently able to learn a great deal about friendship patterns in an urban community.[25]

In other cases, respondents are asked to discuss their friendships, marriages, or love relationships in much greater detail. Sociologist Mirra Komarovsky used such intensive interviews to explore the affectional patterns to be found in the marriages of a sample of American working-class couples. One of the techniques that she used to find out about husbands' and wives' attitudes toward communicating with one another was to ask them to react to the following story:

A couple has been married for seven years. The wife says that her husband is a good provider and a good man, but still she complains to her mother about her marriage. She says he comes home, reads the paper, watches T.V., but doesn't talk to her. He says "he doesn't like to gab just for the sake of talking." But she says he is not companionable and has nothing to say to her.—*What do you think of this couple?*[26]

Komarovsky reports that her respondents' reactions could be grouped into two major categories. Some of the individuals interviewed thought that the lack of conversation represented a genuine problem ("There is something wrong if he has nothing to talk about. If something is bothering him, he shouldn't hide behind a paper"), while others denied that the wife had a legitimate grievance ("Gee, can you tie that? He's generous, don't bother her, he just keeps out of the way, and she's fussing and wants him to sit there and entertain her"). Komarovsky was able to make use of these reactions to gain insight into the patterns of communication in the respondents' own marriages.

In our attempt to learn more about the ways in which interpersonal relationships develop, a particularly valuable research technique is the *longitudinal* survey or interview study, in which the same people are followed up at two or more points over a period of months or years. My own current research, for example, is a longitudinal study of college dating couples in the Boston area. My students and I began in the spring of 1972 with a sample of couples who had been going together for relatively short periods of time, and we are now proceeding to trace and recontact the same people. Some of the couples in our initial sample have already broken up. In these cases we want to find out what caused the breakup, and how each of the ex-partners reacted to it. Many other couples will stay together for longer periods of time, and some will eventually marry. By following up these couples over a period of years we hope to construct a more complete picture of the development of opposite-sex relationships.

Naturalistic Observation

Surveys and interviews can tell us a great deal about patterns of attraction in real-life situations, but only to the extent that people are able and willing to describe these patterns on questionnaires or to interviewers. Much of the time people are unaware of the behaviors that underlie liking and loving, however, and it requires systematic observation of their encounters with one another to gain a fuller understanding. One of my former students, John Morihisa, spent much of his junior year at Harvard observing people from behind a beer at several Boston area dating bars, and he came up with detailed reports such as the following:

> . . . At 9:24 Bob sat down next to Sarah on an adjacent stool. They appeared to have a lively talk for about 40 minutes. Then at 10:02 Sarah turned to a male who was sitting opposite the bar table from them, and whom we will call David. Sarah continued to talk to David in what appeared to be a friendly and animated manner for 12 minutes. During this 12-minute period Bob appeared to become increasingly agitated. (In the first two minutes Bob appeared to be listening to the conversation between Sarah and David, and sat quietly. In the last two minutes Bob exhibited a great deal of body movement, touching his hair five times and picking up his glass without drinking four times. He frequently glanced back and forth between Sarah and David and the television set across the room.)
>
> At the end of this 12-minute period an interesting change in behavior occurred. Without taking her eyes off David, Sarah reached below the bar table and touched Bob's knee. This action was not visible to David because he was on the opposite side of the table. Sarah began stroking Bob's leg slowly and this continued intermittently for

five minutes. During this five-minute period Bob's behavior appeared to change significantly. He spent almost the entire five minutes looking at Sarah or a space in between Sarah and David. He did not touch his hair at all and his hands remained folded on the table. He appeared to be following the conversation between Sarah and David, smiled several times, and contributed to the conversation four times.

After this five-minute period Sarah turned to Bob and said that it was getting late and she should be going. Bob said that he would take her home. Sarah said good night to David. David said good night to Sarah. Bob appeared to avoid any eye-contact with David and did not say anything to David as he left. Sarah and Bob left at 11:15. David went to Bar Area One and bought a beer.[27]

One of Morihisa's conclusions was that a great deal of dating-bar behavior is regulated by subtle rituals which enable people to approach and to take leave of one another without excessive embarrassment or loss of self-esteem. Although his observations were careful, they remained primarily on an impressionistic level. It may also be useful, however, for such naturalistic observations of everyday interactions to be quantified. For example, one investigator recently adopted the procedure of counting the numbers of embracing, hand-holding, and nontouching couples as a function of their race (Caucasian, Oriental, or mixed) at strategic locations on the University of Hawaii campus as a means of illuminating some of the cultural mores of courtship.[28]

Archival Data

In addition to experimenting, surveying, and observing, the social scientist can profitably pore over existing archival material, ranging from marriage records to inscriptions on toilet walls, in his attempt to learn more about liking and loving. An illustration of the application of archival material to the analysis of changing courtship patterns is a recent comparison of the rock lyrics of the 1950s with those of the late 1960s. Contrasting the earlier refrains with the later ones, sociologist James Carey came to the following conclusion about romantic patterns, *circa* 1970:

In the idealized sequence revealed by rock and roll lyrics today, one actively searches out and becomes involved with someone else rather than passively waiting for an affair. Relationships are initiated on the basis of initial attraction, which includes both physical and spiritual elements. When these elements disappear, the expectation is that the relationship will be terminated. Relationships can also be ended if one or both of the parties diagnose it as "unhealthy." Usually this means that it is tainted by dishonesty. Love is not placed in the hands of fate, but is actively controlled by the lovers. Consequently, rock and roll lyrics are no longer likely to talk about "falling in love," since that phrase refers to a romantic conception of boy–girl relationships which is rejected.[29]

These observations do not directly address the question of the correspondence between actual courtship patterns and the ideology of courtship manifest in popular culture, a question to which we will return in Chapter 9. Nevertheless, the popular culture of any place and time invariably forms a significant part of the setting within which actual affairs and relationships are played out. If we are fully to understand the reality, we must understand the ideals and the myths as well.

Experiments, surveys and interviews, naturalistic observations, and archival studies are the major methodological weapons that we will bring along with us on our hunt. Some researchers take the imperialistic position that one technique is inherently superior to the others. Thus two laboratory experimenters recently pronounced, "One must thoroughly understand the determinants of attraction as measured, for example, by two seven-point scales before expecting to understand the determinants of love and hate in the real world."[30] Many survey researchers or naturalistic observers feel quite as much disdain for the laboratory experimenter. But such an attitude would put us in the disadvantageous position of the golfer who undertakes to par the course with only a driver or only a putter in his bag. Throughout this book we will examine research that makes use of a wide variety of approaches. It is by considering the results of contrasting approaches side by side that our hunt is most likely to make significant progress.

The Shape of an Interdiscipline

The phenomena of liking and loving are by no means the only concerns of the social psychologist. The territory that the social psychologist has staked out may be defined as *the ways in which people's thoughts, feelings, and behavior are affected by other people*. This is an extremely large ballpark to play in. It includes not only patterns of interaction in two-person relationships, but also patterns of interaction in larger groups and organizations; not only people's feelings about other people, but also their feelings about virtually all conceivable ideologies, causes, and issues; not only the ways in which people attract and repel one another, but also the ways in which they persuade and influence, help and hurt, flatter and deprecate. Social psychologists investigate not only the individual need to affiliate with others, but also the needs to achieve, to nurture, and to aggress; not only the ways in which children are trained (or "socialized") to play the roles of friend, lover, or spouse, but also the ways in which they are socialized to play roles of male or female, black or white, law-abider or delinquent. More broadly, social psychologists are interested in the ways in which patterns of human interaction affect people's conceptions of themselves, on the one hand, and the structure of their societies, on the other.

Although the concerns of the social psychologist range widely, they are closely interconnected. The readers of this book will soon discover that it is impossible to make progress in our exploration of liking and loving without at the same time considering many other aspects of human social life. In Chapter 3, for example, our consideration of the need to affiliate with others will encompass not only two-person relationships but also larger groups and crowds. In Chapters 6 and 7 we will consider the roles of proximity and similarity in intergroup relations as well as in friendship and mate selection. And in Chapter 9 our investigation of courtship patterns in contemporary America will necessarily be intertwined with an examination of other aspects of the American social structure.

Because of the breadth and nature of its concerns, it will also become clear that social psychology is not so much a single, well-bounded discipline as it is an *interdiscipline*. Because social encounters and relationships are shaped by the thoughts, feelings, and motives of the individuals who take part in them, the student of social behavior must depend to a large degree on psychological approaches to the individual's cognition, emotion, and personality. Because social interaction also takes place within the frameworks of norms, roles, and group memberships that characterize human societies, the social psychologist must also attend carefully to the work of the sociologist. Although there are many "psychological" or "sociological" social psychologists who would differ with me on this issue, my own view is that social psychology is not a subarea of psychology or of sociology, but rather the interface of the two. And in some cases, when we are concerned with patterns of social behavior across space and time, the field of social psychology intersects with anthropology and history as well. Liking and loving provide particularly good testimony to the interdisciplinary nature of social psychology, for they are at once individually experienced sentiments, dyadic patterns of interaction, social institutions, and cultural products. Consequently, although much of the research that we will explore has been conducted by investigators who call themselves "social psychologists," our search will not be bound by traditional disciplinary lines. Now that the social psychologist has finally arrived at the party, we will be concerned less with what he calls himself than with the relevance of what he does.

Chapter 2
HOW DO I LIKE THEE?
Let Me Count the Ways

I never met a man I didn't like.

—WILL ROGERS

In *The Lonely Crowd*, sociologist David Riesman characterized modern American society as obsessed with liking and, especially, being liked. "While all people want and need to be liked by some of the people some of the time," Professor Riesman wrote, "it is only the modern other-directed types who make this their chief source of direction and chief area of sensitivity."[1]

What Riesman called the "other-directed type" is epitomized by the desperately approval-hungry character of Willy Loman in Arthur Miller's *Death of a Salesman*, which opened on Broadway in 1949, the year before the publication of Riesman's book. Liking, for Willy Loman, is the key to success. "The whole wealth of Alaska passes over the lunch table at the Commodore Hotel," he tells his sons, "And that's the wonder, the wonder of this country, that a man can end with diamonds here on the basis of being liked!"[2]

In large measure Willy Loman was right. It is only in modern America, I suspect, that men and women could make an all-time best seller out of a book like Dale Carnegie's *How To Win Friends and Influence People*, devoted to such homespun suggestions as "Six Ways To Make People Like You." The most common problem or desire listed by high school students in nation-wide surveys conducted in the 1940s and 1950s was "[I] want people to like me more." According to the pollsters,

> ... The passion for popularity translates itself into an almost universal tendency to conformity among our younger generation. It runs

through all social classes. American teenagers show substantial class differences in many aspects of their behavior, but in their desire for popularity . . . they are as one: low-income or high-income, their highest concern is to be liked.[3]

Even the results of political elections are determined to a large extent by liking. When asked to explain their preferences for President in 1956, 7 percent of a national sample of American voters did not allude to parties or issues at all, only to their personal feelings toward the candidates. "I just like him, the way things have gone," said one Texas woman who planned to vote for Eisenhower, "that's all I really know."[4]

Affection and Respect

What does it mean to like another person? As do many of the words that we use to refer to our attitudes and emotions, it can mean different things at different times. Compare the following usages:

1. "I like Mama's Boy in the seventh"; "I like International Conglomerate for the long term."
2. "Gee Betty Sue, you're just so much fun to be with, I mean it really makes me feel good when you tell funny stories and smile that way, I mean you're just a really nice person—I guess what I'm trying to say is that I really like you a lot."
3. "I've never had a boss whom I liked better than Mr. Snodgrass. It's true that he's solemn and humorless most of the time, but he always has a good grip on the situation, and he can be absolutely relied on to come through in the clutch."

In the first examples, "liking" Mama's Boy or International Conglomerate is simply another way of saying that one has a particular preference. "Liking" in this sense is a commonly used synonym for "choice." These examples do not involve liking another person, but they illustrate an element that is always present in interpersonal liking. Liking always connotes a preference or choice. The distinctions to be drawn between one type of liking and another boil down to distinctions between the various reasons for which other people are chosen.

As a result, there are as many kinds of liking as there are reasons for choosing other people. In *The Adolescent Society*, sociologist James Coleman notes:

Anyone can be popular, if he exhibits the right qualities, and the "right qualities" are determined by the culture. In a farming culture, the farmer who helps his neighbor in time of need is popular; in a hunting culture, the bravest hunters are popular; among little girls playing dolls, the girl with the fancy doll house is popular.[5]

Coleman illustrates his point by demonstrating that the bases for popularity among high school students depend on the school's ideological climate. Whether beauty or brains, sports or studies, are the keys to being liked depends on the particular culture that the students have established.

Not only the characteristics of popular people, but the very meaning of "popularity" varies from one instance to another. Liking someone because he helps you out in times of need is a sentiment somewhat different from liking someone because he is a brave hunter. Liking a girl because she is beautiful is a phenomenon different from liking a girl—even the *same* girl—because she is brainy. These shades of difference have important consequences for our behavior. The particular way in which we like someone will determine whether we help him or expect him to help us; whether we embrace him, kiss him, or shake his hand; whether we approach him closely or keep a respectful distance. It would not do to try to discuss every conceivable variety of liking individually. This would be not only impossible but also wasteful since all of the varieties have much in common with one another. There are two fundamental dimensions of liking, however, that seem to summarize many of the differences among the varieties. I will call them *affection* and *respect*.

Affection is liking that is based on the way another person relates to you personally, and it is experienced as an emotional warmth and closeness. The speaker's fondness for Betty Sue in the second example is a case of affection. Respect is liking that is based on another person's admirable characteristics or actions in spheres other than personal relations. It is a cooler, more distant sort of liking, such as the way the speaker feels toward Snodgrass in the third example.

It sometimes seems as if the world is divided into three types of people: those who receive affection, those who receive respect, and those who receive neither. At least, this is the conclusion we would reach if we were to generalize from studies of small problem-solving groups conducted by Robert Freed Bales and his colleagues at Harvard.[6] In these groups the person who is seen by his fellow group members as contributing the "best ideas" for solving the problem is rarely the person who is rated as "best liked." In this context it seems appropriate to assume that the "best idea" ratings (which also tend to coincide with ratings of "leadership") reflect respect, while the "best liked" ratings reflect affection.

Bales and his colleagues code with considerable precision each of the communicative acts that take place during the group discussion, making use of such categories as "shows solidarity," "gives opinion," and "asks for suggestions." When we compare actions of the best-liked person with those of the person rated as having the best ideas, we find that the best-liked person more often shows and receives solidarity, while the idea man more often gives suggestions and opinions. These differences help to demonstrate that the group members' ratings have an objective basis. More surprisingly, the best-liked person also disagrees, shows tension, and shows antagonism more frequently than the idea man.

In Bales's terms, the idea man is a "task specialist." He is adept at directing the group toward a solution of the problems, and he is respected for it. But because the task specialist dominates much of the discussion and gives directions to the other group members, he frequently arouses hostility. Another member of the group must play the role of "social–emotional specialist"—someone who can smooth over disagreements and who can express negative as well as positive sentiments on behalf of the group as a whole. While the task specialist will continue to receive the group's respect, it is the social–emotional specialist who will receive their affection.

It is only rarely that a leader arises, whether in a small laboratory group or in a nation, who has that peculiar combination of qualities that enables him to receive both respect and affection. The ability to elicit both may indeed be regarded as one of the central marks of greatness. Other lesser men and women may receive differently weighted combinations of the two types of liking, such as much respect but little affection, or middling amounts of both. Respect and affection are, in other words, coexisting dimensions of liking. I should like to consider the behavioral consequences of respect and affection later in this chapter. An empirical approach to this issue presupposes, however, that we can measure the two dimensions accurately.

Measuring the Unmeasurable

The distinction between affection and respect has not generally been reflected in social psychologists' measurement techniques. The focus to date has been on measuring liking in a less differentiated way. A large number of laboratory experiments, for example, have measured liking by means of the following two-item scale: *

1. Personal Feelings (check one)
    —I feel that I would probably like this person very much.
    —I feel that I would probably like this person.
    —I feel that I would probably like this person to a slight degree.
    —I feel that I would probably neither particularly like nor particularly dislike this person.
    —I feel that I would probably dislike this person to a slight degree.
    —I feel that I would probably dislike this person.
    —I feel that I would probably dislike this person very much.
2. Working Together in an Experiment (check one)
    —I believe that I would very much dislike working with this person in an experiment.
    —I believe that I would dislike working with this person in an experiment.
    —I believe that I would dislike working with this person in an experiment to a slight degree.
    —I believe that I would neither particularly dislike nor particularly enjoy working with this person in an experiment.
    —I believe that I would enjoy working with this person in an experiment to a slight degree.
    —I believe that I would enjoy working with this person in an experiment.
    —I believe that I would very much enjoy working with this person in an experiment.[7]

It might be suggested that the first of these questions reflects the subject's affection for "this person," while the second question reflects his respect. The fact of the matter is not known, however, because responses on the two questions are almost never treated separately. Instead, the subject's scores on each of the two items—each ranging from an extremely negative 1 to an extremely positive 7—are added up to produce a single, undifferentiated meas-

* Social scientists who specialize in attitude measurement use the word "scale" to mean two different things: (a) the entire set of questions or items that makes up a measuring instrument, and (b) the response continuum (for example, from 1 to 7) that is used to express one's reaction to any individual item. Thus we can have two-item, ten-item, or fifty-item scales (referring to the entire instrument), and we can have two-point, ten-point, or fifty-point scales (referring to the response continuum accompanying an individual item).

ure of liking. There is logic behind this procedure. Although the two questions are apparently getting at two somewhat different dimensions of liking, subjects' responses to the two questions tend to be highly correlated. It is extremely rare for a subject to indicate that he "would probably dislike this person very much" and at the same time that he "would very much enjoy working with this person in an experiment," or, conversely, to couple extreme liking with an aversion to working together. In adding together the individual item scores, researchers feel that they are combining two aspects of what is essentially the same entity. The net result is an index of "liking" that is more reliable than scores on either item taken alone.

As part of my own recent research I made up a thirteen-item "liking scale"[8] for use in assessing boyfriends' feelings toward their girlfriends, and vice-versa. (The history of this "liking scale" and of the "love scale" that accompanied it will be chronicled in Chapter 10.) The liking scale consisted of the following statements:

1. When I am with _____, we are almost always in the same mood.
2. I think that _____ is unusually well adjusted.
3. I would highly recommend _____ for a responsible job.
4. In my opinion, _____ is an exceptionally mature person.
5. I have great confidence in _____'s good judgment.
6. Most people would react very favorably to _____ after a brief acquaintance.
7. I think that _____ and I are quite similar to each other.
8. I would vote for _____ in a class or group election.
9. I think that _____ is one of those people who quickly wins respect.
10. I feel that _____ is an extremely intelligent person.
11. _____ is one of the most likable people I know.
12. _____ is the sort of person who I myself would like to be.
13. It seems to me that it is very easy for _____ to gain admiration.

I told my subjects, all members of dating couples who volunteered to take part in the research, that the blank space in each statement referred to one's boyfriend or girlfriend. A response continuum that looked like this appeared beneath each item:

| Not at all true; disagree completely | Moderately true; agree to some extent | Definitely true; agree completely |

The subjects were asked to respond to each statement by placing a check on the most appropriate point on the line. Later I divided the lines into nine equal segments and assigned scores ranging from 1 ("Not at all true") to 9 ("Definitely true") on the basis of the location of the subject's check.

As in the case of the two-item measure, each of the thirteen items reflects a somewhat different facet of liking. Once again, however, no attempt was made to explore these distinctions or their consequences. Instead, the subject's scores on all thirteen items were added to produce a single summary index of "liking." Once again responses to the individual items were sufficiently consistent with one another to justify the assumption that they were all reflecting shades of difference within what was essentially the same sentiment.

The two measures that we have examined so far differ from one another in length and format, but they share the same basic strategy. Both of them presume that we can determine how much one person likes another by the straightforward technique of *asking* him. Although this self-report approach to measurement has much to recommend it, it is also subject to an important criticism. Particularly when we are concerned with people's feelings toward close friends or lovers, we are often dealing with deep and private sentiments—and these may not be the sorts of things that people can easily report by putting checks on lines. It is possible that a person does not even know how much he "likes" a particular other person. And if he does know, he may not want to tell a researcher about it. Consequently, we would not always want to take a person's own statement of how much he likes another person as an accurate reflection of the true state of affairs.

One of the most influential contemporary social–psychological theorists is a German emigré, a professor in the United States since 1933, named Fritz Heider. Heider makes the point about questionnaire measures of liking in the following terms: "If somebody says that he dislikes another person O, but it is obvious that whenever he is with O he experiences great enjoyment, then something is felt to be wrong. In order to make the pieces fit . . . re-evaluation takes place. We may decide, for instance, that he really likes O but doesn't realize it."[9] Instead of taking people's self-reports of liking at face value, we are inclined to interpret such statements in the light of whatever other evidence is available.

In the parlance of the social scientist, like is an *attitude*. Since the "attitude" is probably the most frequently employed concept of the social psychologist, a textbook definition seems in order:

The term *attitude* refers to certain regularities of an individual's feelings, thoughts, and predispositions to act toward some aspect of his environment. Feelings are often referred to as the *affective* component, thoughts as the *cognitive* component, and predispositions to act as the *behavioral* component. One may hold attitudes toward concrete objects, such as Coca-Cola, or toward abstract entities, such as democratic government. Attitudes may pertain to remote, impersonal entities, such as foreign aid, or they may be extremely personal, such as feeling that one's nose is too big.[10]

People can also hold attitudes toward other people, one basic variety of which is commonly called "liking."

Like most scientific constructs, whether they be atoms, gravitational fields, or superegos, attitudes are invisible. Feelings, thoughts, and predispositions to act are all inherently private experiences. As Freud has taught us, sometimes they are so private that the feeler or thinker himself is unaware (or "unconscious") of them. The only way in which an attitude can be assessed, therefore, is by means of its visible manifestations, the effects it produces on behavior.

When we say that a person has a particular attitude, we are saying, in effect, that we expect to find certain consistencies in his behavior with respect to the object of his attitude. Verbal reports, such as those provided on paper-and-pencil scales, represent but one manifestation of an attitude. In the case of liking, other manifestations might include smiles and other "positive" nonverbal expressions, physical approach, and helpful acts. But any one of these behaviors may be produced for a variety of reasons that are unrelated or even negatively related to liking. The check on a scale may reflect faking or misunderstanding; the smile may represent uneasiness rather than affection; the approach may really be an attack; the helpful act may be an attempt at appeasement. In consequence, no single report or observation can be taken as a fully adequate assessment of an underlying attitude, even though for reasons of convenience social psychologists are often prompted to pretend that it can.

As a result, the social psychologist's attempts to measure liking may sometimes seem to be quixotic efforts to measure an entity that is inherently unmeasurable. The best way around this impasse is to attempt to measure liking in any given instance in a variety of ways, both verbal and nonverbal. If the different indices obtained contradict one another, we can then try to discover the underlying reasons for the contradiction. If several reports and observations are consistent with one another, on the other hand, our confidence about inferring the attitude in question will legitimately rise. With this introduction, let us examine some alternative measures of liking.

Liking without Words

The importance of nonverbal signals of liking has long been acknowledged. "The minutest movements accompany every process of thought," psychoanalyst Theodore Reik wrote in *Listening with the Third Ear.* "Muscular twitchings in the face or hands and movements of the eyes speak to us as well as words. No small power of communication is contained in a glance, a person's bearing, a bodily movement, a special way of breathing. . . . There are variations in tone, pauses, and shifted accentuation, so slight that they never reach the limits of conscious observation, which nevertheless betray a great deal to us about a person." Reik felt that the analyst must learn to decipher these "signals of subterranean emotions and impulses" if he is truly to understand his patient.[11]

The study of nonverbal communication is sometimes divided into such subareas as "paralanguage" (voice quality), "Proxemics" (the use of space), and "kinesics" (facial expressions and body movements). Our systematic understanding of the ways in which liking and loving are expressed through these channels is still rudimentary, but it is advancing at a rapid pace. For example, the emotional connotations of vocal tone can be assessed by first electronically filtering the higher tone frequencies from recorded speech, so that the words become unintelligible but the tones remain. By playing such filtered tapes to subjects, it is possible to assess reactions to the purely vocal aspects of spoken messages, independent of their verbal content.* Using this method, psychologist Albert Mehrabian has concluded that a speaker's tone of voice is more important than the content of his message in determining whether the listener feels liked or disliked. "If someone calls you 'honey' in a nasty tone of voice," Mehrabian observes, "you are likely to feel disliked; it is also possible to say 'I hate you' in a way that conveys exactly the opposite feeling."[12]

A doctoral thesis recently completed at Harvard by Shirley

* An alternative method, recently introduced by Klaus Scherer, involves cutting a stretch of recording tape into tiny pieces and splicing them back together in a random order. The resulting voice samples retain all of the speaker's voice qualities but are completely unintelligible.

Weitz suggests that someone's tone of voice may be a better indication of his liking or disliking of another person than his self-report on a questionnaire.[13] In her experiment each of the white male subjects was given a written description of a black man who was to be his partner in the experiment, and who was ostensibly waiting in an adjoining room. The subject was then given several opportunities to express his reaction to his unseen partner on the basis of the written information. First, he filled out a paper-and-pencil measure of liking for the partner. Second, he read task instructions to the partner over an intercom system. Tape recordings of these statements were later scored by a panel of raters for their warmth of tone. Third, the subject was asked to indicate how many additional hours he would be willing to return to the laboratory during the following week to take part in further experiments with the same partner. Such a commitment to future interaction with a person would be a particularly convincing manifestation of liking.

After collecting these measures, Weitz computed the extent to which they correlated with one another. She found that whereas warmth of tone and commitment to future interaction correlated positively with one another, each of these measures correlated *negatively* with the questionnaire measure of liking. Those subjects who expressed the most positive attitudes toward their black partner on the questionnaire had the *least* friendly voice tone and were *least* willing to interact with him further. Weitz suggests that this dramatic inconsistency may stem from a tendency of whites within the liberal college environment to repress their negative or conflicting feelings toward blacks by overreacting in a positive direction on the questionnaire. Their questionnaire responses, she suggests, may be a case of the "doth protest too much" syndrome.

Researchers have also begun to explore the ways in which body postures signal liking. In one study conducted by Mehrabian, male and female subjects were asked to act out the ways in which they would sit while speaking to men and women whom they liked or disliked in different degrees. Both men and women leaned forward to express liking, but their body language differed in other respects. When speaking to men whom they disliked intensely, men held their bodies more tensely and adopted a more direct shoulder orientation than women did. Mehrabian speculated that intensely disliked males pose more of a threat to men than to women and therefore elicit a greater degree of tension and vigilance.[14]

We not only lean forward toward people whom we like, but we also move our entire bodies closer to theirs. An experiment conducted by Donn Byrne and his colleagues at the University of Texas helped to document the link between liking and physical approach.[15] As part of a study of "computer dating," previously unacquainted couples were briefly introduced and then sent to the Student Union for a research-sponsored Coke date. When the couples returned for further instructions, the experimenter surreptitiously recorded the distance between the two as they stood in front of his desk. The subjects were then separated and asked to indicate their liking for one another on a questionnaire. The results were clear: The more subjects indicated that they liked one another, the closer together they stood.

Another nonverbal manifestation of liking may be derived from behavior of our eyes.[16] Experiments have shown that people who are cooperating make more eye-to-eye contact than people who are competing, and that subjects spend more time looking at others from whom they expect approval than those from whom they expect disapproval. The amount of eye contact engaged in by subjects has also been found to correlate positively with their self-reports of liking.

As in the case of the other measures we have discussed, these results are not always easy to interpret. Making eye contact may indeed be an indication of liking or an expression of love. Eye contact can be hostile as well as affectionate, however, and it is not always an easy matter to distinguish the loving gaze from the hostile stare. Yet just this sort of distinction is necessary if we are to treat nonverbal expressions as indications of liking. A stare accompanied by a scowling face or a tense posture may mean something quite different from a gaze accompanied by an easy grin and a relaxed posture. Similarly, the meaning of eye contact may depend upon the verbal statements made by the gazer. Eye contact often serves as a "multiplier" of sentiment. If what a person says is friendly or approving, eye contact will make it seem even friendlier. If what a person says is unfriendly or disapproving, on the other hand, eye contact will serve to emphasize the hostility.[17]

One advantage of nonverbal measures of attraction, assuming that we can learn to decipher them accurately, is that they are typically less susceptible to conscious control or to "faking" than verbal measures are. Nevertheless, vocal, facial, and bodily expressions are by no means immune to dissimulation. Psychologist Paul Ekman, who has investigated the facial expression of emotion in cultures throughout the world, notes that the task of discovering the cross-cultural "universals" of facial expression is vastly complicated by the existence of learned "display rules." For example:

> Middle class, white, adult, urban males in the U.S. follow the display rule of neutralizing or masking sadness and fear in almost all public places; their female counterparts, particularly those who are in the pre-matron age bracket, follow the display rule of neutralizing or masking anger. In a business setting where two executives have been competing for a job promotion, the display rule specifies that . . . the winner should de-intensify expressions of happiness, while the loser should de-intensify, neutralize, or mask . . . the facial expression of sadness. At beauty contests the losers at the moment of announcement must mask sadness with happiness.[18]

Thus the use of nonverbal measures of liking shares with the use of self-reports the difficulty of distinguishing between what is really felt and what is presented for public scrutiny.

Are there any measures of liking that are not susceptible to conscious control and thus exempt from this drawback? One approach, best known for its use by practitioners of lie detection, is the measurement of internal physiological responses. The most frequently used index of this sort is the galvanic skin response (GSR), a measure of the electrical resistance of the skin that is typically produced when a person experiences threat or danger. Recent investigations have shown, for example, that whites who express antiblack attitudes on questionnaires also tend to show increases in GSR when they come into contact with blacks. Similarly, there is evidence that the level of free fatty acid in the blood, which is regulated in part by autonomic nervous activity, is greater when people are with groups of strangers than when they are with groups of friends.[19]

Research by psychologist Eckhard Hess also suggests that people's positive or negative attitudes toward objects that are exposed to them are reflected by the widening or narrowing of the pupils of their eyes. In one study Hess found that men's pupils widened most when they were shown female pinups, and women's pupils widened most when they were shown male pinups and pictures of babies. On the other hand, both men's and women's pupils tended to constrict when they viewed pictures of cross-eyed and crippled children. In another study Hess found that the pupils of homosexual men widened more when they looked at pictures of men than when they looked at pictures of women, while heterosexual men showed the opposite pattern. Hess notes that the pupillary response is affected by the sympathetic portion of the autonomic nervous system and thus reflects cognitive and emotional activity. He goes on to maintain, "Embryologically and anatomically the eye is an extension of the brain. It is almost as though a portion of the brain were in plain sight for the psychologist to peer at."[20]

But Hess's assessment is probably too optimistic. In spite of scattered results involving such indices as GSR, free fatty acid, and pupil dilation, the current verdict of experts is that physiological responses have not proven to be reliable indices of attitude or attraction. For each of the studies that has yielded positive results, there are several whose results have been negative or inconclusive. Physiological responses *have* proven to be valuable indicators of some psychological states, such as stress, tension, and arousal. When it comes to liking and loving, however, it is likely that adequate physiological measurement will have to await much more sophisticated tracking of complex brain mechanisms than is currently—or indeed may ever be—possible. This is because liking and loving involve not only arousal or activation, which may be detectable physiologically, but also the pattern of thoughts and interpretations that accompany the arousal.*

* Although physiological measures are not reliable indicators of attitude, it is not too difficult to convince people that they are. Especially because of the mystique of the lie detector, the notion that scientists have a physiological pipeline to people's inner feelings is a plausible one to the general public. This plausibility has provided the basis for an ingenious new approach to attitude measurement which its inventors, social psychologists Edward E. Jones and Harold Sigall, call the "bogus pipeline."[21] The procedure involves three basic steps: first, explaining to the subject that a recent breakthrough in electrophysiological research has made possible the unerring physiological measurement of his attitudes by monitoring his "implicit muscle movements"; second, attaching the subject to an elaborate-looking (but in fact phoney) machine and convincing him of its effectiveness; and third, asking the subject to *estimate* his own electrophysiological reading when he is asked how he feels about various people or groups. The only measure actually collected is the subject's estimate. But in contrast to the usual self-report procedure in which the subject is simply asked to inform the experimenter of his feelings, the bogus pipeline subject is asked to estimate feelings that he believes the experimenter already knows all about. Since the subject typically wants to demonstrate that he is in fact in touch with his own feelings, his responses may well be more accurate reflections of his actual attitude. It is also possible that the bogus pipeline provides a better measure of the affective component of an attitude (*"How do you feel?"*), while standard rating techniques provide a better measure of its cognitive component (*"What do you think?"*). The problem of pinpointing the relative merits of the two techniques once again testifies to the complexity of our attempt to measure the "unmeasurable."

The Politics of Touch

Given the difficulties of measuring liking even in generalized terms, it is not surprising that the nature of more refined dimensions such as affection and respect has gone largely unexplored. Nevertheless, research has progressed far enough in recent years to hint at certain important conclusions about them. These conclusions focus on a comparison of the "likability" of men and women.

Women, like the "best-liked" members of Bales's groups, may be characterized as the "social–emotional specialists" of our society, while men, like the group members with the "best ideas," are the "task specialists." Women are the mediators, conciliators, comforters, and confidantes, while men are the bread-winners, warriors, and heads of state. If we accept the premise that affection is "social–emotional" liking and respect is "task-related" liking, therefore, we would expect women to receive more than their share of the available affection, and men to receive the bulk of the respect. And there is considerable evidence to support these predictions.

One manifestation of men's greater access to respect is the greater influence that they wield, even when it is not justified by greater expertise. Social psychologist Philip Goldberg showed female college students a series of professional articles on topics ranging from nutrition to city planning.[22] Half of the subjects were told that the articles were written by men; half were told that the same articles were written by women. Regardless of the topic, the subjects rated the same articles as less persuasive and of poorer quality when they were thought to be the work of women. Similarly, studies of simulated juries have found that women generally participate less and are less influential than men.[23]

If you glance back at the "liking scale" that I developed (p. 30), you will see that it is really more of an index of respect than of affection. Many of its items are about such task-related matters as responsibility, good judgment, and intelligence. I was initially surprised to discover that although girlfriends and boyfriends *loved* one another about equally on the parallel scale that I developed, girlfriends *liked* their boyfriends significantly* more

---

* The word "significant" has a technical meaning for the social scientist that is somewhat different from its everyday meaning. It means that a statistical test has shown that an obtained result (such as the difference between women's and men's scores on the liking scale) would be unlikely to come about by chance. A "significant" result is not always one of great magnitude or importance. The fact that it is significant implies, however, that it probably reflects a real state of affairs rather than a statistical accident.

than boyfriends liked their girlfriends. Once I realized that the scale was getting at a more circumscribed conception of liking— what we are now calling respect—the finding became much less surprising.

These experimental results are probably not necessary to convince you that American men are typically more highly respected than American women. A cursory glance at a list of congressmen or business executives or college administrators would almost inevitably lead to the same conclusion. The complementary prediction that women should receive more affection than men is also well documented. One such indication is the finding that people of both sexes disclose intimate things about themselves more easily to women than to men.[24] Although self-disclosure may in some instances be a manifestation of respect, as when a person reveals his intimate secrets to a psychotherapist or father confessor, in everyday life it is more often an indication that one feels warmly and affectionately toward the other person. Another indication is that women are physically touched more, again by people of both sexes, then men are.

Let us consider touching in greater detail. Whereas we relate to people whom we respect by regarding them at a distance, we seek close physical contact with those for whom we feel affection. The association of distance with respect is illustrated by Theodore White's description of the events at John F. Kennedy's "hideaway cottage" when his nomination for President became a certainty:

> The others in the room surged forward on impulse to join him. Then they halted. A distance of perhaps 30 feet separated them from him, but it was impassable. They stood apart, these older men of long-established power, and watched him. He turned after a few minutes, saw them watching him, and whispered to his brother-in-law. Shriver now crossed the separating space to invite them over. First Averell Harriman; then Dick Daley; then Mike DiSalle, then, one by one, let them all congratulate him. Yet no one could pass the little open distance between him and them uninvited, because there was this thin separation about him. . . . They could come by invitation only, for this might be a President of the United States.[25]

The affectionate potential of the touch, on the other hand, has been utilized by the new wave of encounter groups and human potential institutes, where exercises involving hugging, stroking, massaging, and lifting are used to help people break down emotional barriers. As William Schutz, a psychologist at the Esalen Institute, explains,

"The methods used to develop the potential for affection rely heavily on the close tie between physical touch and affectionate feelings."[26]

Women's greater touchability is documented by survey data indicating that mothers and daughters are touched more by others within the family than are fathers and sons. Observational data suggest, in fact, that six-month-old girls are touched more by their mothers than are six-month-old boys. And in a sample of instances of opposite-sex touching in public recorded by social psychologist Nancy Henley, almost twice as many involved the man touching the woman as vice-versa. To the extent, then, that touching is a sign of affection, women clearly receive more affection than men do.[27]

But this is not the only way to interpret women's greater touchability. An alternative explanation is that touching is a prerogative of a higher-status, more powerful person in his interaction with a lower-status, less powerful person. Henley presented a persuasive argument to this effect in a paper called "The Politics of Touch," originally presented as part of a panel discussion on "Social Psychology and Women's Liberation."

> To support the argument that touching is a sign of power, I would like you to consider interaction of various pairs of persons that I will name, and to picture who would be more likely to touch the other (e.g., putting an arm around the shoulder, hand on the back, tapping the chest, holding the wrist, etc.): teacher and student; master and servant; policeman and accused; doctor and patient; minister and parishioner; adviser and advisee; foreman and worker; businessman and secretary. If you have had the usual enculturation, I think you will find the usual picture to be that of the superior-status person touching the inferior-status one. In fact, it is often considered an affront, insubordination, for a person of lower status to touch one of higher status.[28]

Sociologist Erving Goffman corroborates Henley's conclusion with observations at a psychiatric hospital: "The doctors touched other ranks as a means of conveying friendly support and comfort, but other ranks tended to feel that it would be presumptuous for them to reciprocate a doctor's touch, let alone initiate such a contact with a doctor."[29]

Henley concludes that male–female touching, rather than simply being a demonstration of affection, is more importantly an assertion of male power. "Touching is one more tool used by a male supremacist society to keep women in their place, another reminder that women's bodies are free for everyone's use." She notes, too, that when a woman touches a man it is much more often interpreted as a sexual invitation than when a man touches a woman. "Because touch is an indication of power, it is acceptable when done by a man; when by a woman, the implication of power is unacceptable and must be denied." The alternative interpretation of sexual intent is a more acceptable one.

Can a single category of behavior, that of touching, simultaneously be an expression of affection and a symbol of domination? The answer is that it can and does. To understand why this is the case we must reinterpret affection and respect in political terms. Respect is an attitude that characteristically flows from people of lower power and status to those of higher power and status. We respect people whom we regard as being in some way superior to ourselves. In a society that emphasizes achievement and success, it is not surprising that respect is highly related to one's assessment of another person's responsibility, good judgment, intelligence, and leadership ability. Affection, on the other hand, is most likely to flow reciprocally between people who are more or less equal in power and status. Equality of status seems to breed the trust and rapport that is necessary for affection.

But if respect is liking that is directed toward persons of higher status and affection is liking that is directed toward people of equal status, how shall we characterize liking that is directed toward persons of *lower* status? The answer seems to be that our positive sentiments toward people of a status lower than our own more closely resemble affection than respect. It is this link between affection and condescension that helps to explain the dual function of touching.*

Whom To Say *Tu* To

The link between affection and condescension is pointed up by an analysis of the ways in which people address one another. In the

---

* These characteristic patterns are not, of course, universal ones. It is in fact quite common for a person to respect someone of lower status or to feel affection for someone of higher status. Examples include a parent's respect for his child, or a child's affection for his parent. And, as pointed out earlier, respect and affection may often coexist. Nevertheless, the association between the two sentiments and relative status is a pervasive one that accounts for many of their connotations.

course of his investigations of linguistic usage, Roger Brown has uncovered what he believes to be a universal norm underlying forms of address.[30] The norm has two parts:

1. Those forms of address that are (or were in earlier periods) used by superiors in addressing subordinates coincide with the forms used reciprocally by people of equal status who are well acquainted or intimate with one another.
2. Those forms of address that are (or were) used by subordinates to address superiors coincide with the forms used reciprocally by people of equal status who are not well-acquainted or intimate with one another.

Several examples of this linkage are diagrammed in Figure 2.1. In French, for example, subordinates used to address superiors with the respectful pronoun *vous*, while superiors addressed subordinates with the more familiar pronoun *tu*. But *vous* also became the form used reciprocally between equal-status strangers or new acquaintances, while *tu* became the form for brothers and sisters, friends, and lovers. The same pattern prevails in German, where the shift from *Sie* to *du* is an important rite of passage in the development of a relationship. In English the pronoun *you* is used

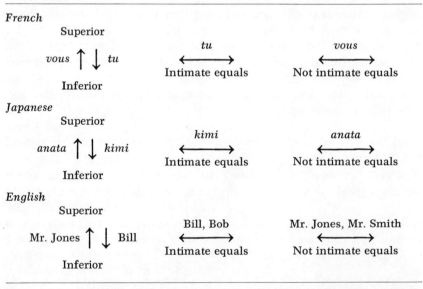

FIGURE 2.1   Examples of the universal norm of address (Adapted from Roger Brown, *Social Psychology*, Fig. 2–6, p. 93, with permission of The Macmillan Company. Copyright © 1965 by The Free Press).

in all cases, but Brown's norm determines whether we call someone by his first name ("Bill") or by a title, followed by his last name
("Mr. Jones"). We use first names in addressing both our em-
ployees and our close friends. We are more likely to use title–last
names in addressing our bosses and our more remote acquaintances. "In the research hospital," Goffman reports, "doctors tended
to call nurses by their first names, while nurses responded with
'polite' or 'formal' address."[31]

Interestingly, the norm that underlies forms of address is
closely paralleled by norms regulating touching and other forms
of nonverbal behavior. As we have seen, people are most likely to
touch others of a status lower than their own, as well as people
with whom they feel close and affectionate. We are least likely to
touch others of higher status or people with whom we do not feel
close. Mehrabian's research on body language has pointed to a
similar pattern. He reports a convergence of the ways in which
subjects act out approaches to a lower-status person and approaches toward a person whom they like very well; in both cases
the subjects seem to let down their guard and adopt a less direct
shoulder orientation than they do when approaching a higher-
status or less-liked person.[32]

There are many other convergences of indices of affection and
of superiority. Men pat children on the head—and also their
wives. We call both our comrades and our elevator men by their
nicknames, and often in the same tones of voice. We call people
whom we love "baby." These convergences are too striking to be accidental. Rather, they reflect basic differences between the motives
that underlie affection and those that underlie respect.

One of the reasons for our tendency to like people who are
similar to ourselves is that they are best able to confirm our own
views and to bolster our self-esteem. We feel warmly and affectionately toward such similar people because they make us feel
comfortable, secure, worthwhile, and on top of things. But this is
often precisely the way we are made to feel by subordinates whom
we like—comfortable, secure, worthwhile, and certainly on top of
things. We compare ourselves to the other person and are reassured when the comparison turns out in our favor. Liking for a
person whom we regard as superior to ourselves seems to be based
on a different sort of motive, however: the motive to improve ourselves either by emulating the other person or, more vicariously,
by observing and identifying with him. It is epitomized by the item
on my liking scale, "_____ is the sort of person who I myself
would like to be." Such respect does not necessarily breed warmth

and comfort. It may sometimes even lead to feelings of threat and inferiority. Thus I see two general families of motives underlying our liking for others: The need for self-confirmation leads to affection for equals *and* inferiors, while the need for self-improvement leads to respect for superiors. And to the extent that affection is linked with feelings of superiority, condescending elements are likely to creep in.[33]

Staying in One's Place

David Riesman, in *The Lonely Crowd*, has written that the other-directed person "seeks not fame . . ., but the respect *and, more than the respect, the affection*, of . . . [his] jury of peers." In a subsequent preface to his book Riesman amplified this point:

> The other-directed man wants to be loved rather than esteemed; he wants not to gull or impress, let alone oppress, others but, in the current phrase, to relate to them; he seeks less a snobbish status in the eyes of others than assurance of being emotionally in tune with them.[34]

For many of us respect alone is indeed unsatisfying, especially to the extent that it implies being held in rather distant awe by people who call us by our titles and last names and do not deign to touch us. But neither is affection alone the panacea. As women, slaves, and members of other underprivileged groups are likely to discover, to be regarded with affection is often to be patronized. To receive affection one must stay in one's place and take care not to threaten one's superiors.

For example, many of the college women interviewed by Mirra Komarovsky[35] in the early 1940s indicated that they "played dumb" on dates—concealing academic honors, pretending ignorance of some subject, or allowing the man the last word in an intellectual discussion. They felt that these tactics helped them to retain their boyfriends' affection. "One of the nicest techniques," one woman reported, "is to spell long words wrong once in a while. My boyfriend seems to get a great kick out of it and writes back, 'Honey, you certainly don't know how to spell.'" Similarly, Negro slaves in the American South were often inclined to feign ignorance, probably in part as a strategy to gain their masters' affection.[36]

As a result of the link between affection and condescension it is sometimes difficult for an oppressed group that has become conscious of its oppression to accept affection freely. A familiar greeting becomes an insult, a gentle touch "one more tool used by a male supremacist society to keep women in their place." What most of us really want, of course, is neither affection nor respect alone, but a degree of both. We want to be regarded warmly by people who also appreciate and admire our strengths.

Chapter 3
STOP WORRYING
AND LOVE THE CROWD
The Psychology of Affiliation

It is not good that man should be alone.
—GENESIS, 2, 18

Konrad Lorenz reports that when a flock of starlings comes within sight of one of their predators, a flying sparrow hawk or hobby, "they press so close together that one can hardly imagine that they can still use their wings." More generally, Lorenz continues, "There is not a single gregarious animal species whose individuals do not press together when alarmed, that is, whenever there is a suspicion that a predator is close at hand."[1] Fear appears to induce clustering among humans as well. In one experiment boys aged nine to twelve were told ghost stories as they sat around a campfire at a Halloween party. "Although the diameter of the circle was about 11 feet at the beginning of the story telling," the researchers noted, "by the time the last ghost story was completed, it had been spontaneously reduced to approximately three feet."[2]

The tendency for individuals to increase their proximity to others of the same species is called affiliation. People must affiliate with one another to realize a large proportion of their practical goals, from playing bridge to building bridges. In this chapter, however, we will focus on less strictly utilitarian functions of affiliation among both humans and lower animals. One of our guiding questions is whether the case of the flocking starlings and

47

the case of the huddling boys are in fact similar in a sense that goes beyond mere metaphor. In this connection we will be led to examine the more general debate between those scientists who are greatly impressed by the relevance of animal behavior to an understanding of human behavior and those who are not.

Affiliation refers to the tendency to associate with other individuals in general, rather than to the formation of attachments to particular others, as in the case of liking or loving. But our consideration of affiliation will help lay the groundwork for our later exploration of liking and loving for two major reasons. First, people must come into contact with one another before they can form individual attachments. Thus, affiliation is in most instances a necessary precondition for attraction. Second, we will discover that the motives that lead people to approach or to avoid others in general often coincide quite closely with the bases of individual attraction and rejection.

Affiliation among Animals:
Safety in Numbers

Lorenz begins his discussion of affiliation among animals by expressing some puzzlement about it. It would seem, he suggests, that animals would often have a better chance for survival if they isolated themselves from their fellows, thereby reducing the competition for food which takes place in dense crowds. But nature seems not to have been much impressed by this line of reasoning. Instead she has made the flock the commonest form of animal association, prevailing among species ranging from squids and insects to buffaloes and baboons. The impulse forcing the animals together is often tremendously strong—so strong that in the case of a bird called the brambling it may even be deadly. Lorenz observes that when there is a particularly good beechnut crop in a certain area, the birds may crowd together to such an extent that the crop cannot sustain them. In the winter of 1951 Lorenz studied an enormous flock of these birds on the Swiss Thunersee. He reports that every day there were many corpses under their roosting trees. Post-mortem examinations revealed that the birds had died of starvation.[3]

In the face of such obvious disadvantages of affiliation, Lorenz is led to conclude that they must be offset by rather compelling advantages. He goes on to explain that in one way or another the flocking together of animals invariably provides a margin of safety from their predators. The precise way in which affiliation protects the animal differs from one species to another. In some cases groups of animals conduct active defensive warfare. Bands of small apes leap after a tiger or leopard from the safety of the treetops; bull buffaloes and baboon males entrench themselves in heavily armed defensive positions. In the case of completely defenseless fish and small birds, affiliation provides a more subtle form of protection by preventing the predator from concentrating on a single target. When the predator's field of vision is occupied by a large number of potential targets, it will often find it impossible to fix upon any single one. It has been experimentally demonstrated, for example, that goldfish catch fewer water fleas when they are offered too many at once than when offered only a few. Lorenz notes that radar-guided missiles can be fooled into acting the same way when aiming at airplanes: The missile heads for the empty space between two targets that are close together and positioned symmetrically on both sides of the missile's trajectory. Thus, herrings swim in close shoal formation for much the same reason that jet fighters fly in close formation—to minimize the chances of a direct hit by an enemy.

The wisdom of affiliation as a defensive tactic is attested to, Lorenz contends, by the fact that none of the large predators ever attacks in the midst of a dense herd of its prey. Big lions and tigers almost never leap onto an African buffalo in the herd, paying proper respect to the herd's defensive powers. Smaller hunting animals adopt a similar policy of trying to isolate a single animal from the group before they attack it. Lorenz cites W. Beebe's observation of corresponding behavior among fish in the sea. Beebe saw a big amber jack trailing a shoal of little porcupine fish, patiently waiting until one of the small fish swam off by itself in pursuit of some still smaller prey. Each time this happened the little fish was snapped up by the big one.[4]

Lorenz adds that the effectiveness of affiliation in staving off attack need not be particularly great for the flocking impulse to be perpetuated in the course of natural selection. "The social defense reaction of jackdaws may not result in saving their fellow from a hawk, but if it is just annoying enough to make him hunt jackdaws a little less eagerly than magpies, and thus to make him prefer magpies as prey, this is enough to give social defense a very strong survival value." Because of this survival value, animals evidently inherit a predisposition to cluster together whenever they are alarmed or fearful. The clustering helps to minimize the danger and, consequently, to reduce the fear. As part of the evolutionary master plan, moreover, the same response pattern is often generalized to situations that are fearful for reasons that do not involve predation.

Recent experiments have documented, for example, that affiliation has a direct fear-reducing effect for laboratory rats. In one study individual white rats were placed in an unfamiliar cage (which in itself is known to be fear-arousing) and observed under five different conditions.[5] Each rat was placed in the cage either alone or with a moving toy (a red Ferrari that kept scooting around the cage), a stationary toy, an anesthetized (and hence stationary) rat of the same sex, or a normal (and hence moving) rat of the same sex. Among rats the frequency of defecation provides a good measure of fearfulness. It was found that whereas from a third to a half of the rats defecated in the isolated and toy conditions, only 13 percent of those paired with the anesthetized rat and 2 percent of those paired with another normal rat did so. Thus, fear was apparently reduced by the presence of another member of the species, especially if he was alive and well. Analogous results have been obtained in studies of other mammals, including goats and monkeys.

The mechanisms by which the presence of a companion reduces fear are not completely clear, but several reasonable explanations have been offered. One is that an inborn propensity for fear to be reduced by the presence of another member of the species is triggered by such characteristics as the other animal's color, texture, shape, smell, and movement. Another is that the animal learns as an infant that its needs are most likely to be satisfied and its fears assuaged in the presence of others who feed and care for it, and that this learning is transferred to other fearful situations. It is possible that both of these explanations are correct, with both nature and nurture contributing to the animal's predisposition to affiliate.

Affiliation among Humans: Waiting for Zilstein

The intensity of people's need to affiliate is dramatically illustrated by the harrowing experiences of men and women who, whether by choice or by coercion, have spent long periods of time in isolation from others. "Gradually the loneliness sets in," wrote one prisoner who had been placed in solitary confinement. "Later I was to experience situations that amounted almost to physical torture, but even that seemed preferable to absolute isolation."

The isolate's need for companionship is often expressed dramatically in his thoughts and actions. Christopher Burney, who was held in solitary confinement by the Germans for eighteen months during World War II, obtained some small measure of relief when he found a snail in the exercise yard. "It was company of a sort," Burney later wrote, "as if it were an emissary from the world of real life." Joshua Slocum, who sailed alone around the world, developed hallucinations of a savior who appeared at times of particular stress. More recently, students at McGill University who volunteered to take part in studies of complete isolation and sensory deprivation reported that "they felt as if another body were lying beside them in the cubicle; in one case the two bodies overlapped, partly occupying the same space." Prolonged experiences of isolation have been known to produce extreme mental and emotional disorders, and even psychotic breakdown.[6]

Human isolation does not invariably produce such extreme effects. The effects tend to be most pronounced when there is some objective cause for fear. Being shipwrecked or being taken prisoner of war is a terrifying experience under any conditions, but when it is endured in isolation, the terror is multiplied. Reports of London children during the wartime blitz, soldiers during battle, and experimental subjects taking hallucinogenic drugs for the first time all concur in the conclusion that the presence of others provided some degree of protection against the otherwise devastating effects of the stressful situation. In many of these cases the other people were in fact unable to take action that would have increased the person's physical safety and would thus have reduced the objective cause for fear. Nevertheless, their mere presence seemed to have had a calming effect.[7]

If the presence of others helps to reduce fear, a logical corollary is that people should have stronger desires to affiliate when they are fearful than when they are not. This prediction was confirmed in a dramatic laboratory experiment conducted by social psychologist Stanley Schachter.[8] Small groups of female undergraduates at the University of Minnesota were greeted at the laboratory by a stern-looking man in a white coat, who identified himself as Dr. Gregor Zilstein of the medical school's departments of neurology and psychiatry. Zilstein told the women that they would be taking part in a study of the physiological effects of electric shock. They would receive a series of shocks while measures of their pulse rate and blood pressure were taken. After an ominous pause, Zilstein informed the subjects in one experimental condition that the shocks would indeed be extremely painful. "If in research of this sort we're to learn anything that will really help humanity," he explained, "it is necessary that our shocks be intense." He added with a tight smile that the shocks would do no permanent tissue damage.

Other groups of subjects came to the same room and were met by the same experimenter, but in these sessions Zilstein was much less alarming. He told the women that the shocks they would receive were to be very mild. "Do not let the word 'shock' trouble you," Zilstein purred to the subjects in this experimental condition. "I assure you that what you feel will not in any way be painful. It will resemble more a tickle or a tingle than anything unpleasant."

Now that some of the subjects had been made considerably more fearful than others, the stage was set for the assessment of their desires to affiliate. The women were told that they would have to leave the laboratory for ten minutes while the equipment was being prepared. During this delay each girl was given her choice between waiting by herself in a private room and waiting in a classroom together with some of the other subjects. She indicated her preference on a questionnaire that listed three alternatives: "I prefer being alone," "I prefer being with others," and "I really don't care." The subjects in the two experimental conditions differed dramatically in their preferences. Two-thirds of the subjects in the low-fear condition either preferred to wait alone or indicated that they had no preference. Two-thirds of the subjects in the high-fear condition, on the other hand, preferred to wait with others.

To Generalize or Not To Generalize?

It seems that among humans, just as among lower animals, fear leads to a strong tendency to flock together with others. But having noted this parallel, let us pause to consider its implications. Does the fact that both humans and jackdaws are predisposed to affiliate when afraid imply that the same underlying mechanisms are at work in both cases? Can we presume to classify both the rat's reaction to an unfamiliar cage and the coed's apprehension about a forthcoming electric shock under the same heading of "fear," or by doing this are we mistakenly putting human words into animals' mouths? More generally, does drawing such analogies across species facilitate or hinder our understanding of human social behavior?

Konrad Lorenz has provided the most persuasive modern re-
statement of King Solomon's advice that man can learn a great
deal about himself by observing the behavior of animals. "Believe
me, I am not mistakenly assigning human properties to the animal," Lorenz assures his readers after describing the "status consciousness" of the jackdaw. "On the contrary, I am showing you
what an enormous animal inheritance remains in man, to this
day."[9] He goes on to argue convincingly for the validity of using the
same psychological and behavioral constructs, such as "fear" or
"affiliation," to refer to observed behavior in a wide variety of
species, including man:

> The more complex and differentiated two analogously con-
> structed and similarly functioning organs are, the more right we have
> to group them in the same functional conception and to call them by
> the same name, however different their phylogenetic origin may be.
> When Cephalopods, like the Octopus, Squid, and Cuttlefish, on the one
> hand and vertebrates on the other have invented, independently of
> one another, eyes built on the same principle of the lens camera, and
> when in both cases these organs have similar constructional units
> such as lens, iris, vitreous humor and retina, no reasonable person
> will object to calling both the organ of the Cephalopods and that of
> the vertebrates an eye—without any quotation marks. We are equally
> justified in omitting the quotation marks when speaking of the social
> behavior patterns of higher animals which are analogous with those
> of man.[10]

Lorenz acknowledges that the existence of such analogous
behavior patterns does not imply that the behaviors of the two
species in question had the same evolutionary origins. The earliest
common ancestors of birds and mammals, for example, were low
reptiles of the Upper Devonian and Lower Carboniferous strata,
which had no highly developed social life and were scarcely more
intelligent than frogs. Thus the behavioral similarities between
geese and men cannot be traced to direct evolutionary links. But
neither are these similarities simply due to chance. They represent, rather, what Lorenz calls "convergent adaptation." Both geese
and men face many of the same tasks in adapting to their environment, including the requirements of food-getting, successful reproduction, and protection from predators. By observing the
analogous behavior patterns that have emerged in the two species,
we can gain insight into these common problems of adaptation and
the ways in which organisms have evolved to cope with them.
"If, in the Greylag Goose and in man, highly complex norms of

behavior such as falling in love, strife for ranking order, jealousy, grieving, etc., are not only similar but down to the most absurd details the same, we can be sure that every one of these instincts has a very special survival value, in each case almost or quite the same in the Greylag and in man. Only in this way can the conformity of behavior have developed."

Other writers have been profoundly critical of Lorenz's reliance on analogy, however.[11] One recent critic branded the Lorenzian approach as characterized by a kind of "word magic" that tries to explain human phenomena simply by attaching labels to them; a smile becomes an "appeasement gesture," athletic events become "rituals," and so on. The critics go on to contend that by grouping overtly similar behaviors of different animals under the same functional headings the similarities between species are exaggerated, while the equally important differences between them are ignored. In addition, Lorenz's approach is seen as putting excessive emphasis on innate behavior patterns and minimizing the equally important role of learning in shaping social behavior.

These criticisms have considerable merit. Lorenz and other members of his school of thought (including Desmond Morris and Robert Ardrey) seem to take their analogies too far, generalizing from animals to men in a seductive style that may distract serious scientific questions about their appropriateness. I believe, nevertheless, that when taken with the necessary grain of salt, such analogies can be greatly enlightening. They serve the function of transporting our own behavior patterns out of their everyday settings, where they are typically taken for granted and therefore not carefully examined, into the unfamiliar environs of the marsh, the jungle, and the stream, where they stand in sharper relief and thus can often be more fully understood. As psychologists D. O. Hebb and W. R. Thompson suggest, studies of animal behavior are comparable to studies of "abnormal" human behavior in their implications for our understanding of "normal" human patterns:

> Finding that a psychotic behaves in a certain way does not prove anything about normal persons, but no one would argue from this that clinical studies have not helped in our understanding of the normal. In principle, study of animals has exactly the same status.[12]

It must also be recognized, however, that there are few, if any, instances in which a fully adequate account of human social behavior can be provided in terms that could reasonably be applied to any nonhuman species. Human social behavior is unique in its reliance upon self-conscious reflection about its meaning and the ways in which it will be interpreted by others, instead of being more or less directly governed by physical cues. In the next section we will see that it is necessary to postulate such cognitive processes in order to account for some of the observed aspects of human affiliation. But to the extent that the behavior of humans and of lower animals can be explained in identical terms, the more general law thus derived provides a useful baseline for the further examination of human behavior. The general principle that fear leads to affiliation is an example of such a baseline generalization.

Labeling One's Own Feelings

With the above baseline generalization, we have taken our comparison of human and animal affiliation about as far as we profitably can. Beyond this, there remain several aspects of human affiliation that have no apparent parallels in the animal world. Whereas fear often gives rise to affiliation among men and women, another psychological state seems to have this effect even more consistently. This is the state of *uncertainty*, both with regard to one's external environment and especially with regard to one's view of oneself. It is a state that seems distinctively human. Although I have tried, I find it difficult to conjure up an "uncertain" jackdaw or white rat without at the same time investing it with other human capacities such as self-conscious reflection and the use of language.

Human beings have a strong need to make sense out of the world and of their own reactions to it. We want to be able to validate our perceptions and assumptions, to distinguish the true from the false, the real from the illusory. Although most of us can comfortably live with a great deal of ignorance, few of us can tolerate much ambiguity. In many cases our own senses are sufficient to accomplish the reality tests that we require. If we believe that it may be raining, we stick our hands out the window and find out. If we think that we are capable of bending an iron bar, we attempt it and discover whether or not we were right. In many other cases, however, "reality" can be discovered only by means of social appraisal. There is no physical test with which to assess the correctness of our views about the greatness of a work of art or the existence of an afterlife. But since our need for certainty is just as intense in these situations as in the former ones, we must still attempt to validate these beliefs—not against the yardstick of physical reality, but by continual consultation and comparison with other people. It is this desire for social validation of our perceptions and opinions that directs much of human affiliative behavior.[13]

One of the most reliable ways of producing affiliative behavior is to create a mystifying event that people are unable to explain for themselves. Stanley Schachter provided a demonstration of this effect, with the assistance of the principal of a girls' school.[14] The principal simply entered several classrooms at the beginning of the day, pointed to a single girl, and said, "Miss K., get your hat, coat, and books and come with me. You will be gone for the rest of the day." In the wake of this unprecedented event the remaining girls spent almost the entire school day in intensive social contact, attempting to reduce their uncertainty about what had happened.

We are often just as confused and uncertain about events within ourselves as we are about the events around us. At the most global level, we have a need to come to terms with our own identity. The link between this need and affiliative behavior has been discussed by the psychoanalyst Frieda Fromm-Reichmann:

> Perhaps the explanation for the fear of aloneness lies in the fact that, in this culture, people can come to a valid self-orientation, or even awareness of themselves, only in terms of their actual overt relationships with others. "Every human being gets much of his sense of his own reality out of what others say to him and think about him," as Rollo May puts it. While alone and isolated from others, people feel threatened by the potential loss of their boundaries, of the ability to discriminate between the subjective self and the objective world around them.[15]

While Fromm-Reichmann's analysis is to the point, most of the systematic research on the link between the need for self-evaluation and affiliation has been concerned with people's desire to identify or confirm their own reactions in more specific situations. In discussing Schachter's electric-shock experiment, we have labeled the relevant stimulus "fear." It may well be, however, that Schachter's subjects found themselves in a highly ambiguous situation. What *should* one's reaction be when faced with the prospect of receiving a series of painful shocks? Fear for one's safety? Anger at the diabolical Dr. Zilstein? Philosophical acceptance? Gratitude for being allowed to suffer in the name of science? It may be that subjects in this situation really didn't know what their own emotions were, and they elected to affiliate with others in order to find out. Thus, the relevant stimulus may be reinterpreted from fear to *uncertainty*.

Schachter was able to derive some additional evidence for this reinterpretation. He reasoned that if the desire to reduce fear was the primary motive underlying the subjects' preference to affiliate with others, it should not matter too much just who the others are. As long as the others are members of the same species, according to our baseline generalization, they should do. If, on the other hand, the subjects' main desire was to reduce uncertainty by comparing their reactions with those of others, affiliation should be more selective. Not all people should be good comparison points for classifying one's own reactions, but only others who are in the same situation. Thus, the uncertain women should desire to affiliate with fellow subjects, but not with anyone else.

Schachter confirmed this prediction of selective affiliation in a second experiment.[16] All of the subjects in this study were told that they would receive painful shocks. Half of them were given the choice between waiting alone and waiting with fellow subjects, as in the initial experiment. The other half of the subjects were given the choice between waiting alone and waiting in a room where other girls were waiting to see their academic advisors. As Schachter had predicted, the subjects indicated a preference to wait with others only when these others were fellow-subjects. "Misery doesn't love just any kind of company," Schachter observed, "only miserable company."

At the conclusion of the experiment Schachter's subjects were also asked to write down why they had chosen to wait alone or together with others. The comments of several subjects who chose to affiliate reflected the need for self-evaluation. "I wanted to wait with other people to see how they would react while waiting for the experiment," one subject wrote. Another woman explained, "I thought that the others probably had the same feelings toward the experiment that I had, and this thought made me want to be with someone." The preference for affiliating with others in the same predicament was found even in a condition in which subjects were told in advance that they would not be allowed to talk to one another. The subjects presumably recognized that social comparison of one's emotions does not necessarily require verbal communication. Simply glancing at the facial expressions of others in the same boat may be sufficient to help a person who is uncertain about his own reactions decide how he himself should feel.

A subsequent study by Harold Gerard demonstrated more directly that uncertainty about one's reactions motivates human affiliation.[17] Gerard employed the same fear-inducing procedure as Schachter, but he also found a way to manipulate directly subjects' certainty about their own reactions. When the subject arrived at the laboratory, the experimenter escorted him to a private room and connected electrodes to his hand and forearm. A meter labeled "Emotionality Index" was placed in front of the subject. The experimenter explained in an authoritative tone that this meter would provide an accurate reading of the subject's degree of emotionality, based on his skin resistance and muscle tremor. The meter's dial was calibrated from 0 to 100, with higher numbers indicating greater emotional arousal. Immediately after being told that he was to receive painful electric shocks, each subject in the "uncertain" condition saw the needle on his meter fluctuating widely on the scale, with an average reading of 75. Subjects in the "certain" condition also saw an average reading of 75, but in their case the needle was quite steady. After several minutes the subject was asked whether he wanted to wait for the shocks with other subjects or alone. As Gerard had predicted, subjects who had been made uncertain about their own feelings reported a stronger desire to affiliate than subjects in the "certain" condition. The latter subjects presumably already had "reliable" information about their own reactions and accordingly felt less need to compare their reactions with those of others. Although the wavering and steady meter readings in Gerard's study were artificially manufactured by the experimenter, they may provide meaningful parallels to people's actual experiences of emotion. The evidence suggests that we are more likely to seek out others when our feelings are changeable and confused than when they are constant and clear-cut.

Schachter's research on affiliation was a central impetus to his subsequent development of the theory of emotion that we outlined in Chapter 1, in connection with our discussion of the Ovid–Horwicz phenomenon.[18] The theory holds that the experience of any given emotion, whether it be fear, anger, or love, is jointly determined by the experience of physiological arousal and the labeling of that arousal as being due to a particular cause. Schachter and Jerome Singer found that when subjects were given injections of adrenalin without being warned of its arousing effects, they tended to "catch" whatever emotion was displayed by a confederate of the experimenter whom they were with. When the confederate acted boisterously, playing with a hula hoop, flying paper planes, and generally laughing it up, the subjects began to exhibit a similar euphoria. When, in another condition, the confederate expressed hostility toward the experimenter, the subjects tended to pick up his angry mood. Notably, these contagious reactions did not take place when the subjects were informed in advance of the effects the adrenalin would have—a racing heart, flushing, and tremor. In these "informed" conditions, the subjects could confidently attribute their physiological arousal to the injection they had received. But when such attribution of their arousal to the drug was impossible, the subjects apparently identified their emotional states by comparing their reactions with those of their fellow subject and deciding that they must be reacting to the same things that he was reacting to. In many real-life situations, as well as in the laboratory, people may often feel agitated or stirred up without knowing why. In these instances we compare ourselves with others in order to identify our own emotions.

Losing Oneself in the Crowd

In addition to the fear-reducing and uncertainty-reducing functions of affiliation, people also affiliate with others in order to lose themselves. The similarity between human and animal flocking behavior often seems most striking in riots, revival meetings, rock concerts, and other crowd situations. In all of these cases there is a strong tendency for people to cease behaving as individuals and to be taken up instead by the spirit of the crowd. The usual restrictions on the individual's behavior are loosened, and what may seem to be his more bestial impulses come to the surface. Tom Wolfe analyzed the behavior of the teeny-bopper audience at a 1966 Beatles concert:

> Control—it is perfectly obvious—they have brought this whole mass of human beings to the point where they are one, out of their skulls, one psyche, and they have utter control over them—but they don't know what the hell to do with it, they haven't the first idea, and they will lose it . . . suddenly GHHHHHHWOOOOOOOOOWWWWW-WWW, it is like the whole thing has snapped, and the whole front section of the arena becomes a writhing, seething mass of little girls waving their arms in the air, this mass of pink arms, it is all you can see, it is like a single colonial animal with a thousand waving pink tentacles;—vibrating poison madness and filling the universe with a teeny agony torn out of them—it is *one being*. They have been transformed into one being.[19]

The description reminded me of Lorenz's description of certain species of small fish which, when alarmed, "crowd together to form a body so that they look like one big fish, and since many of the large, rather stupid predators such as the Barracuda meticulously avoid large prey for fear of choking, these tactics may be special protection."[20] For the fish the flocking together is a defense against predators. For the human crowd, it may instead represent a rejection of individual restraints.

The impulse that rises to the surface in the midst of a crowd is sometimes exultant, as in the above example, but it is all too often violent. Lynch mobs, firing squads, and urban riots all illustrate the power of the crowd to bring out aggressive instincts. In his classic analysis of the crowd, the French sociologist Gustave LeBon argued that people who compose a crowd take possession of "a sort of collective mind which makes them feel, think, and act in a manner quite different from the way each individual of them would feel, think, and act were he in a state of isolation."[21] The characteristics of each individual are reduced to those he holds in common with all other crowd members, resulting in a least common denominator of impulsiveness, irritability, and irrationality.

LeBon goes on to argue that, because of the size of the crowd, the individual within it feels invincible, anonymous, and unaccountable for his own behavior. The member of a firing squad—or, analogously, the member of an army company firing at a group of civilians—feels such a lack of responsibility. No one can call the individual soldier a murderer, for he was but one of the crowd. The net effect of these forces, coupled with the "contagion" of emotion among the crowd members, is to encourage the individual to yield to his baser instincts.

What attracts people to crowds in the first place? Often it is simply a matter of curiosity, a desire to be "where the action is." Consequently, regardless of the initial reason for its formation, a crowd, once formed, is likely to attract additional members. Social psychologist Stanley Milgram and two of his students at the City University of New York experimentally investigated the "drawing power" of crowds of various sizes.[22] The researchers had anywhere from one to fifteen students form crowds on New York's 42nd Street and look up at a building across the street as though something interesting or unusual was taking place. The only interesting or unusual thing actually happening was that Milgram's assistant was unobtrusively taking movies of the scene from a sixth-floor window. The obtained result was that the percentage of passers-by who attached themselves to the crowd was a direct function of the size of the "stimulus crowd." Carnival barkers, sidewalk salesmen, and other entrepreneurs have long been aware of this principle. They commonly employ small boys or other shills to hang around looking interested, thereby hoping to draw others to the group.

In addition to such curiosity, however, social psychologist

Philip Zimbardo believes that people join crowds precisely because of their ability to reduce individual constraints and to liberate primitive impulses.[23] Zimbardo sees crowd behavior as dictated by the "urge to be deindividuated." He describes this urge as "a universal need to shatter all formal controls," having mythical counterparts in "the ageless life force, the cycle of nature, the blood ties, the tribe, the female principle, the irrational, the impulsive, the anonymous chorus, the vengeful furies." Once it has begun, Zimbardo maintains, deindividuated behavior tends to increase in intensity until it either reaches a frenzied peak or the person collapses in fatigue. The behavior itself seems to serve as a stimulus for increasingly intense behavior of the same sort. For example, a journalist provided the following account of police behavior at the ill-fated 1968 Democratic convention in Chicago:

> The ones who actually got arrested seemed to have gotten caught up among the police, like a kind of human medicine ball, being shoved and knocked back and forth from one cop to the next with what was obviously *mounting* fury. And this was a phenomenon . . . which we were to observe consistently throughout the days of violence—that rage seemed to engender rage; the bloodier and more brutal the cops were, the more their fury increased.[24]

Zimbardo stresses that deindividuated behavior is not always violent. The extremely conforming behavior of members of such diverse groups as armies and religious orders shares with mob outbursts the tendency to replace one's personal identity with that of the group. Whether for lower impulses or for higher goals, there is a sacrifice of individuality in favor of partaking in a collective experience. Zimbardo argues that such deindividuation is not inherently opposed to human values of individual growth and development. "Individuals who normally live controlled lives need such revels," he contends, "so that they can experience both the pleasure derived directly from such expression and the greater pleasure of becoming *reindividuated* following a period of abandon or running amok." Whether it is for good or for evil, all of us are at least occasionally motivated to associate with others so as to shed the vestiges of our individuality. "I live in the crowd of jollity," Dr. Johnson wrote, "not so much to enjoy company as to shun myself."

The Spaces between People

We have seen that people tend to huddle together when they are fearful, when they are uncertain, and when they wish to shed their individuality for the anonymous security of the crowd. But affiliation has its costs as well as its benefits. There are times when the presence of others is burdensome or threatening rather than rewarding. At such times we reject the company of others in favor of retreat or communion with ourselves.

Whereas fearful and uncertain situations typically spur affiliation, *extremely* fearful or uncertain feelings sometimes lead to precisely the opposite reaction. Several days after President Kennedy's assassination, the National Opinion Research Center conducted a nation-wide survey of reactions to the tragedy. A majority of those surveyed reported that immediately after hearing that the President had been shot they felt a desire to talk to others. But 40 percent of the sample indicated instead that they desired to be alone at this time. Significantly, the desire for privacy was most prevalent among those categories of people who reported that they admired President Kennedy the most. The feelings that these Americans experienced may have been so painful that they did not wish to expose them to others or to clarify them through social comparison.[25]

A variation of the Schachter experiment conducted by Irving Sarnoff and Philip Zimbardo yielded analogous results.[26] Their experiment included conditions characterized by either a high or low degree of "oral anxiety"—a Freudian concept referring to the fear that one's repressed wish for one's mother's breast will return to the surface. Sarnoff and Zimbardo's subjects were male undergraduates at Yale, recruited for a study of the "physiological effects of tactile stimulation." Those in the high-anxiety condition were told that while the physiological measures were being obtained they would be required to suck on a collection of baby bottles, pacifiers, breast shields, and oversized nipples that was arrayed in front of them. Subjects in the low-anxiety condition were also told that they would have to mouth various objects, but they were innocuous ones like pipes and whistles. The threatening word "suck" was not used in the instructions to these subjects. Then, as in Schachter's study, the men were asked whether they wanted to wait for the experience with other subjects or by themselves. Whereas Schachter had found that high fear strengthened his subjects' desire to affiliate, Sarnoff and Zimbardo found that high oral anxiety strengthened their subjects' desire to wait alone. The possibility that one will reveal to others—or to oneself—an extremely threatening emotion seems to dampen the desire to affiliate.

The opposition between the benefits and the costs of affiliation is graphically reflected in the ways in which people space themselves. Experiments have shown, for example, that women characteristically sit closer to one another when they are conversing than men do, that extroverts approach others more closely than introverts do, and that students expecting to be praised by an instructor place their seats closer to him than do students who expect to be censured. Each of these findings makes sense in terms of the struggle between the forces of approach and the forces of avoidance. Men, who typically find it more difficult to disclose their feelings to others than women do, may be more highly motivated to keep an appropriate distance from others so as to minimize the possibility of revealing themselves. Similarly, introverts are often people who find others threatening and wish to avoid their scrutiny, whereas extroverts are less likely to have such fears. And, like laboratory rats who quickly learn to approach the end of the alley where they are fed and withdraw from the end where they receive electric shock, we learn to come close to others whom we expect to reward us and to distance ourselves from those whom we expect to punish us.[27]

As we noted in Chapter 2, physical closeness often signals people's feelings of affection. But the physical approach that oversteps conventional bounds is interpreted as an invasion rather than an expression of affection. Experiments have shown that a person's degree of emotional arousal, as measured by the galvanic skin response, steadily increases as he is approached more and more closely by a stranger.[28] Studies conducted by social psychologist Robert Sommer and his students have indicated that the best way to get a library table or a park bench to yourself is simply to sit extremely near the person already occupying it.[29] More often than not he will first turn away, then try to shield himself with his hands, and finally take flight. In crowded buses and subways escape is generally impossible. Instead, anthropologist Edward Hall observes, "The basic tactic is to be as immobile as possible and, when part of the trunk or extremities touches another person, withdraw if possible."[30] In elevators and other enclosures people typically space themselves as far as possible from one another, much as molecules of a gas disperse themselves equidistantly within a closed container.*

* Anthropologist Hall also notes, however, that reactions to physical closeness vary widely among cultures. For example, the characteristic "personal distance" is smaller for Middle Easterners than for Americans. Thus, Middle Easterners in public places do not express the outraged reaction to being touched by strangers that Americans do.

Glenn Lym, an urban designer who is now completing his doc-
torate in social psychology, has perceptively commented on the
opposing functions of physical approach:

Coming together in space can be a mixed blessing. Let's consider
Jill and Bill. The closer and more directly face to face Jill comes to
Bill, the more Jill can see Bill. At 15 feet, she cannot discern Bill's
smile. At 6 feet she can discern that smile and maybe even the degree
of retraction of Bill's lower lip which in the past has normally indicated if Bill is in a happy or pensive mood. But at 6 feet she cannot
touch him or hold hands. At 2-½ feet Jill can touch Bill, but the
chances are she won't be able to smell him. So she moves to full body
contact distance. Here at 0 to 1-½ feet from Bill, Jill's sight of Bill is
confined to details of his skin and face. She can bite him, hug him,
or smell him if she wants. Let's say Jill has just had a very disturbing
experience; she has had her purse snatched. She is shaken by the
incident. Coming back to Bill eases her tension and gives her a sense
of security in being with someone she trusts and loves. Coming together in space facilitates types of affiliations that are impossible if
one is distant in space.

Coming together in space has a double edge, however. Jill has come
close to Bill to affiliate, to momentarily lose herself in him. But imagine another situation. Jill and Bill are on the verge of separation. He
has beaten her up in the past, and their argument now portends the
same. At 1-½ feet Bill can discern if she is sweating, a reaction in her
that he cannot stand. She knows this and moves to a point 2-½ feet
from him. Her sweating is less apparent, but he can still slug her with
his fist at this distance. And besides, he can look her straight in the
eye at 2-½ feet and scream his head off. If he does then she will feel
spellbound by him. His screams carry more weight eye to eye. Jill
moves further away from Bill. At 6 feet he cannot easily manhandle
her and he certainly cannot monitor her nervous sweating. But his
yelling is still potent. She moves to 18 feet away. Bill's yell is less
potent; he cannot harm her unless he tries to throw an object at her.

With Jill and Bill we have the two archetypal patterns of coming
together vs. moving apart, of proximity for affiliation vs. distance
from someone for protection from that person, of incorporation vs.
individuation.[31]

Our competing motives to come close to others and to move
away from them sometimes create what psychologists call an
approach–avoidance conflict.[32] Remember the young man standing against the wall at the party described in Chapter 1. He sees an
attractive girl near the opposite wall. His emotions are mixed. On
the one hand, he would like to move toward her and strike up a
conversation. On the other, he is afraid of being rejected and

hence would like to stay away. At first his approach tendency is the stronger, and he begins to move across the floor. As he gets closer to his goal, the avoidance tendency gains in strength. Like a rat heading toward a goal box where it has sometimes been fed and sometimes been shocked, the young man slows down and vacillates. If he is outgoing and secure, the approach tendency will win out. If he is shy and insecure, the avoidance tendency will be the victor. In borderline cases, the young man may spend much of the evening glancing at his watch and looking foolish on the middle of the floor. The distances that we establish between ourselves and others in a wide variety of situations are often determined by similar tugs of war between competing forces. The distance finally arrived at is the resultant of the two forces. "Like the porcupines in Schopenhauer's fable," Robert Sommer concludes, "people like to be close enough to obtain warmth and comradeship but far enough away to avoid pricking one another."[33]

There is a very general principle about liking and loving that will underlie much of our exploration. It is that people are attracted to those others who are rewarding to them, who fulfill their needs and gratify their desires. The study of affiliative behavior helps us to identify some of the ways in which particular people are rewarding. Just as we tend to affiliate when we are afraid, we are attracted to those others who we feel can provide us with protection and security. Just as we seek the company of others in the same situation when we are uncertain about our own reactions, we are attracted to those others who are similar to ourselves and can thus be counted upon to provide us with a yardstick for self-confirmation. And just as we tend to avoid contact with others when we fear their scrutiny or when we are unwilling to come to grips with our own potentially threatening feelings, we shun those others who we are afraid will reject us or whose qualities remind us of things we do not wish to recognize in ourselves. We will return to each of these themes in later chapters. First, however, it is necessary to state some general principles of attraction more precisely, in terms of the trading rules of the interpersonal marketplace.

Chapter 4
THE INTERPERSONAL MARKETPLACE
An Investor's Guide

My true-love hath my heart, and I have his,
By just exchange one for the other given.
　　　　　　　　—SIR PHILIP SIDNEY

You look up from your menu in an exclusive restaurant to see an unlikely couple enter. The woman is a strikingly attractive blonde in her late twenties. She has bright eyes, a flawless complexion, an outstanding figure. She is smiling down at her escort, who is a short, balding man some fifteen years her elder, with small, beady eyes and protruding ears. If you are the sort who puzzles over such mysteries, you will quickly reduce the situation to several possibilities.* He might be a visiting cousin from Kansas City, but that doesn't seem too likely. You notice that both of them are wearing wedding rings. They seem, in fact, to be married to each other. This inference is soon confirmed when the headwaiter greets them deferentially as Mr. and Mrs. Pennypacker. You entertain the possibility that he might be an internationally known poet or philoso-

---

* A recent experiment by Harold Sigall and David Landy demonstrated the prestige value that may result from being seen with a physically attractive partner. Subjects briefly met a man who was sitting next to, and presumably going with, a woman who was, in one experimental condition, extremely attractive or, in another condition, rather unattractive. The subjects were then asked to record their initial impressions of the man. When the man was paired with the attractive woman, he was liked more and tended to be viewed as friendlier and more self-confident than when he was paired with the unattractive woman. (Harold Sigall and David Landy, "Radiating Beauty: Effects of Having a Physically Attractive Partner on Person Perception," *Journal of Personality and Social Psychology*, 1973, 28, 218–224).

pher who swept her off her feet when she was in his class at Sarah Lawrence. But much more likely in your mind is the remaining possibility that he is extremely rich—the heir of the Pennypacker Department Stores or the Pennypacker Copper Mines or both.

The chances are good that you would be right. Both the beautiful woman and the wealthy man have something of value to offer one another. She can please him aesthetically, and, perhaps more importantly, she can enhance his esteem in the eyes of others. As Thorsten Veblen put it in *The Theory of the Leisure Class*, attractive women "enable successful men to put their prowess in evidence by exhibiting some durable result of their exploits."[1] He, in turn, can provide her with a standard of living that she would not otherwise be able to attain. The result, following the trading rules of the interpersonal marketplace that we will explore in this chapter, is that attractive women and successful men are likely to become paired with one another—and that, moreover, the more attractive the woman, the more successful the man is likely to be. North Carolina sociologist Glen H. Elder, Jr., recently documented this principle statistically. Elder analyzed data on the marriages of a group of women whose physical attractiveness had been rated many years earlier, when they were still in high school. He found that the girls rated as better looking were more likely than their less attractive classmates to end up marrying higher-status men.[2]

A group of my students at the University of Michigan also obtained evidence for people's tendency to pair off with others of approximately their own level of "social desirability." They surreptitiously rated some fifty coeds on their physical attractiveness and asked each of them to complete a questionnaire about their dating preferences. A man's occupation made a great deal of difference in the women's ratings of how acceptable he would be as a date. Virtually all of the girls felt that men in high-status occupations— physicians, lawyers, chemists—would be highly acceptable dates, almost all of them agreed that men with low-status jobs—janitors and bartenders—would hardly be acceptable. When it came to rating men whose occupations were in the middle of the status hierarchy—electricians, bookkeepers, plumbers—the attractive and unattractive girls differed. The unattractive girls felt that they would be at least moderately acceptable dates, while the attractive girls felt they would not be.[3]

A woman's beauty and a man's wealth are by no means the only relevant commodities in the interpersonal marketplace. In many contexts, in fact, these commodities are much less important than other characteristics. In the small towns of eastern Europe, wealthy Jewish merchants would try—often with the help of the local matchmaker—to marry their daughters off to poor but talented scholars from the local *yeshiva*. In such a case the woman's economic status was being exchanged for the man's intellectual and spiritual distinction.[4] Other exchanges involve the social status of one partner and the economic status of another. As part of the marriage settlement between Consuelo Vanderbilt and His Grace the Ninth Duke of Marlborough, the Duke was reportedly guaranteed for life the income from $2,500,000 of Beech Creek Railway stock.

In this chapter we will be concerned less with the particular commodities which are bartered than with the processes of social exchange themselves. We will ultimately discover that whereas the principles of the interpersonal marketplace can explain a great deal about the establishment and structure of interpersonal relationships, they cannot explain them in their entirety. Especially after a relationship has gained a certain degree of intimacy, it is necessary to look beyond exchange toward economically "unsound" principles that involve not only self-interest but also concern for others.

Man as Pigeon

As I write this, I am sitting in my office on the fourteenth floor of William James Hall, Harvard's center for the behavioral sciences. Seven floors below me, several large rooms are filled with many rows of glass-and-chrome cages. Each cage contains a pigeon, and each pigeon is going through an interesting ritual. It is repeatedly pecking at a key situated at the front of its cage. Some of the pigeons are pecking energetically at a rate of several pecks per second; others are pecking at a more leisurely pace. In all cases, after the pigeon has pecked for a while, there is a clicking sound, and a food pellet is automatically deposited in a cup just beneath the key. The pigeon does not seem at all surprised to receive the food. It calmly bends down, picks up and devours the pellet, and then with hardly a pause returns to his pecking.

The pigeons are the property of the behaviorist psychologist B. F. Skinner and his disciples, and their pecking demonstrates the principles of what Skinner calls "operant conditioning."[5] Because the pigeon gets fed only after it has pecked the key a certain number of times, it quickly learns to peck if it wants to get fed. The hungrier it is, the more rapidly it pecks. The food pellet, in Skinner's terminology, is a "reinforcer"—it rewards the pigeon for its past pecks, and it motivates the pigeon to continue pecking in the future. If the psychologist has regularly reinforced the pigeon's pecks and then abruptly stops doing so, the pigeon will appear to become angry, flapping its wings and cooing hurriedly. And then, after a while, it will stop pecking. Pigeons peck only as long as they are being reinforced. If the reinforcement is permanently discontinued, the pecking is "extinguished."

Sitting at his desk three floors below Skinner's laboratory, on the fourth floor, is Sociology Department chairman George Caspar Homans.[6] Professor Homans can fairly be characterized as a Skinnerian sociologist, for he believes that all of human social behavior is determined in more or less the same way as the pecking of Skinner's pigeons. Men and women rarely peck, but they emit such other activities as assisting one another, expressing love and approval, and conforming to social norms. And each of these behaviors on the part of one person may serve as another person's reinforcement. Whether or not a person will emit such potentially rewarding activities depends on whether or not he is getting sufficient rewards in return. As the noted sociologist Georg Simmel put it over fifty years ago, "All contacts among men rest on the schema of giving and returning the equivalence."[7]

In Homans's view, men—like pigeons—are basically profit-seeking creatures. We seek to obtain the greatest possible reward at the least possible cost. If a pigeon can get all the food it wants by pecking once every ten seconds, it will not push itself to peck any more frequently. Similarly, if a student can get all the help he needs from his generally inaccessible professor by seeking him out twice a term, he will not expend the time and energy necessary to seek him out any more often. Unlike laboratory pigeons, however, people often have more than one alternative source of the social rewards they require. If it is too difficult or demeaning to get all the love we need from one person, we may turn to someone else whose love proves to be less costly. Man as profit-seeker is always seeking the best bargain that he can get. It is this continuing bargain-hunt that underlies the operation of the interpersonal marketplace.

An excellent illustration of Homans's "exchange theory" of social interaction is provided by sociologist Peter Blau's study of a group of sixteen agents working in a federal law-enforcement agency. The agents' task was to investigate firms and to prepare reports on their compliance with the law. The task was a difficult one, and the agents often had questions about which of many regulations should be applied to a particular case. The official procedure was for the agent to take such questions to their supervisor, but many of the agents were reluctant to do this. They feared that turning to the supervisor would reflect badly on their competence and thus hurt their chances for promotion. Instead, the agents often turned to one another for advice. The more competent agents were often consulted by the less competent ones, and, as a rule, they were willing to help out. For whereas they had to take time off from their own work in order to assist others, they received in exchange the approval and esteem of their fellows. Blau summarized the exchange process as follows:

> A consultation can be considered an exchange of values: both participants gain something, and both have to pay a price. The questioning agent is enabled to perform better than he otherwise could have done, without exposing his difficulties to his supervisor. By asking for advice, he implicitly pays his respect to the superior proficiency of his colleague. This acknowledgment of inferiority is the cost of receiving assistance. The consultant gains prestige, in return for which he is willing to devote some time to the consultation and permit it to disrupt his own work. The following remark of an agent illustrates this: "I like giving advice. It's flattering, I suppose, if you feel that others come to you for advice."[8]

Thus the human pigeons keep pecking—one of them by giving assistance, the other by paying his respect—as long as it is profitable for both of them to do so. At some point, however, it becomes increasingly costly for a competent agent to continue to take time off from his own work to provide help and increasingly costly for a less competent agent to continue to admit his inferiority to his colleague. In the latter case, Blau reported, "The repeated admission of his inability to solve his own problems . . . undermined the self-confidence of the worker and his standing in the group." In economic terms, both the help-givers and the help-seekers experience diminishing marginal returns. As a result, many of the less competent agents established mutual partnerships, in which they consulted one another for most of their run-of-the-mill problems. Homans analyzed this solution as a profit-maximizing strategy: "The advice a man got from his partner might not be of the highest value, but it was purchased at low cost since a partner was apt to be his social equal. And thus he was able to save his really difficult problems for the most competent agents, whose advice, since it did come high in confessed inferiority, he did not want to ask often."[9]

The same principles of social exchange are applicable to cases of pairing in courtship and marriage, such as the ones with which we began this chapter. An unattractive man or woman may often be able to secure the affection of an attractive partner, but to do so is likely to involve a great deal of personal cost. He or she will have to provide a higher quality of rewards to the partner than the partner can receive from anyone else. And since the more attractive partner, being highly desirable, has many other available alternatives, the less attractive partner may have to work very hard to provide him or her with sufficient benefits.

Consider the following description provided by a physically unattractive and unpopular young woman of her affair with an older man:

> I accepted his structuring of our relationship. When he chose to deal in wit rather than in real information, I followed suit. When he acted casual about sex, so did I. I wanted something real from him, an honest encounter of mutual understanding and trust; even when I knew this was impossible on my terms, I went ahead with it in his way, thinking I might get what I wanted by using his channels. I didn't back off, because I thought the potential was there, and a dateless summer had taught me that opportunities didn't come up all that often.[10]

The woman, Margaret, was apparently more dependent upon her partner for social rewards than he was dependent upon her. Because of her greater need, she had to work considerably harder than he to sustain the relationship. At some point, however, Margaret may come to feel that the rewards provided by her boyfriend are not sufficient to justify the costs that she must bear to obtain them. She may discover, in other words, that she is taking an interpersonal loss rather than making a profit. In such an event Margaret may well abandon the relationship in favor of either another "dateless summer" or a relationship with a less demanding (even if less desirable) man.

The late sociologist Willard Waller discussed cases like Margaret's under the heading of the "principle of least interest," which states that whichever partner is less involved in the relationship is the one who is able to set its terms.[11] Waller noted that relationships in which one partner is considerably more dependent and involved than the other tend to be unstable. In such asymmetrical relationships both partners may ultimately find themselves to be incurring excessive costs. The more dependent partner may suffer the costs of being exploited, while the less dependent partner may feel guilty and uncomfortable in the role of exploiter. As a result, we would expect relationships in which there is a lopsided balance of involvement and power to be short-lived. Relationships that survive for longer periods of time are likely to be those in which the relative desirability and relative involvement of the two partners is more or less equal.

Appraising One's Own Market Value

People generally have a pretty good idea of where they stand on the scale of social desirability. An expert agent in an agency like the one Blau studied will soon realize that he has resources of great value to his fellow workers and that if he occasionally takes the time to help them out, he will be held in high esteem. Similarly, pretty girls learn from the time they are very small that they can expect to receive the approval of others without working very hard to get it. When they grow up, they find that they are able to get more dates—and with a wider variety of men—than their less attractive classmates. Such experiences make it clear to the attractive woman that she is a desirable social partner. To some extent they determine her personality; she becomes more self-confident, choosy, even conceited. These dispositions, in turn, affect her romantic inclinations. As my students' study at the University of Michigan demonstrated, for example, attractive women tend to aim higher and more selectively in their ratings of prospective dates.

But people's estimates of their social desirability are rarely if ever fully objective. Many people continually overestimate their value on the interpersonal marketplace, wishfully aspiring to social rewards that they cannot in fact command. Only after long periods of trial and error do they finally bring their self-evaluations down to realistic proportions. Other people have the opposite tendency of underestimating their social desirability. A highly attractive person may overreact to a single disappointment or rebuke, deciding that he is a pitiable creature whom no one could love, even though this is in fact far from the case. Particularly extreme forms of such faulty self-perception are found in cases of emotional disturbance.

A person's appraisal of his own desirability—or his self-esteem —may have a characteristic overall level, but it also tends to vary from day to day or even from hour to hour, as dictated by the person's recent experiences of approval or disapproval, success or failure. These fluctuations are in turn likely to influence who the person will approach on the interpersonal marketplace. A junior executive's mood on a given day may determine, for example, whether he boldly takes a seat across from the company president at lunch or whether he sits with the assistant bookkeepers. The analogous impact of self-esteem on romantic choice was investigated in a dramatic laboratory experiment conducted at Yale.[12] In the first part of the experimental session the Yale man was shown results that made him think that he had done either exceptionally well or exceptionally poorly on an intelligence test that he had taken. The subject was then escorted to a small canteen for a coffee break, where he was maneuvered into a carefully staged encounter with a Connecticut College girl who "happened" to be in the area. In half of the cases the girl was stunning, and in the other half she was quite plain-looking. (The same girl played this Mata Hari role in both conditions. She was extremely attractive to begin with, but was able to make herself look plain when she tried.) Once the encounter had been set up, the experimenters simply waited to see what the subject would do. The pattern of results generally corresponded to the researchers' predictions. Men whose self-esteem was high—they had just proved themselves to be among the brightest men on campus—were more likely to make romantic advances when the girl they encountered was highly attractive. Subjects with low self-esteem, on the other hand, were more likely to approach the plain-looking girl. In both cases the subjects' assessment of their own desirability had an apparent impact on their level of romantic aspiration.

Although the Yale study confined itself to a single encounter, the same processes of self-evaluation are at least as relevant to longer-term relationships. As sociologist Erving Goffman has written, "A proposal of marriage in our society tends to be a way in which a man sums up his social attributes and suggests that hers are not so much better as to preclude a merger or a partnership in these matters."[13] Only the timid will undersell themselves on the interpersonal marketplace because by doing so they will get less of a bargain than they might otherwise obtain. Up to a point, indeed, it is good strategy to *oversell* oneself. If a person believes that he is more desirable than he really is—or if he can act as if he feels this way—he may in fact succeed in increasing his market value. The very temerity of the commoner who dares to approach the princess may ennoble him in her eyes. But if the trader on the interpersonal marketplace overvalues himself too much, his strategy will backfire. He will set his sights too high and end up paying the costs of rejection.

Trading in Social Approval

Pigeons can be trained to peck, to prance about, and even to play ping-pong, all for the sake of obtaining food pellets. In the interpersonal marketplace people praise others, give them assistance, and cater to their whims, all—or, at least, in large measure—for the sake of social approval. We exert tremendous amounts of time and energy, often at the expense of our own material well-being, in order to receive such intangible rewards as "Thanks" or "Good job, Bob," or "I love you." In Professor Homans's terms, social approval is a "generalized reinforcer." It can be effectively used to reinforce a wide variety of human social behaviors, just as food pellets and money serve to reinforce a wide range of behaviors in their respective spheres.

The generalized importance of social approval is a lesson learned by children very early in life, when they discover that the approval of their parents is closely related to the receipt of other more tangible rewards like hugs, desserts, and presents. As we grow older, we continue to find that the approval of our peers is a virtually unerring indicator of the extent to which we can expect to receive other valued goods, such as other people's compliance to our wishes and their assistance in times of need. In addition, experiencing the approval of others is one of the prime ways in which we come to respect ourselves. Psychotherapist Carl Rogers emphasizes that the "positive regard" of others makes an important contribution to a person's mental health.[14]

You can demonstrate the use of social approval as a reinforcer the next time you are on the phone with a friend simply by saying "Mm . . hmm . ." or "Yeah . . ." or making other approving sounds every time he states an opinion.[15] Before long you will probably find him offering opinions more frequently than he was at the start of the conversation. If you ask him about it later on, he may or may not be aware of the fact that his verbal behavior was being shaped by your approval. But in either case it clearly was, much in the way that a pigeon's behavior can be shaped by the psychologist's food pellets. If you continue the experiment long enough, however, you may well find that your friend's rate of offering opinions begins to drop off again. If this happens, your friend will be behaving like the pigeon who becomes temporarily satiated and hence less strongly motivated to keep pecking. Social approval, like food, tends to have diminishing marginal utility. As Homans puts it, "The more often a man has in the recent past received a rewarding activity from another, the less valuable any further unit of that activity becomes to him."[16]

By the same logic, social approval should have its greatest impact when one is starved for it—when one has gone for a long time without receiving expressions of love or esteem, and particularly when one has recently been disapproved of. Such a principle might help to explain psychoanalyst Theodor Reik's observation that people are especially likely to fall in love soon after a rejection.[17] A dramatic experimental demonstration of this principle was provided by social psychologist Elaine Walster.[18] Walster's subjects were undergraduate women attending Stanford University and nearby Foothill Junior College. As the laboratory drama opened, the subject arrived at an empty reception room, where a sign asked her to wait for the experimenter. A few minutes later a smooth, well-dressed graduate student named Gerald Davison— now a professor of psychology at the State University of New York at Stony Brook—came on stage and explained that he was waiting for another experimenter. Davison then casually began a conversation, and the dialogue proceeded something like this:

DAVISON: It's really kind of thoughtless of them to make us wait out here so long.
SUBJECT: It certainly is.
DAVISON: I don't even know what I'm supposed to be doing here.
SUBJECT: I don't either, really.
DAVISON: You see, I just got into town last week. I graduated from Harvard last June, and now I'm starting grad school at Stanford.
SUBJECT (IMPRESSED):   Oh!
DAVISON: I don't really know anyone out here yet.
SUBJECT (HOPEFUL):   Ohhhh!
DAVISON: Say, I heard that there's a good play in San Francisco. Would you have dinner with me Saturday night, and then we could go to the show?
SUBJECT (ECSTATIC):   I'd love to!

Davison was well chosen for his matinee-idol part, for 32 of the 37 subjects accepted his invitation, casting any previous commitments to the winds. What he had done, of course, was to provide the women with a massive dose of social approval.

In the next act of the drama Dr. Walster arrived, escorted the happily deluded subject to another room, and explained that the purpose of the study was to compare various personality tests. The subject, who had previously taken the test, was now shown what purported to be an evaluation of her personality prepared by "a therapist in San Francisco." Half of the girls got the reassuring news that they possessed, among other things, "sensitivity to peers, personal integrity, originality, and freedom of outlook." The remaining girls received far less approving reports: "Although she has adopted certain superficial appearances of maturity," the "therapist" had written, "her basically insecure drives remain. . . . She shows a weak personality, antisocial motives, a lack of flexibility and originality, and a lack of capacity for successful leadership. . . ." The evaluations were, of course, fabricated. Their purpose was to vary the girls' self-esteem and, as a result, the extent to which they would be likely to value Davison's approval. And the variation had the predicted effect. When the women were subsequently asked to rate Davison, those who received the negative evaluation indicated that they liked him considerably more than did those who received the positive evaluation. In other words, the girls who had the greatest need for approval were most attracted to the person who provided it.*

If social approval has diminishing marginal utility, it also follows that we should value more highly the approval of a person who initially disliked us than that of a person who expresses approval consistently. Consider the following example, conjured up by social psychologist Elliot Aronson.[19] You are at a cocktail party and have a conversation with a person you have never met before. Later that evening, while standing behind a potted palm, you overhear him talking about you. In fact, you encounter the same person at several consecutive parties and manage to overhear his comments about you each time. There are at least four interesting possibilities:

1. He is always saying positive things about you.
2. He is always saying negative things about you.
3. At the first one or two parties he seems down on you, but at subsequent parties his comments become more and more positive.
4. At the first one or two parties he seems quite favorably impressed by you, but at subsequent parties his comments become more and more negative.

In which of these cases would you like the person the most? Aronson suggests that it would be in Case 3, in which an initially

* After the session was concluded, Dr. Walster spent close to an hour with each subject, carefully explaining the deceptions employed and the reasons for them. She reports that when the girls finally left, none of them remained disturbed by the false personality report or the broken date.

disapproving person gradually comes to be approving, rather than in Case 1, in which he is approving all the time. Similarly, Aronson proposes, you would like your evaluator the *least* in Case 4, in which his initial approval turns into disapproval. Aronson and Darwyn Linder obtained support for these predictions in a laboratory experiment in which subjects were exposed to sequences of evaluations like the ones described above.* Although it is rewarding to be approved of, constant approval gradually loses its reinforcing power. It becomes predictable, stale, even boring. Approval that follows disapproval, on the other hand, comes like food to the hungry pigeon. It satisfies a need that has been accumulating over a period of time and thus serves as a more potent social reward.

Aronson's finding has some disconcerting implications for ongoing relationships. It implies that once we have learned to expect frequent approval from another person, these rewards will become less valuable to us. When a husband compliments his wife's appearance after ten years of marriage, she may simply yawn. She already knows that her husband thinks she is attractive, so his compliment does not provide her with any particular boost in esteem. When a stranger offers her a similar compliment, however, she is extremely flattered. The compliment may in fact increase her attraction to the rewarding stranger, even though it had no effect on her liking for her doting husband. These possibilities have led some of Aronson's students to dub his principle "Aronson's Law of Marital Infidelity," and simple observation indicates that there is some truth to it. People often do get bored—in pigeon talk, "satiated"—with others who have served as consistent, long-term reinforcers, and they are often lured by the prospect of approval from new and unfamiliar sources.

Aronson's Law probably operates to some extent in most close relationships. But it is usually offset by two more powerful considerations. The first is that although a close friend or spouse cannot always provide a "boost" in approval, his disapproval is particularly potent. The hurt that we feel when a loved one expresses his disappointment in us often motivates us to reestablish the intensity of the relationship. Short absences and separations may also have such an intensifying effect. The second consideration is that, unlike food pellets or money, the value of approval depends to a large degree on whom it comes from—how close we feel to-

* It should be noted, however, that at least one recent replication of Aronson and Linder's experiment failed to obtain this pattern of results. Instead, subjects liked a consistent approver (Case 1) better than an initial disapprover (Case 3). (Jerome Tognoli and Robert Keisner, "Gain and loss of esteem as determinants of interpersonal attraction: A replication and extension," *Journal of Personality and Social Psychology,* 1972, *23*, 201-204.)

that, unlike food pellets or money, the value of approval depends to a large degree on whom it comes from—how close we feel toward him, how much we trust him, the degree to which our lives are intertwined. Once an intimate relationship has been established, even frequent, constant, *repetitious* approval remains an amazingly potent reinforcer. In at least this respect the approval of someone who is close to us—a commodity that we often call "love" —can be clearly distinguished from bird seed.

In less intimate relationships, however, we may often do better on the interpersonal marketplace by dispensing our approval sparingly. A man can be consistently loving and approving to his wife with impunity, but if he dispenses his compliments too freely to his boss he will be seen as ungenuine and ingratiating. Even when he is thoroughly sincere in his praise, it will be discounted as undiscriminating. The dilemma of when to express approval and when to hoard it for future use is particularly acute during courtship. A person who feels that he is falling in love is typically eager to express his deepening affection. Yet, if he is to maintain the interest and esteem of his partner, he must hold back. Peter Blau has gone as far as to suggest, "A woman who readily gives proof of her affection to a man . . . provides presumptive evidence of her lack of popularity and thus tends to depreciate the value of her affection for him."[20] (Although Blau has a way of adopting the male perspective in his writing, the same is equally true for a man's demonstration of affection to a woman.)

To the extent that Blau's analysis is applicable, prospective lovers may sometimes find themselves in the position of trying as best they can to conceal the extent of their affection. Sooner or later, of course, the prospective lover will have to express the affection that he has been saving up or he will never be able to take advantage of its accumulated value. People do crave approval, and they will return it either in kind or with other material or social commodities. And if they do not get enough of it, they will break off the exchange and seek greener pastures. Like pigeons in studies of "extinction," they will stop pecking. The trader in approval, like the trader in stocks and bonds, must learn the art of good timing. He must learn just when to invest his social resources in order to maximize the returns they will bring.

How To Be a "Rewarding" Person

Almost anyone is capable of dispensing social rewards, but some of us seem to be more capable of it than others. Even when the time and effort invested is identical, the interest, approval, and assistance of some people is worth more than that of others. Of the first sort of person we are likely to say, "I found him to be very rewarding," or, "I got a great deal out of him." Of the second sort we are more likely to say, "He's not too valuable a friend," or, "He doesn't have much to offer." In most of the examples that we have employed in this chapter we have been presuming that there is a single scale of social desirability that people agree on. One is potentially rewarding to the extent that he or she is good-looking or wealthy, intellectually gifted or socially pedigreed. It cannot be denied that such hierarchies of social desirability exist in many spheres of society. Willard Waller studied the "rating and dating" system of a midwestern state university in the 1930s, and concluded that one's standing in the social hierarchy was determined by a handful of generally agreed-upon criteria:

> Young men are desirable dates according to their rating on the scale of campus values. In order to have Class A rating they must belong to one of the better fraternities, be prominent in activities (of which some carry vastly more prestige than others), have a copious supply of spending money, be well-dressed, "smooth" in manners and appearance, have a good line, dance well, and have access to an automobile. . . . The factors which appear to be important for girls are good clothes, a smooth line, the ability to dance well, and popularity as a date. . . . And, above all, the coed who wishes to retain Class A standing must consistently date Class A men.[21]

Many of these criteria would be more or less irrelevant on today's campuses, where fraternities and sororities are dead or decaying, "good clothes" have become square, and "smooth manners" have been supplanted by the value placed on open communication. But whereas the criteria for prestige may differ from one time and place to another, each time and place nevertheless has its social hierarchy. Whether it is on the basis of dancing well or being well-informed, having access to a car or coming from a "good family," some people in any social grouping will rate higher than others.

When it comes to assessing someone's potential "rewardingness" as a potential friend, lover, or spouse, however, the general prestige hierarchies that we have been discussing do not tell the whole story. For although it is true that within a given society or subculture some people tend to be more generally admired than others, it is equally true that within any social circle each individual finds somewhat different things to be rewarding. When people within a given culture are asked to rate the physical attractiveness of others, for example, their judgments never agree completely.* More importantly, individuals within any social circle invariably differ about the relative value of specific combinations of looks, skills, attitudes, personality traits, and other qualities in their personal hierarchies of rewards. In many instances we are most rewarded by people who resemble ourselves, especially in their basic attitudes and values. In other cases we are most rewarded by people who differ from us in complementary ways. An assertive person, for example, may receive his most valuable social rewards from a submissive, unquestioning partner. A masochist will get his biggest kicks from whomever can hurt him the most. Thus, one's value on the interpersonal marketplace cannot be fixed solely in terms of general social standards. It can be ascertained only when we know the individual preferences and needs of the prospective buyer.

The qualities that any given person finds to be rewarding in another also depend to a large degree on the sort of relationship in question and the stage of development it has reached. What makes someone a rewarding friend or business associate will not necessarily have great value on the market for dates and spouses. And as a relationship progresses from initial acquaintance to casual interaction to a deeper level of intimacy, the qualities that each of the partners finds most rewarding in the other are likely to change. Social psychologist George Levinger asked college students to indicate the relative importance of each of thirty-three characteristics of another hypothetical individual in affecting one's feelings toward that person.[22] The characteristics listed ranged widely, from "height" to "how loving" or "how dominant" the other person is.

* Systematic research is just beginning to identify the personality traits which underlie such differences in people's physical preferences. Some interesting but highly tentative findings come from a study of college men's preferences for female body types conducted at the University of Illinois. The subjects were shown silhouettes of women's bodies in which the size of the breasts, buttocks, and legs were systematically varied. Each of fifteen silhouettes was paired with each of the others, and in each case the subjects indicated their preference on a scale ranging from "Strongly Prefer A" to "Strongly Prefer B." There was a tendency for men who preferred a large female figure to be high on a measure of achievement needs and also to be drinkers. Those who preferred small figures tended to persevere in their work and to be of upper-class background. And men who preferred the figures with the largest busts were likely to be readers of *Playboy* magazine. (Jerry S. Wiggins, Nancy Wiggins, and Judith Conger, "Correlates of heterosexual somatic preference," *Journal of Personality and Social Psychology*, 1968, *10*, 82–90.)

These characteristics were rated for both same-sex and opposite-sex others, and for six different levels of interpersonal involvement, ranging from mere awareness of the other to a level where an already established relationship is to be maintained. Not surprisingly, the subjects rated easily visible characteristics, such as the other person's height or physical attractiveness, as more important at a first contact than after the development of a closer relationship. Conversely, the other person's "deeper" characteristics, such as his considerateness or his need to give or receive love were rated as unimportant for one's early impressions, but very important at later stages.

As Blau has noted, there is also a sense in which human commodities are more like artistic creations than like economic goods. Economic goods like diamonds or potatoes are judged to be more or less valuable in terms of established standards of beauty or quality, but artistic creations involve the establishment of new standards. Great paintings or symphonies create values that previously did not exist at all. Similarly, each individual has qualities that cannot be assessed with reference to existing criteria. Blau writes, "The woman who can convince men that her distinctive style makes being in her company a more desirable experience than being with other women has made herself attractive by the creative act of investing her style with value."[23] It should be clear, then, that one's value on the interpersonal marketplace is never frozen. Like stocks and bonds, the value of personal commodities is constantly fluctuating in response to changing market conditions.

Beyond Exchange

The notions that people are "commodities" and social relationships are "transactions" will surely make many readers squirm. Exchange theory postulates that human relationships are based first and foremost on self-interest. As such, it often seems to portray friendship as motivated only by what one person can get from another and to redefine love as a devious power game. Such characterizations contrast sharply with what many of us would like to think of friendship and love, that they are intimate relationships characterized at least as much by the joy of giving as by the desire to receive. But although we might prefer to believe otherwise, we must face up to the fact that our attitudes toward other people *are* determined to a large extent by our assessments of the rewards they hold for us.

It is difficult to imagine that there has ever been a human society in which some generally agreed upon standards of a person's worth and desirability did not exist. And as long as there are such standards, our interpersonal preferences and relationships will share some of the features of the marketplace. We will typically want to associate with those people who are "valuable" and to shun those who are not. As a result, people's relative value on the marketplace will often structure their relationships, with the more desirable member of a pair also being the one who exerts the greater power. Much of the time these effects will take place more or less automatically, like the operation of the economic laws of supply and demand. In at least some cases, however, conscious tactical considerations play a demonstrable role on the interpersonal marketplace, just as they do in the financial world. It is ultimately more valuable, in my view, for us to recognize these marketplace features of liking and loving—to "raise our consciousness" of them—than to blind ourselves to them wishfully. Understanding the interpersonal marketplace as it operates would seem to be particularly useful for those who would like to see some of its procedures changed.

Having said all this about the value of exchange theory, however, it is time to consider its limitations. For the fact is that, even when presented in its most enlightened form, a theory that presumes an overriding human desire to maximize one's own—and only one's own—profits inevitably falls short of providing a complete understanding of human relationships. Contrary to the guiding assumption of the exchange perspective, human beings are sometimes altruistic in the fullest sense of the word.[24] They make sacrifices for the sake of others without any consideration of the rewards they will obtain from them in return. Such selfless concern for the welfare of others may emerge even in interactions among strangers, but it emerges most often and most clearly in close interpersonal relationships.

The skeptic will correctly observe that many behaviors that pass as "altruistic" are in fact motivated by basically self-serving inclinations. For example, the wealthy businessman will make a large contribution to a university so as to receive the benefits of social approval and prestige for his generosity. The adulation and publicity that may accrue from having one's name emblazoned on "Moneymaker Hall" suggests that such a contribution will not necessarily be a wholly altruistic one. The man who spends the day painting his girlfriend's apartment or the woman who volunteers to wash her boyfriend's clothes may not be totally altruistic either. In each case, they may be investing their time and energy largely because of the prospect of the reciprocal rewards they will bring. Such transactions are facilitated by what sociologist Alvin Gouldner calls the "norm of reciprocity," the unspoken but implicit agreement between people that one good turn will sooner or later be repaid with another.

But not all acts of service or helpfulness can be so glibly explained away as self-serving. There are many recorded instances— and countless other unrecorded ones—of people making great sacrifices for the sake of other people's welfare. During the Nazi era, many Christians risked their lives by concealing Jews in their homes and helping them to flee from Nazi-occupied territory. In the American civil rights movement, thousands of people, both black and white, devoted tremendous amounts of time and energy —and in several cases gave their lives—in order to fight conditions of injustice. In the daily newspaper we read of people who rush into blazing buildings or plunge into freezing rivers to save the lives of others. On a less dramatic level, many of us contribute large amounts of money, often anonymously, to alleviate the plight of the poor and hungry. We donate our blood for the benefit of others whom we don't even know. Laboratory experiments have demonstrated that people will willingly exert considerable time and effort to help partners who will never even know the identity of their benefactor.

In these cases it is difficult to argue that we come to the aid of others for the sake of prestige, publicity, or the desire to get something in return from the person we help. There are still *rewards* involved in such acts of altruism, but they are not the sorts of rewards that play a role on the interpersonal marketplace. Rather, they are the internal rewards that we experience when we can do something to improve the plight of another person. Two concepts that help to explain the operation of such self-mediated rewards are those of *empathy* and of *responsibility*.

Empathy refers to one person's vicarious experience of another person's presumed emotional state. In a recent doctoral dissertation at Harvard, Dennis Krebs found that subjects who watched another person being alternately rewarded (with money) and punished (with electric shocks) showed significant changes in their own heart rate and skin conductance.[25] These physiological changes were greatest when the other person was described as being similar to the subject himself. Apparently the perception of similarity heightened the subjects' sensitivity to the reactions of the other person, perhaps by making it easier for them to imagine that they were in the other person's position. As two people come to know one another and to play increasingly important roles in one another's lives, their capacity to experience one another's feelings is also likely to increase. As Spinoza wrote in the seventeenth century, "He who conceives that the object of his love has been affected pleasurably or painfully will himself be affected pleasurably or painfully."[26] Whereas at an earlier stage of their relationship the two people may have been motivated to help one another only by virtue of what they expected to get from the other in return, they will now help one another because they get pleasure from the very act of doing so.

People may also feel a basic moral duty to help those who are in need of help. There is some disagreement about how such a sense of responsibility develops, with popular explanations ranging from Freud's concept of the superego to Lawrence Kohlberg's more recent theory of the stages of moral development. Regardless of how the sense of responsibility develops, its presence explains acts of heroism that would otherwise be entirely inexplicable. When we help someone who is in need, we experience the internal rewards of knowing we have done "the right thing"—the rewards of good conscience. When we fail to take such action, we may feel the pangs of guilt. And, as in the case of empathy, our sense of responsibility is likely to be strongest for relatives, friends, and others with whom we have established close relationships.

Closely related to both empathy and responsibility is the phenomenon of people in close relationships beginning to define themselves not only as individuals, but also as members of the couple. By helping one's partner, one is helping the *partnership* and thus helping oneself as well. Here again there is a reward involved, but it is not a reward to be gained at someone else's expense. It is, rather, a reward gained by and for the collective unit. "Perhaps the simplest way of describing this wholeness is by saying it is a 'we,' " sociologist Charles Horton Cooley wrote over sixty years ago. "It involves the sort of sympathy and mutual identification for which 'we' is the natural expression."[27]

Elizabeth Douvan characterizes the sort of relationship that goes beyond exchange as "integrative" or "heroic." In such relationships, she maintains, there is no simple way to assess and equate the rewards obtained by each of the two parties:

> Examples here include the mother–infant relationship, kinship relationships, relationships between close friends, good neighbors, and the relationship of man to God. . . . In these relationships the rewards are enormous for each partner, but they are not comparable.

They cannot be reduced to a single dimension and reasonably compared. In the heroic relationship apprehension of the joys and comforts of the other person requires empathy, an imaginative leap into the reality of the partner. The parent of a tiny child benefits enormously from the love and growth of that child, but there is no way to reduce the joys of parenthood to a scale that allows comparison with the joys of a nurtured, comfortable, normal infancy. Nor does anyone try to do so. The mother does not say to the infant, "I give you fifteen units of maternal care so that you will return to me fifteen units of filial devotion, smiles, coos, contented gurgles." The birth and growth of a human infant . . . is a joy in itself aside from any comparison or measurement against other values. It is a positive good in and of itself.[28]

We need to know much more than we currently do about the psychological processes that make such a "heroic" relationship possible. In very recent years an upsurge of research on empathy and altruism has begun to address this question. But we already know enough to be able to say with assurance that such relationships do occur and, as such, stretch the limits of any approach to liking and loving that is based solely on self-interest and exchange.

What are we to make of the interpersonal marketplace? Is it cold, calculating, and impersonal, as some critics of exchange theory (or "economic pigeon theory," as one critic put it) often make it out to be? The answer is that it sometimes is, but that it need not be. Whether the interpersonal marketplace is to be warm or cold, mercenary or spiritual, depends in large measure on the nature of the commodities that the traders find to be valuable. As long as people are trading in relatively superficial commodities, the interpersonal marketplace will remain a relatively superficial place. In certain sectors of society and in certain sorts of relationships, this may be precisely the present state of affairs. But the recognition that people enter into mutually rewarding relationships is by no means a negative commentary on human social life. The suggestion that the behavior of men and of pigeons follows many of the same principles—that we too exchange "pecks" for "pellets"—does not reduce men to pigeons. It all depends on what kinds of pellets we are pecking for.

The principles of the interpersonal marketplace are most likely to prevail in encounters between strangers and casual acquaintances, and in the early stages of the development of relationships. As an interpersonal bond becomes more firmly established, however, it begins to go beyond exchange. In close relationships one becomes decreasingly concerned with what he can get *from* the other person and increasingly concerned with what he can do *for* the other. But even in the closest of relationships, the principles of the interpersonal marketplace are never entirely repealed. As we shall see later, even in the case of love the dual themes of what we can get and what we can give remain closely intertwined.

Chapter 5
THE RISE AND FALL
OF FIRST IMPRESSIONS
How People Are Perceived

Master, shall I begin with the usual jokes
That the audience always laugh at?
—ARISTOPHANES, *Frogs*

The acknowledged superstar of the 1971 baseball season was a twenty-one-year-old Oakland Athletics pitcher named Vida Blue. Signed for his first full major league season for the comparatively paltry salary of $14,750, Blue proceeded to leap to the heights, winning the starting assignment in the All-Star Game, the American League's Most Valuable Player Award, and the Cy Young Award for the best pitcher in the league. After a prolonged holdout he finally signed for the 1972 season for a reported salary of some $60,000, representing an annual raise of about 300 percent. Some writers were calling him the greatest lefthanded pitcher who ever lived—better than Grove, better even than Koufax.

There is no doubt that Blue had a superb 1971 season, finishing the year with a won–lost record of 24–8 and leading the league with an earned-run average of 1.82. But his meteoric rise to fame seemed to be based not only on what he did, but also on *the order in which he did it*. Beginning the season in relative obscurity, Blue proceeded to win ten of his first eleven decisions, four of them with shutouts. By late May he was leading the league in earned-run average (1.01), strikeouts (78), shutouts (4), and complete games (8). He continued on the same course through June, July, and early August, accumulating an amazing won–lost record of 22–4. His chances to become a thirty-game winner looked excellent. In late August and September, however, Blue's fortunes took a downward turn. After winning his first three games in August, he proceeded to lose four of his last five decisions. During the stretch between August 15 and September 26, three days before the end of the season, he managed to win only a single game. Whereas he had led the league in four major categories in late May, he ended the season on top in only one, earned-run average—and even this index had worsened over the course of the season.[1] (In 1972 Blue's performance continued to decline. Although the Athletics won the American League pennant and World Series, Blue's record was a disappointing 6–10, and he did not pitch well in the series.

There are many possible explanations for Blue's decline toward the end of the 1971 season, including the facts that his teammates were not getting as many runs for him and that he was pulled out of several games that he might have won. But without denying Blue's legitimate right to the acclaim he received, one might well speculate that it would not have been quite so great if his season had progressed in the reverse order, starting with a mediocre record of 5–4 after the first two months and only gradually building up to his final 24–8. Blue's tremendous acclaim at the end of the 1971 season illustrates what social psychologists call a "primacy effect" in person perception. The general principle is that first impressions establish the mental framework in which a person is viewed, and later evidence is either ignored or reinterpreted to jibe with this framework.

But whereas first impressions are often extremely powerful, they do not always determine our ultimate opinions of people. In the fall of 1971 a college quarterback named Gary Wichard was widely reported to be near the top of the draft lists of several professional football teams. Although Wichard played for a small college, C. W. Post, he had performed outstandingly through most of his college career. A month before the professional draft, however, Wichard played in the Senior Bowl game and performed poorly. As a result, he was not selected until the sixteenth round of the pro draft, by the Baltimore Colts. George Young, the Colts' personnel director, explained the management's reasoning: "One of our maladies is that we tend to overlook consistency and Gary had that. Like any other business, it's a matter of what you have done lately."[2] The case of Gary Wichard illustrates what social psychologists call a "recency effect," in which later information outweighs or replaces a previously formed impression.

Primacy and recency effects are of importance not only to the baseball or football scout, but also to the student and practitioner of liking and loving. As sociologists George J. McCall and J. R. Simmons observe, "we interact, not with individuals and objects, but with *our images* of them."[3] These images go beyond our perception of the other person's physical characteristics or overt actions to our inferences about his underlying personality traits and abilities. These inferences are never perfectly objective or reliable, but they are necessary to allow us to predict the other person's future behavior and to develop our own strategy of relating to him. In this chapter we will survey research on the ways in which people perceive other people. A central focus will be the attempt to distinguish between the cases of Vida Blue and of Gary Wichard—that is, to specify the factors that lead to the perpetuation of first impressions and those that lead to their downfall.

Reputations and Stereotypes

We often begin to form our impression of another person even before we meet him. Before going out on a blind date, people are briefed about the date's characteristics by their fixer-uppers. Before attending the first lecture of a course, students learn something about the professor from students who took the course the previous year. Professors similarly obtain advance information about their students. In each case the other person's reputation, regardless of whether or not it is in fact justified, is likely to shape the way the person is perceived when he is later encountered. In most cases, the direction of this impact is that of the primacy effect—that is, we are primed to see a person as living up to his reputation.

In a pioneering experiment conducted in the late 1940s, social psychologist Harold Kelley[4] arranged to have students in a social science course at M.I.T. told that their class would be taken over for the day by a new instructor, whom they would be asked to evaluate at the end of the class period. Before the instructor was introduced, the students were given a biographical note about him to read. Unbeknownst to the students, two versions of the sketch were employed. The sketch that was distributed to half of the students read as follows:

> Mr. _____ is a graduate student in the Department of Economics and Social Science here at M.I.T. He has had three semesters of teaching experience in psychology at another college. This is his

first semester teaching Economics 70. He is 26 years old, a veteran, and married. People who know him consider him to be a rather warm person, industrious, critical, practical, and determined.

The other half of the students read the following description:

Mr. _____ is a graduate student in the Department of Economics and Social Science here at M.I.T. He has had three semesters of teaching experience in psychology at another college. This is his first semester teaching Economics 70. He is 26 years old, a veteran, and married. People who know him consider him to be a rather cold person, industrious, critical, practical, and determined.

The two descriptions differ in but a single word: In the first sketch the instructor is described as "warm" and in the second as "cold." After the students had read the sketch, the instructor appeared and led the class in a twenty-minute discussion. During the discussion an observer recorded how often each student made a comment or asked a question. After the instructor had left the room, the students were asked to rate him on a set of adjective scales and to write a brief description of him. The results were striking. Although all of the students had been exposed to the same person at the same time, those who had been told that he was reputed to be "warm" rated him as substantially more considerate, informal, sociable, popular, good-natured, humorous, and humane than those who had been forewarned that he was "cold." Identical behaviors of the instructor were apparently interpreted quite differently by the students in the two conditions. Kelley noted, for example, that "several 'cold' observers describe him as being '. . . intolerant: would be angry if you disagree with his views . . .'; while several 'warm' observers put the same thing this way: 'Unyielding in principle, not easily influenced or swayed from his initial attitude.' "

The instructor's reputation also influenced the students' willingness to interact with him: 56 percent of the "warm" subjects entered the class discussion, while only 32 percent of the "cold" subjects did so. As this result suggests, once a negative first impression of another person is formed, we may avoid further contact with him. Such avoidance, in turn, is likely to foreclose our opportunity to revise or correct the impression. Theodore Newcomb has labeled this unfortunate phenomenon "autistic hostility," and suggests that it applies to relationships between groups as well as between individuals.[5]

There are many analogous examples of the impact of a person's reputation upon our impression of him. If a girl is told in advance that her blind date is extremely witty, she will be primed to categorize his remarks as witty ones. If the same date were billed as solemn and humorless, the same "witty" remarks might well fall flat. This is the secret of many comedians. Since they have the reputation of being uproariously funny, people are predisposed to laugh at practically everything they say. Similarly, in the first game of the recent world chess championship, an overeager Bobby Fischer made a "beginner's blunder," seizing a pawn in a way that trapped his own bishop behind enemy lines. But for some time afterward the commentators, awed by Fischer's reputation, insisted that the move was part of a winning combination that was simply too deep for anyone else to fathom. (Unfortunately for Bobby, then-champion Boris Spassky did not make this interpretation. After an initial double-take, he coolly proceeded to capture the bishop and win the game.) "In social perception," Fritz Heider writes, "the act is in many cases assimilated to the origin. Acts or products are colored by the qualities of the person to whom they are ascribed."[6]

The impact of a person's reputation on the way we view him is mirrored in the way we view entire groups of people. Black people are often expected to be musical, Italians to be emotional, football players to be unintelligent. In some cases these group expectations, known as *stereotypes*, have a factual basis, in the sense that on the average members of the group conform to the expectation to some degree. In other cases they have no factual basis whatsoever. In any event, when it comes to forming impressions of an individual member of the group, the expectations produced by knowledge of his group membership are all too frequently dead wrong. Nevertheless the expectations persist, with powerful effects upon our evaluations of individuals. Ex-pitcher Jim Bouton made this observation in his diary of a major league season:

> I'm not sure I'm going to like Don Mincher. It's prejudice, I know, but everytime I hear a Southern accent I think: Stupid. A picture of George Wallace pops into my mind. It's like Lenny Bruce saying he could never associate a nuclear scientist with a Southern accent.[7]

In addition to their membership in religious, ethnic, occupational, or regional groups, people may be stereotyped on the basis of their physical appearance. In his *Eminent Victorians*, Lytton Strachey described Dr. Thomas Arnold in the following terms:

> Such was the man who, at age 33, bcame headmaster of Rugby. His outward appearance was the index of his inward character: everything about him denoted energy, earnestness, and the best intentions. His legs, perhaps, were shorter than they should have been; but the sturdy athletic frame, especially when it was swathed (as it usually was) in the flowing robes of a Doctor of Divinity, was full of an imposing vigor; and his head, set decisively upon the collar, stock, and bands of ecclesiastical tradition, clearly belonged to a person of eminence. The thick, dark clusters of his hair, his bushy eyebrows and curling lower lip—all these revealed a temperament of ardour and determination. His eyes were bright and large; they were also obviously honest. . . .

As social psychologists Albert Hastorf, David Schneider, and Judith Polefka note, "Many of the characteristics noted are the results of inferences by the author, yet they are cast as if they were just as clear and as given in experience as the individual's physical height."[8] Vigor is inferred from a sturdy frame, determination from a firm lip, honesty from bright eyes. Jim Bouton makes the same sort of inferential leap: "Before the first workout, Joe Schultz, the manager (he's out of the old school, I think, because he *looks* like he's out of the old school, short, portly, bald, ruddy-faced, twinkly-eyed), stopped by while I was having a catch."[9]

As in the case of other stereotypes, the assumed links between appearance and personality may be wholly idiosyncratic, as when a person encounters someone who looks like an old friend and assumes that the physical resemblance extends to his temperament as well. In other cases the links have achieved a large degree of cultural acceptance. Fat people are often assumed to be jolly, men with moustaches to be villainous, women with bowed lips to be seductive. Sometimes the stereotypes can be traced to metaphorical or functional assumptions. People with thin lips ("tight-lipped") may be typecast as reticent, people with "coarse" skin as insensitive, and people with high foreheads (and therefore presumably more brain room) as intelligent.[10] I have a rather low forehead myself and look forward to growing bald as a means of gaining an aura of intellect.

In its most general form the stereotyping process refers to our pervasive tendency to fill out our impressions of other people on the basis of assumptions about which characteristics tend to co-occur.

When some people are told that someone is unsuccessful, for example, they may assume that he is unintelligent as well, even though they have no direct evidence for the assumption. A woman may be attracted to tall men not because she values tallness itself, but because she has somewhere along the line acquired the notion that tall men are more likely to be successful. Psychologists call a person's set of assumptions about which characteristics of others are likely to co-occur his "implicit personality theory." Each of us has such a theory, even though we may be unable to spell it out explicitly. As a result, each of us, whether consciously or not, engages in stereotyping to a greater or lesser degree. We go beyond the information directly known about another person to a mental construction of what he must be like.

Social psychologists Seymour Rosenberg and Russell Jones recently made use of a computational technique called multidimensional scaling to explore in detail one man's implicit personality theory. The person they chose was the American novelist Theodore Dreiser.[11] They began by carefully recording each description of a physical, social, or psychological trait applied by Dreiser to each of 241 different characters in his collection of sketches, A *Gallery of Women*. They proceeded to construct an elaborate map of the dimensions underlying Dreiser's descriptions, based on an analysis of which combinations of traits tended to be applied to the same characters. One of the most central dimensions that emerged from their mapping was that of "male–female." In other words, one would know a good deal about all other aspects of a Dreiserian character's personal traits if one knew only the character's sex. Female characters were likely to be described as attractive, charming, defiant, intelligent, cold, and clever. These characteristics may reflect Dreiser's own predilection "attractive, unconventional women" and his reliance on female literary agents. On the other hand, the mapping revealed that Dreiser reserved for men the traits of sincerity, genius, and greatness, perhaps revealing something of the novelist's conception of himself.

Rosenberg and Jones also discovered a notable absence of a basic split between the positive and negative aspects of people in Dreiser's descriptions. "Good" and "bad" traits were as likely as not to co-occur in the same characters. This conclusion jibes with Granville Hicks's observation that "there are no contemptible persons in Dreiser's novels. Although at times he professed a Nietzschean scorn of the masses . . . he instinctively made the best case possible for any person he wrote about."[12] Former Green

Bay Packer guard Jerry Kramer illustrated a similar transcendence of the good–bad polarity when he described his coach, the late Vince Lombardi, as "a cruel, kind, tough, gentle, miserable, wonderful man whom I often hate and often love and always respect."[13]

Kramer's description is probably a good deal more accurate than any description that stressed only Lombardi's toughness or only his compassion. Nevertheless, it violates a basic organizing principle inherent in most people's implicit personality theories. The principle is that the "social personalities" of other people, as created by our thoughts about them, should be tied up in neat, uncontradictory packages. It is summed up in Heider's influential theory of cognitive balance:

> We want to attain orderly and stable evaluations; we want to find the good and the bad distributed in a simple and consistent fashion. The codification in terms of positive and negative value is simpler when the positive features are grouped into one unit and the negative ones in another unit. For instance, there is a tendency to see only the positive traits in a person we like. . . . If we hear that a person we like has done something we dislike, we are confronted with a disharmonious situation, and there will arise a tendency to change it to a more balanced situation; for example, we can refuse to believe that the person performed this negative action.[14]

Several studies have documented Heider's proposition that we tend to see the people we like as having almost exclusively positive traits and those whom we dislike as having almost exclusively negative traits. For example, college students in Kentucky and California were recently asked to describe "liked" and "disliked" persons with whom they were well acquainted by choosing words from a list of two hundred adjectives.[15] There proved to be quite general agreement among the students that liked people were energetic, considerate, happy, intelligent, and truthful, whereas disliked people were complaining, insincere, narrow-minded, quarrelsome, and self-centered. Thus we may view liking and disliking as themselves giving rise to stereotypical images of others, sometimes known as positive and negative "halo effects." There is, to be sure, a chicken-and-egg problem here. Do we consider another person to be energetic, considerate, and intelligent because we like him, or do we like him because we value his qualities of energy, consideration, and intelligence? The evidence suggests that in fact the causal link goes in *both* directions: from liking to favorable evaluation, and from favorable evaluation to liking.

*"It's like everything else; there are good
Samaritans and there are bad Samaritans."*

Seeing What You're Looking for

The decision as to which pigeonhole to put a person in depends
not only on expectations based on his reputation or group membership, but also upon the perceiver's own needs and values.
Studies of the perception of physical objects have proven that perception is an active, constructive process, rather than a passive
one in which external stimuli automatically impinge themselves
upon our consciousness. This process is powerfully affected by our
physical and psychological needs. Men who have not eaten for
long periods of time, for example, display the "mirage effect" of
seeing hazy objects as food or eating utensils. Poor children—for

whom we may suppose that the value of money is greater—reportedly see coins as being larger than rich children do. As explained by psychologist Jerome Bruner, our needs and values have the effect of making certain of our mental pigeonholes more available for use than others.[16]

The tendency to see what you are looking for, sometimes called "perceptual accentuation," becomes even more striking when it comes to forming impressions of other people. The link between value and perceived size documented in the coin-size study also applies to the perceived size of other people. Two-thirds of a sample of Californians who planned to vote for John F. Kennedy in 1960 perceived him as being *taller* than Richard M. Nixon, while more than half of those planning to vote for Nixon perceived Nixon as being at least as tall.[17] A man's height indeed seems to be associated with his ascribed value in our society, a phenomenon which one sociologist has recently denounced as "heightism."[18] (The association between women's heights and their value is less clear. One study found that there was a significant correlation between students' expressed liking for President Johnson and their estimates of his height, but that no such link between height estimates and liking existed for Lady Bird.)[19]

A recent experiment conducted by social psychologists Walter Stephan, Ellen Berscheid, and Elaine Walster probed the impact of sexual arousal on perceptual accentuation.[20] The subjects, male undergraduates at the University of Minnesota, thought they were taking part in two unrelated experiments. In the "first experiment," half of the subjects read a description of a highly arousing seduction scene. The other subjects read a highly nonarousing description of the sex life of herring gulls. In the "second experiment," each of the young men was asked for his impressions of an attractive coed on the basis of her photograph and a rather uninformative self-description that she had purportedly provided on a questionnaire. As Stephan and his colleagues had predicted, the sexually aroused subjects rated the girl as being significantly more attractive than unaroused subjects did. The men indeed "saw" what they wanted to see.

The Minnesota researchers also varied whether or not the subject anticipated that he would actually meet the girl he rated, as part of a research program on dating. Half of the men in each of the arousal conditions were told that the girl they were to rate was their randomly assigned blind date, while half were told that they had been assigned to a date with someone else. The coed was perceived as most sexually receptive—the specific traits rated included "amorous," "willing," and "non-inhibited"—by men who were sexually aroused and also expected to have a date with her. Thus the men's impressions were influenced not only by their sexual needs, but also by their expectations as to whether the coed might be able to satisfy them.

Our needs and values seem to have two interrelated effects on person perception. First, one focuses attention on those aspects of the other person that are relevant to what one is looking for and consequently ignores other less relevant characteristics. Football scouts sort prospects in terms of size and speed and ignore most of their other human characteristics. Cabdrivers notice little about a fare other than cues related to the amount of his probable tip. "A young man may think of females almost exclusively as objects possessing some degree of the multidimensional attribute 'desirability,' " McCall and Simmons write. "He is surprised to learn that they must also budget their money, defecate, and have dental checkups, as he himself does."[21] Second, one tends to magnify or accentuate those characteristics of the other person that are relevant to one's needs. Just as hungry people may perceive food as tastier, sexually aroused people may perceive available sexual partners as sexier. An especially striking instance of perceptual accentuation goes by the name of "idealization," and is associated with the state of being in love. The process has not been well researched by social scientists, but it was described by Stendhal a century and a half ago:

> Why is one so carried away by each fresh beauty that one discovers in the person one loves?
> The reason is that each fresh beauty gives you the full satisfaction of a desire. If you want her to be sentimental, she is sentimental; later you want her to be proud like Corneille's Emilie, and although these qualities are probably incompatible, she immediately seems to acquire the Roman spirit.[22]

It may be speculated that in love, especially in its early stages, we tend to see what we are looking for to the fullest degree.*

The perceptual tendencies that we have examined so far often lead to perceptual distortions. By placing people in pigeonholes, we obscure the fact that people's personalities typically do *not* form neat, consistent packages. All of us in fact share with

---

* "To be in love," H. L. Mencken wrote, "is merely to be in a state of perceptual anaesthesia—to mistake an ordinary young man for a Greek god or an ordinary young woman for a goddess."

Vince Lombardi the human characteristic of inconsistency: We are good in some respects, bad in others, and vastly changeable in many. Nevertheless, as Heider suggests, we are strongly motivated to form consistent, stable impressions of others. When we categorize people on the basis of reputations and stereotypes, we sacrifice some degree of accuracy for the sake of efficient information storage and retrieval. "Too often it happens," a cab-driving sociologist admitted, "that a fare tabbed as a Sport (big tipper) turns out to be a Stiff (non-tipper), that a Blowhard matches his words with a generous tip, or that a Lady Shopper will given fifteen or even twenty cents."[23] Nevertheless, the imperfect predictive system provided by our stereotypes is in many instances preferable to no predictive system at all. As McCall and Simmons suggest, "We must . . . inquire into the *quality*, not the existence, of stereotyping."[24]

The process of perceptual accentuation may also have its uses. It may in fact be profitable for a hungry man to perceive food as more appetizing than it "really" is, or for a sexually aroused person to overestimate the receptiveness of a prospective partner. These distortions may help the aroused person to marshal his best efforts in pursuit of his goal. In other cases, however, we are motivated to see not what we most desire but what we are most afraid of. The paranoid makes "sense" out of his environment by viewing friendly people as hostile and taking smiles for scowls. The anti-Semite is especially likely to perceive other people as being Jewish, even when they are not. As Gordon Allport has suggested, "It is important to the prejudiced person to learn the cues whereby he may identify the enemy."[25] We may also see the opposite of what we are looking for as a hedge against our failure to obtain it. Thus I would predict that especially timid or insecure men would be likely to *underestimate* the sexual receptiveness of their assigned dates in the Minnesota study, as a means of shielding themselves against possible rejection.

From Acts to Dispositions

In forming impressions of people, we are commonly called upon to make inferences about people's underlying abilities and dispositions on the basis of their overt actions. But the degree to which such inferences can safely be made depends on the context in which the action takes place. Imagine that you are observing another person pacing back and forth. He takes ten steps in one direction, pauses momentarily, turns around, takes ten steps in the other direction, and continues the process uninterruptedly for over an hour. If you observed the person behaving this way in his home or office you might well conclude that he is an extremely nervous sort of fellow, perhaps with a host of personal problems to boot. Having inferred this much about his underlying disposition, you would not be too surprised to find him shaking slightly the next time you were to see him, and you would be inclined to approach him, if at all, with some trepidation. But if you observed the pacing man in a different situation—the waiting room of a hospital maternity ward, for example —he would no longer seem to be a basically nervous person. It would be apparent only that his wife was having a baby, probably her first, and that he was behaving as any prospective father would under such circumstances. And if you observed the same pacing man in a guard's uniform outside of Windsor Castle, his pacing would convey even less information about him. In such a case you would know what he does for a living, but would be able to make no inferences at all about his personality.

Making inferences from acts to dispositions involves processes of *attribution*.[26] Specifically, the perceiver must decide to what extent the action is caused by qualities of the actor himself and to what extent it is caused by the role or situation in which the actor finds himself. A basic attributional principle which is illustrated by the case of the pacing man is that the less socially desirable or "appropriate" a person's actions, the more informative they are about his enduring personal dispositions. "Deviations—almost any deviation—from the rules of propriety," sociologist Gerald Suttles observes, "leave us with the impression that someone has behaved out of choice. Such actions are almost invariably attributed to something basic and essential to the individual; a sort of unalterable and irrepressible force."[27] When a person behaves in ways that are fully appropriate to the situation he is in, on the other hand, the perceiver is more likely to see his actions as constrained by his circumstances rather than as revealing his distinctive personal qualities.

An experiment conducted by social psychologist Edward Jones and his colleagues demonstrated the operation of the principle of appropriateness.[28] Subjects listened to a taped interview between a psychologist and a student applying for a job. On two versions of the tape the applicant presented himself to the interviewer as the sort of person who would be personally well suited to the listed job requirements. On two other versions he presented himself as having a rather different sort of temperament from that called for by the job. The subjects perceived the applicant who behaved

"appropriately" in neutral and uncertain terms. They found it difficult to form any confident impressions about his underlying personality. When the applicant behaved "inappropriately," on the
other hand, subjects were confident that his "real personality" corresponded to the way he had presented himself in the interview.

We can often deal quite successfully with other people on the
level of social roles or standards of propriety. The cabdriver and
his fare do not need to know much about one another to insure a
successful interaction. But especially when we are considering
more permanent relationships, it becomes important to keep an
eye out for inappropriate, "out-of-role" behaviors from which the
other person's dispositions can be reliably inferred. Observing that
a girl is well dressed at a debutante ball or stoned at a pot party
does not provide much information about how she will behave
under other circumstances. If the girl was wearing bluejeans at
the ball or smoking only cigars at the pot party, her actions would
provide better clues of her underlying dispositions.

In general, we are more highly motivated to attribute a person's acts to his enduring dispositions than to situational factors
because such dispositional attributions best serve our desire to predict his future behavior. Our desire to make dispositional attributions often gets the better of us, leading us to underestimate the
importance of situational factors. The sociologist Gustav Ichheiser
provides one such example:

> We are passing by the army barracks and see how a sergeant is
> handling his subordinates. He barks his commands, snaps at any
> attempted questions on the part of his men, listens to no excuses
> or explanations and is downright rude. Now, confronted with this
> type of behavior, we are not, as a rule, inclined to say to ourselves
> or to others, "This man is performing certain functions defined by
> the context of military regulations and standards. He is behaving in
> a way which corresponds to expected and stereotyped norms of
> behavior in this type of social role." Rather, we tend to react in a way
> which, on the verbal level, would sound something like this: "The
> man is rude," or "The man has such-and-such personality charac-
> teristics which make him behave in this way."[29]

This underestimation of situational factors reflects what
Heider called "behavior engulfing the field." We are led to believe
that the debater really believes his arguments or that the athlete
endorsing hair tonic is really sold on the brand, even when their
behavior can be more adequately accounted for by such situational
factors as debating rules or large fees. "We take raw material too

literally," Heider writes, "without taking into account additional factors that may influence it."[30] In doing so we are led to infer enduring dispositions from actions that in fact reflect responses to special conditions. This perceptual bias, as we shall see, has the effect of bolstering the primacy effect.

Getting Off on the Right Foot

What can you say about a person who is intelligent, industrious, impulsive, critical, stubborn, and envious? That he is a walking mass of contradictions? That he has a split personality? That he is just an ordinary guy with a run-of-the-mill mixture of "desirable" and "undesirable" characteristics? The last of these possibilities would probably be most accurate, but none of them corresponds to what most people actually say about such a person. Instead they attempt to integrate all of the person's traits into a single, unambivalent impression. And the overall impression that is formed often depends on the order in which the information about him is obtained. Social psychologist Solomon Asch initiated research on such "order effects" in the 1940s, utilizing a procedure in which adjectives describing a hypothetical person are read one at a time to subjects.[31] Asch found that a person described as "intelligent, industrious, impulsive, critical, stubborn, and envious" was evaluated by subjects in considerably more positive terms than a person introduced as "envious, stubborn, critical, impulsive, industrious, and intelligent." The descriptions provided by two of Asch's subjects illustrate what happened:

> A. *"Intelligent . . . envious."* The person is intelligent and fortunately he puts his intelligence to work. That he is stubborn and impulsive may be due to the fact that he knows what he is saying and what he means and will not therefore give in easily to someone else's idea which he disagrees with.
> B. *"Envious . . . intelligent."* This person's good qualities such as industry and intelligence are bound to be restricted by jealousy and stubbornness. The person is emotional. He is unsuccessful because he is weak and allows his bad points to cover up his good ones.

These subjects apparently used the earlier adjectives in the list to create a framework within which the later adjectives were interpreted: The stubbornness of a man who is already known to be intelligent and industrious is interpreted as integrity, while the stubbornness of a person already known to be envious is seen in a much less favorable light. Thus, Asch obtained a primacy effect.

Psychologist Abraham Luchins, employing fuller descriptions of a person's behavior, provided a further demonstration of the primacy effect.[32] Luchins constructed two paragraphs about a young man named Jim. They read as follows:

> *Paragraph E.* Jim left the house to get some stationery. He walked out into the sun-filled street with two of his friends, basking in the sun as he walked. Jim entered the stationery store which was full of people. Jim talked with an acquaintance while he waited for the clerk to catch his eye. On his way out, he stopped to chat with a school friend who was just coming into the store. Leaving the store, he walked toward school. On his way out he met the girl to whom he had been introduced the night before. They talked for a short while, and then Jim left for school.

> *Paragraph I.* After school Jim left the classroom alone. Leaving the school, he started on his long walk home. The street was brilliantly filled with sunshine. Jim walked down the street on the shady side. Coming down the street toward him, he saw the pretty girl whom he had met on the previous evening. Jim crossed the street and entered a candy store. The store was crowded with students, and he noticed a few familiar faces. Jim waited quietly until the counterman caught his eye and then gave his order. Taking his drink, he sat down at a side table. When he had finished his drink he went home.

When high school and college students were given either Paragraph E by itself or Paragraph I by itself they had no trouble forming an unambivalent impression of Jim. Students who read Paragraph E (for "extraverted") unanimously viewed Jim as a sociable, outgoing, and friendly person. They visualized him as physically well developed and athletic, as walking erect and briskly, and as thinking well of himself. When asked what Jim would do when he was bypassed in favor of another customer at a barber shop, they indicated that he would stand up and assert his priority. Students who read Paragraph I (for "introverted"), on the other hand, viewed Jim as shy, reserved, and unfriendly. They pictured him as having an average or below-average build, as walking slowly or with poor posture, and as feeling inferior to other people. When ignored at the barber shop, he would just sit there and wait. In the crucial conditions of his experiment, Luchins presented subjects with *both* paragraphs, run together to form a single continuous passage. One group of subjects read the new paragraph in the E-I order, another group in the I-E order. They were then asked to answer the same set of questions about Jim. The subjects in the E-I condition consistently described Jim as an extraverted, friendly person, while subjects in the I-E condition described him as shy and introverted. The subjects apparently attributed a stable disposition to Jim on the basis of his initial actions. His later contradictory actions could then be written off to special circumstances. Some of Luchins's E-I subjects decided, for example, that Jim was essentially a friendly person, but that he had had an unusually bad day at school.

A recent series of experiments by Edward Jones and his colleagues also documented the power of first impressions.[33] Subjects observed a fellow student (the "performer") attempt to solve a series of multiple-choice problems, of the sort that appear on tests of intellectual ability. The items were described as being of equal difficulty. The performer, in fact a confederate of the researchers, always answered fifteen of the thirty problems correctly. In one experimental condition, however, his successes were concentrated among the earlier items, and his performance tapered off toward the end. Jones called this the "descending" condition. In the "ascending" condition, on the other hand, his performance steadily improved over the course of the trials. Afterward the subjects were asked to recall how many correct answers he had given and predict how well he would do on a second series of trials. In four experiments conducted along these lines, primacy effects were consistently found. On the average, subjects judging the "descending" performer—the laboratory analogue of Vida Blue—recalled him as solving more of the problems than did students observing the "ascending" performer, even though the number of problems actually solved in the two conditions was identical. The "descending" performer was also expected to do better on a second series of trials than his "ascending" counterpart, and was judged to be the more intelligent.

As Jones and George R. Goethals note, intellectual ability is generally viewed as a stable disposition rather than as a changeable state.[34] Since the subjects were told that the problems were of equal difficulty, they probably expected the performer's successes and failures to be more or less equally spaced over the course of the trials. The proportion of successes in the first few trials could be taken as a good indication of the performer's ability and thus provide a basis for pigeonholing him. The subjects then apparently distorted or ignored the later evidence which contradicted their initial expectations.

Given the power of first impressions to shape lasting opinions, it is often wise for a person who wishes to make a particular impression to present himself in that way from the outset of the relationship. Having done so, he may later be able to reveal other sides of himself with greater impunity. Erving Goffman notes that some teachers take this view:

> "You can't let them get the upper hand or you are through. So I start out tough. The first day I get a new class in, I let them know who's boss. . . . You've got to start off tough, then you can ease up as you go along. If you start out easy-going when you try to get tough, they'll just look at you and laugh."[35]

The strategy of getting off on the right foot is sometimes complicated, however, by the fact that a person who initially presents himself *too* positively will be regarded by others as immodest or intimidating. Sociologist Peter Blau observes that in group situations "impressive qualities make a person attractive in one sense and unattractive in another, because they raise fears of rejection and pose a status threat for the rest of the group."[36] In terms of the distinction drawn in Chapter 2, other people may respect the highly impressive person, but they will find it hard to work up much affection for him. A common technique for handling this problem is for the person to begin by letting his impressive qualities be known, but once he has done so to reveal some of his shortcomings. "Having impressed us with his Harvard accent and Beacon Hill friends," Blau writes, "he may later tell a story that reveals his immigrant background."[37] Johnny Bench, the star catcher of the Cincinnati Reds, has mastered the essentials of this strategy:

> As a rule, Bench does not subscribe to baseball's unwritten code of modesty, but he is nicely measured about it: He is given to understatement ("I've got a little ability") when he thinks you know better, and to fervid overstatement when he thinks you do not ("I can throw out any runner alive").[38]

Even outright blunders may increase the attractiveness of a person if his admirable qualities have already been documented. Elliot Aronson and his co-workers asked Minnesota students to listen to a tape recording of a fellow student trying out for the school's College Bowl team.[39] The contestant performed either brilliantly or at a mediocre level, and then—as enacted on the tape heard by half of the subjects—clumsily spilled his cup of coffee all over himself. The blunder had the effect of decreasing the subjects' rated liking for the mediocre contestant, but it increased their liking for the brilliant contestant. When imposing people reveal weaknesses they emphasize their common ties with the rest of us mortals and may be liked better as a result. One of the least predictable consequences of the Bay of Pigs fiasco was an upsurge in President Kennedy's popularity rating in the polls. As the coffee-spilling experiment suggests, however, when an ordinary person blunders it only makes him appear ignorant or clumsy. It is only after a person has gotten off on the right foot that he can afford to stumble.

But What's He Done Lately?

For all of the importance of first impressions, our images of other people are nevertheless highly susceptible to change. "A playwright's only as good as his last play," and the same standard is often applied to racehorses, boxers, and psychological researchers. Even the opinionated Jim Bouton is capable of changing his mind, and admitting it:

> One of the dumb things I do sometimes is form judgments about people I really don't know. Case history: Jack Hamilton, pitcher, Cleveland Indians. He was with the Angel organization last year and played with me in Seattle, which is where I got to know him. Before that I played against him in the minors and considered him stupid, a hard-throwing guy who didn't care whether or not he hit the batter. In the majors I figured him for a troublemaker because he used to get into fights with Phil Linz. Nobody fights with Phil Linz.
>
> Then, when Hamilton hit Tony Conigliaro in the eye a couple of years ago and put him out for the season, I thought, boy, this guy is some kind of super rat. But when I played with him in Seattle I found he was just a guy like everybody else, honestly sorry he'd hit Conigliaro, a good team player, a friendly fellow who liked to come out early to the park and pitch batting practice to his kids. All of which made me feel like an ass.[40]

It is in part because admitting that one's first impression of another person was wrong makes one "feel like an ass," to borrow Bouton's felicitous phrase, that first impressions are often so impervious to change. The desire to achieve consistent evaluations of others may stem not only from the desire for perceptual harmony, as stressed by Heider's balance principle, but also from our reluctance to admit that our initial opinions were mistaken. Consequently, it may sometimes be possible to minimize the impact of first impressions by reminding people to keep their minds open, that all the evidence is not yet in. Luchins found, for example, that the strength of the primacy effect in subjects' evaluations of Jim was reduced when they were advised in advance to be sure to take into account all of the information to be presented.[41] Paradoxically, it is sometimes the case that the most recent information one has obtained about another person is weighted most heavily when it contrasts sharply with one's previously formed impression. Thus, Jim Bouton may end up perceiving Jack Hamilton as *especially* friendly precisely because he had previously considered him to be a super rat. Against the sinister background of Bouton's initial impression, Hamilton's otherwise unremarkable actions, like pitching batting practice to his kids, take on an aura of virtual saintliness.

A central determinant of whether one's impressions of other people will be governed by primacy or recency is one's set of assumptions about which characteristics of people tend to be stable and which are susceptible to change. We typically view other people as capable of growth, development, or modification in at least certain respects. We may not be too surprised, for example, to note large shifts in interests, personality, and abilities from one year to the next among children or adolescents. In such cases our evaluation of the other person is likely to rely heavily on the most recent information, which, in effect, supersedes any previous evidence. The fact that Senator Edward Kennedy was able to overcome his undergraduate cheating incident and may even be able to rise above the stigma of Chappaquiddick suggests that in at least some instances people are willing to view moral lapses as temporary or mutable. On the other hand, the difficulties encountered by many ex-mental patients in finding jobs, recently illustrated in the recent case of Senator Thomas Eagleton's removal as the Democratic vice-presidential candidate, may reflect an implicit theory that mental and emotional illnesses reflect stable and inherently unchangeable predispositions.

The cases of Vida Blue and Gary Wichard may also be distinguished on the basis of such attributions of stability. The early information on Vida Blue may in fact have been more easily generalizable to predictions about his later performance than the early information on Gary Wichard. After all, Blue's early string of victories had been in the majors, against the very teams that he would continue to face in the future. He had demonstrated that he could do it. For a healthy twenty-one-year-old pitcher, such a demonstration might well be construed as evidence of an underlying ability that would persist for a considerable period of time. As a result of this dispositional attribution, the contradictory later information could not easily offset the power of the first impression. In the case of Gary Wichard, on the other hand, the early impression was based on his performance at C. W. Post, against relatively weak opponents. Thus, it might be attributed to the situation, that of small-college football, rather than to a stable ability that would continue to be displayed in the professional ranks. When it came to dealing with the pass rush of gargantuan professional linemen, Wichard might rise to the occasion, get even better, or fall by the wayside. In light of this perception of changeability, the safest course for the perceivers of Gary Wichard was to give heaviest weight to what he had done lately.

The Self-Fulfilling Prophecy

The importance of impressions of other people goes far beyond their role in the perceivers' own mental lives. Like secret wishes at a birthday party, our impressions of others have ways of making themselves come true. If, for example, we perceive another person as friendly, we are likely to behave warmly toward him. And this behavior on our part may in turn have the effect of *making him* friendly. If, on the other hand, we perceive another person or group of people as being hostile, we may well react toward him in such a way as to make him so. Ichheiser notes that individuals often have no choice but to play the social roles that are assigned to them by others:

> The ex-convict . . . may return to his community with a new view of himself and a determination to become a good citizen, [but] the opinions the people of the community hold of him and ex-convicts in general often prevent his accomplishing his good aims. Instead, in bitterness and resentment, he often gives up the struggle and becomes what the community expected—a hardened criminal. Sometimes, too, the situation is reversed. The ex-convict comes back hardened, embittered, and with his worst characteristics emphasized. Some one or several persons take an interest in him, play up his better qualities, and through encouragement he comes to be what they see him as—a good citizen.[42]

A more personal example is provided by J. R. Simmons:

> . . . My informant rented a room for several days from a middle-aged woman. After seeing her only briefly, and before he had spoken with her, he "intuited" that she was a warm, accepting person who was filled with psychic strength and goodness. When he first talked with her a couple hours later, his manner was far more friendly and patronizing than usual. He showed interest in her collection of antiques, asked about her children, and ended up by saying he felt she was a wonderful person and he wanted to rent from her, partly because they would have a chance to talk together. During the next few days, the writer had a chance to question other tenants and neighbors about the landlady. They described a fairly caustic gossiper who was unreasonably strict about the use of electricity, and of her property and grounds. Her attitude toward the writer was taciturn. But she responded graciously to my informant's open friendliness. She sought him out to talk with on several occasions, she inquired if there was enough light in his room for late reading and supplied him with a table lamp, etc. In her behavior toward him, my informant's intuition certainly seemed correct.[43]

A striking experimental demonstation of the impact of images upon reality was provided by Robert Rosenthal, a social psychologist, and Lenore Jacobson, an elementary school principal.[44] At the start of a school year teachers were given lists of those students in their classes who had been identified by a special aptitude test as probable academic "late bloomers." The lists were in fact entirely unrelated to any test results. They were arrived at by a process of random selection. At the end of the year the children's intelligence was tested. It was found that those children who had been identified as "late bloomers" in fact showed significantly greater gains in I.Q. scores than those children who had not been listed. The teachers had unwittingly given differential treatment to their "late bloomers," perhaps encouraging them more, or listening to them more attentively. Whatever it was that the teachers did, it had the effect of making their expectation come true. For obvious ethical reasons Rosenthal and Jacobson did not create parallel experimental conditions in which teachers were told that particular students had been identified as dullards. But just such conditions are often created in educational situations in which teachers hold the expectation that children in particular schools, particular tracks, or of particular backgrounds lack the ability to go far academically. This expectation, too, bears the seeds of its own fruition.

The sociologist Robert Merton has labeled this phenomenon

the "self-fulfilling prophecy." He defines it as "a false definition of the situation evoking a new behavior which makes the originally false conception come true." Merton continues, "The specious validity of the self-fullling prophecy perpetuates a reign of error. For the prophet will cite the actual course of events as proof that he was right from the very beginning."[45] The self-fulfilling prophecy thus lends further weight to the power of first impressions to shape the course of interpersonal relationships. On balance, first impressions seem at least as likely to confirm and perpetuate themselves than to decline and fall under the weight of later information. As a result, the process of repudiating unearned reputations and smashing erroneous stereotypes is often an exceedingly difficult one. The case is not a hopeless one, however. In the next chapter we will consider some of the necessary ingredients for accomplishing such breakthroughs in our relations with others.

Chapter **6**
FAMILIARITY BREEDS CONTENT
The Effects of "Mere Exposure"

I've grown accustomed to her face.
—ALAN JAY LERNER

Leonard Bernstein's "Mass," first performed publicly in 1971 at the opening of the Kennedy Center for the Performing Arts in Washington, was a monumental exercise in musical eclecticism, combining strains ranging from acid rock to Roman liturgy in a two-hour mixed-media extravaganza requiring a total of over two hundred musicians, singers, and dancers who fanned out through the stage, wings, and audience. The general attitude toward the novel work on first hearing was a sort of respectful befuddlement. But Mrs. Joan Kennedy, who had heard the Mass several times previously in rehearsal, was more unambiguously positive. "Every time I hear it I grow to appreciate it more and more," Mrs. Kennedy declared. Her mother-in-law, Mrs. Rose Kennedy, expressed a variant of this reaction. With only a trace of doubt in her voice the elder Mrs. Kennedy pronounced the composition "simply wonderful," but quickly added that "you can't absorb it all the first time," and that she intended to see the work "again and again and again."[1]

That initially confused, neutral, vaguely positive, or even vaguely negative reactions to objects and events can be converted to enthusiastic approval as a result of repeated exposure has been demonstrated in studies of aesthetic appreciation. In 1903, a psychologist named Max Meyer played students unfamiliar selections of oriental music twelve to fifteen times in succession. He found that most of them reported liking the pieces more on the last than on the first presentation. In the 1920s, J. E. Downey and G. E. Knapp played students a variety of selections once a week for five weeks and with only one exception found that they were liked better at the close of the sessions. The lone exception was "Columbia, the Gem of the Ocean." In the 1930s, Abraham Maslow, later to become better known as a founding father of the "humanistic psychology" movement, projected fifteen paintings of great masters to a group of students on four successive days. Six days later the fifteen paintings were presented once again, together with fifteen paintings by the same artists, which the subjects had never seen. Maslow found that there was an unmistakable preference for the familiar paintings. In a masterful review of these early studies as well as in an ingenious series of experiments of his own, social psychologist Robert Zajonc has called the general principle underlying these phenomena the effect of "mere exposure." In his terms, "Mere repeated exposure of the individual to a stimulus is a sufficient condition for the enhancement of his attitude toward it. By 'mere exposure' is meant a condition which just makes the given stimulus accessible to the individual's perception."[2]

Does the mere exposure principle apply when the "given stimulus" is another person? Zajonc and two of his students, Susan Saegert and Walter Swap, conducted an experiment to demonstrate that it does.[3] To accomplish their goal of "merely exposing" their subjects to one another specified numbers of times, the researcher disguised their study as an investigation of the psychophysics of taste. The subjects, undergraduate women at the University of Michigan, were shuttled in and out of small cubicles, where they were to taste various liquids and rate them on such dimensions as saltiness, sweetness, and sourness. The shuttling was arranged in such a way that each subject was exposed to one other member of her six-person group ten times, another member five times, another twice, another once, and another not at all. Since the subjects were total strangers before the start of the experiment, these carefully managed exposures represented the only contact of any sort that they had with one another. And to insure that the contacts constituted "mere exposure" and nothing more, the subjects were cautioned not to talk to one another or even to communicate with facial expressions or gestures. After the tasting sessions, the entire group was shifted to a larger room, where they filled out a further questionnaire about their reactions to the tasting. The crucial measure of how much the subject liked each of her fellow subjects was smuggled into this questionnaire. The researchers found that these ratings of liking were dramatically affected by the number of exposures between each pair of subjects. On the average the subjects expressed greatest liking for the woman to whom they had been exposed ten times, next most liking for the woman to whom they had been exposed five times, and least liking for the women to whom they had been exposed only once or not at all.

If the principle of mere exposure is to have practical importance, however, we must be able to specify the conditions under which it is applicable to real-life situations, as well as to brief contacts in the laboratory. We would be particularly interested in knowing whether repeated contact between people of different races, religions, or social backgrounds is in itself sufficient to break down unfavorable stereotypes and to promote positive feeling. In this chapter we will proceed from a further examination of research on the effects of mere exposure in the laboratory to the consideration of instances in the real world in which *mere* exposure may or may not suffice to enhance interpersonal attitudes.

From Rats to Elections

Psychologists are still not certain about the mechanisms that underlie the principle of mere exposure, but whatever they are they do not seem to depend upon the subtleties of human intelligence. A team of psychologists at Texas Technological College has demonstrated that mere exposure can produce sophisticated musical preferences among newborn rats.[4] The psychologists raised three groups of rats under three different conditions. One group of animals lived in a chamber equipped with a speaker that for fifty-two days and twelve hours each day broadcast selections from Mozart, such as Symphonies No. 40 and 41, Violin Concerto No. 5, and *The Magic Flute*. A second group was exposed to a fifty-two-day program of the atonal music of Schoenberg, including *Pierrot Lunaire, A Survivor from Warsaw, Kol Nidre,* and *Verklaerte Nacht.* The third group of animals received no musical training at all. After the fifty-two-day concert all of the rats were given a fifteen-day rest, and were then tested for their musical preferences during a period of sixty days. Since rats can neither hum nor fill out attitude scales, an ingenious alternative means of assessing their tastes was devised. The animal being tested was placed in a chamber whose floor was hinged at the center and suspended over two switches, one on each side of the hinge. The rat's weight was enough to push down one or the other side of the floor and thus activate a switch. Needless to say, one switch turned on music by Mozart, the other music by Schoenberg. By moving from one side of the cage to the other the rat was able to regulate its own musical diet.

The preference test supported the mere exposure principle: Previous exposure to one or the other kind of music led the animals to prefer that kind. The selections played to the rats during the testing period, incidentally, were not the same as the ones to which they had previously been exposed, but selections by the same composers that they had not heard before. Thus, repeated exposure did not simply acclimate the animals to particular selections. It had the more far-reaching effect of producing a preference for a particular musical style or mode. It may be noted, finally, that the preference of Mozart-reared rats for Mozart was stronger than the preference of Schoenberg-reared rats for Schoenberg, and that the rats who received no prior musical training spent more time listening to Mozart than to Schoenberg. This overall victory of Mozart has led at least some observers to revel in the knowledge that their musical tastes are shared by untrained rats.

Although Zajonc's systematic formulation of the principle of mere exposure was not published until 1968, the principle has long been utilized by advertisers and politicians. In radio and television ads a common strategy is to repeat the name of the product as frequently as possible within the allotted thirty-second or one-minute spot. Even if the audience never learns precisely what the product is good for, the theory goes, they will still be most attracted to products with familiar (that is, frequently exposed) names when they see them in the supermarket. And it sometimes works. In a recent experiment women were shown slides of various syllables like "BIJ" and "WUG" varying numbers of times and then offered their choice among "brands" of stockings bearing the nonsense names. In accord with the principle of mere exposure, the women preferred the stockings whose brand name had been viewed most frequently.[5] Political campaigners often refer to themselves by their proper names rather than in the first person not only because of vanity, but also to increase the electorate's exposure to this stimulus. Zajonc reports on a related exposure strategy for political success:

> A man by the name of Hal Evry will elect you to office if you can follow his formula. You must not make speeches, not take a stand on issues. In fact, you must not appear at all in the campaign. But his

organization guarantees that your name will be as familiar to voters as Tide or Ford. Evry mounted an extensive saturation campaign on behalf of one unknown fellow, by flooding the city with signs saying *Three Cheers for Pat Milligan*. That was all. The voters saw these words on billboards, in full-page newspaper ads, on facsimile telegrams sent through the mails. The advertisement of the slogan went on for months, and on election day Pat Milligan was the undeniable winner. What else but the effects of mere exposure?[6]

Both the experiment with stockings and the Pat Milligan strategy suggest that people's attitudes toward particular objects may be enhanced by repeatedly exposing them to *symbols* of those objects—specifically, the names that the objects go by. This makes sense when one considers that it is often the name rather than the object itself to which the audience responds, whether it is by selecting a box from a supermarket shelf or by pulling a lever in the voting booth. This phenomenon has the disquieting consequence that popularity is sometimes conferred upon or withheld from people as an unintended effect of the names they happen to bear. Albert Harrison randomly selected 50 men's and 50 women's given names from a metropolitan telephone directory. He asked one group of students to rate each name for how familiar it sounded, thus reflecting how frequently they had been exposed to each name in the past. Another group of students was asked to indicate how much they thought they would like or dislike a person bearing each name. The results were perfectly in line with the mere exposure principle. Those names which were rated as most familiar were also the best liked, and those which were rated as least familiar were the least liked. The overall correlation between the two sets of ratings was .87 (1.00 would indicate a perfect association), indicating a remarkably strong relationship between familiarity and liking.[7]

In a recent study of actual popularity among Florida gradeschool pupils, strong relationships were found between children's ratings of how much they liked particular first names and how much they liked classmates who bore those names.* In accord with Harrison's results, the "undesirable" names tended to be the least common ones. The psychologists who conducted the study, John McDavid and Herbert Harari, were led to caution that "a par-

* The same result was obtained when the first names were rated by children from another class. This finding helps to rule out the possibility that the subjects' attitudes toward their classmates led to their evaluations of their names, rather than vice-versa.

ent might appropriately think twice before naming his offspring for great Aunt Sophronia."[8] Perhaps if Hubert Humphrey Sr. had foreseen that his first-born son would one day find himself in an important popularity contest with a kid named Dick, he would have thought again, named him something common like Joe or Jim, and thus altered the course of history. "What's in a name?" More, apparently, than most of us realize. A rose by some other name—if it were a name that we had never heard before—might not smell quite so sweet.

Coming to Terms with the Unknown

At least part of the explanation for the principle of mere exposure seems to be the pervasive animal fear of the strange and unknown. Although the unknown has its fascination as well, we remain unlikely to form positive attitudes toward unfamiliar objects until they are thoroughly explored. It is through repeated exposure that familiarization takes place. We gradually learn that the object can be safely approached or dealt with, and our initial confusion as to how to respond to it is slowly overcome. This process is equally applicable to our reactions to other people. Several years ago a mysterious student attended a speech class at Oregon State University every Monday, Wednesday, and Friday for two months enveloped in a big black bag, with only his bare feet showing. The instructor of the class, who knew the identity of the person inside the bag, reported that the students' attitude toward "the Black Bag" was initially hostile. But over the course of time it changed to curiosity and finally to a feeling of genuine friendship.[9]

Even when the people we encounter are not wearing black bags, increasing familiarity will often enhance our attitudes toward them. When a stimulus is novel, we lack the usual guidelines of habit or culture to shape our response to it. Instead we are thrust into a confused state of "response competition," in which a variety of possible reactions struggle against one another for supremacy. Our reactions become slower and less certain, and we may exhibit such bodily symptoms of anxiety as increased sweating and quickening of the pulse. Because such response competition and its accompanying anxiety are unpleasant experiences, we try to avoid the objects and people who give rise to it, much as a rat will initially shy away from an unfamiliar object thrust into its cage. And to justify our desire to avoid the novel stimulus, we develop a distaste for it, telling ourselves that it—or he or she—has little of value to offer. Gordon Allport succinctly summarized the process in his classic book on *The Nature of Prejudice*:

See that man over there?
Yes.
Well, I hate him.
But you don't know him.
That's why I hate him.[10]

When we are repeatedly exposed to a novel stimulus, however, our fear gradually abates, and our reactions become quicker and more certain. Albert Harrison has found, for example, that when American subjects are asked to provide free associations ("Say the first thing that comes into your mind . . .") to Chinese characters, the responses come quicker the more frequently the particular symbol has been exposed to them.[11] The bodily symptoms of anxiety also diminish with repeated exposure. Zajonc reports that there is a steady decrease in the magnitude of subjects' galvanic skin response with successive exposures to nonsense syllables.[12] The net result of this acclimation is a reduced desire to avoid the stimulus and an enhanced attitude toward it. The only problem, it would seem, is to keep the rat or the student in contact with the new stimulus long enough for the familiarization process to take place.

But the anxiety-reduction explanation for the effects of repeated exposure seems at best a partial one. It suggests that repeated exposure to novel stimuli will neutralize attitudes that are mildly negative, but provides no rationale for the possibility that repeated exposure will lead to more strongly positive sentiments of liking or love. Yet there is at least anecdotal and musical evidence that people can "grow on us," that we become enthusiastically "accustomed to her face," that "to know him is to love him," and so on. Exchange theorist Homans has put such views into the form of a general proposition, suggesting that "If the frequency of interaction between two or more people increases, their degree of liking for one another will increase."[13] Homans does not see this link between interaction and liking as inevitable, but as an outcome that is much more likely than not to occur.

The basic assumption behind Homans's proposition is that there are usually many ways in which any two people can reward one another. The possible rewards span a wide range, from material assistance to moral support to simply providing a way to pass the time. Given that such rewards are possible, they are obtained most *cheaply* from those with whom we are in frequent contact, such as next-door neighbors, co-workers, or classmates. Our proximity to such people saves us the time and effort that would be needed to obtain the same rewards elsewhere. "Suppose that two persons are, as we say, thrown together," Homans explains, "that interaction between them is made easy and likely because they live near one another or work on the same job. If they interact at all, they emit activities to one another; and if no special factor is present that might bias systematically their values or their activities, the chances are that each one will find some of the other's activities valuable, if only because they may be obtained at less cost from him than from a third party at a greater distance. . . . And to the extent that each finds the other's activity valuable, each is apt to express favorable sentiment toward the other. For this reason, an independent increase in interaction between persons is apt to be associated with an increase in liking between them."[14]

The Architecture of Friendship

Homans's proposition is supported by the results of two studies that explored the links between physical proximity and friendship, one of them in an M.I.T. housing project and the other in a University of Chicago dormitory. In both cases the investigators found that the closer two dwelling units were to one another, the more likely it was that their occupants would be friends. The first study was conducted by social psychologists Leon Festinger, Stanley Schachter, and Kurt Back, and it focused on a married-student housing complex at M.I.T. just after World War II. Housing in Cambridge was extremely scarce, and the students, many of whom were returning veterans, were assigned almost at random to housing units as soon as they became available. Almost none of the residents of the project knew each other before moving in. Thus, preexisting friendships could play no part in determining how close families lived to one another. Instead, the investigators could focus directly on the effects of proximity on the formation of friendships. One part of the housing complex, called Westgate West, consisted of seventeen separate two-story buildings, each containing ten apartments. All of the wives living in these apartments were asked to name the three closest friends they had made in the project. People living in the same building comprised fully 65 percent of the friends mentioned. Fewer friends lived in other buildings in the same quadrangle, and fewest of all lived in other quadrangles. Even more striking, the women's choices within their own building were highly related to the distance between apartments. More than two-thirds of the within-building choices were for others living on the same floor. And even within one's floor, people living next door were more likely to be friends than people two doors away, and these in turn were more likely to be friends than those living three or four doors away.

In introducing their highly consistent results, Festinger and his colleagues suggested that the primary importance of spatial arrangements in facilitating friendship lies in the ways in which it makes possible passive, unintended contacts between people. As they suggest, "In hanging clothes out to dry, or putting out the garbage, or simply sitting on the porch, one is much more likely to meet next-door neighbors than people living four or five houses away." The likelihood that passive contacts will take place does not depend on absolute physical distance alone. It depends even more directly on what Festinger and his colleagues call "functional distance," those elements of design and position that determine the specific patterns of paths that people take and, consequently, which people will meet one another. Although physical distance and functional distance are usually highly associated with one another, a clear distinction between the two can be drawn:

> For example, two back-to-back houses which are 30 feet apart and have neither back doors nor back yards would be considered functionally farther apart than two back-to-back houses, also 30 feet apart, which do have back doors and yards. Thus we can have varying functional distances while physical distance remains constant.[15]

Figure 6.1 suggests that in the Westgate West houses Apartments 1 and 5 on the first floor were functionally closer than any of the other first-floor apartments to apartments on the second floor. The left-hand stairway to the second floor passes directly in front of the doorway of Apartment 1, and the right-hand stairway passes close by, though not directly in front of, the doorway of Apartment 5. In addition, the cluster of five mailboxes that serves all the upper-floor apartments is adjacent to the doorway of Apartment 5. The impact of these functional features was revealed in the residents' friendship choices. Residents of Apartments 1 and 5

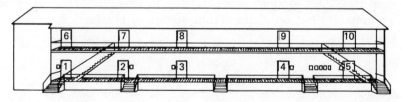

FIGURE 6.1   Schematic diagram of a Westgate West building. (Reprinted from *Social Pressures in Informal Groups* by Leon Festinger, Stanley Schachter, and Kurt Back with the permission of the publishers, Stanford University Press. © 1950 by Leon Festinger, Stanley Schachter, and Kurt Back.)

chose people on the upper floor more often than did residents of any of the other first-floor apartments, and were chosen by the upper-floor residents more often in return. Evidence of the importance of functional distance also came from the neighboring project of Westgate:

> In order to have the street appear "lived on," ten of the houses near the street had been turned so that they faced the street rather than the court area as did the other houses. This apparently small change in the direction in which a house faced had a considerable effect on the lives of the people who, by accident, happened to occupy these end houses. They had less than half as many friends in the project as did those whose houses faced the court area. The consistency of this finding left no doubt that the turning of these houses toward the street had made involuntary social isolates out of the persons who lived in them.[16]

The M.I.T. results document the impact of spatial arrangements on friendship even when the distances involved are quite small.* (The distance between any two apartments on the same floor in Westgate West ranged from twenty-two to eighty-eight feet.) A recent study conducted in a large student dormitory at the University of Chicago obtained very similar results with respect to still smaller distances.[17] Even though rooms in this case were only eight feet apart from one another, students still displayed a striking tendency to like, on the average, the person next door more than the person two doors away, and so on. When the distances involved are as small as this, it seems difficult to account for the effects of proximity simply in terms of physical or functional distance. After living for six months in a dormitory, one is certainly likely to have met the person who lives three or four doors away and to have as much opportunity as he wants to continue interacting with him. Robert Priest and Jack Sawyer, who conducted the Chicago study, suggest that in this and other cases we must consider not only the actual distances involved but also the ways in which people *perceive* them.

---

* William H. Whyte, Jr., came to a similar conclusion in his study of the suburban community of Park Forest, Illinois. "In suburbia friendship has become almost predictable," Whyte wrote. "Despite the fact that a person can pick and choose from a vast number of people to make friends with, such things as the placement of a stoop or the direction of a street often have more to do with determining who is friends with whom." (William H. Whyte, Jr., *The Organization Man*, New York: Simon & Schuster, 1956, p. 330.)

Although distances between people can be measured in terms of miles and feet, Priest and Sawyer argue, they are not always perceived that way. Instead, perceived distance often seems to depend on the number of others who intervene. In a rural area people living a half-mile away may be considered neighbors, while in a city those living a hundred feet away may not be. In a university dormitory a room five doors away may represent more than ten seconds of added travel time. It also represents five *closer* opportunities passed by. One of the results of this perception is that the farther a door is from one's own, the more purposive one's approach must be and the more justification it tends to require. Thus to solicit change for the Coke machine from someone five doors away may raise the question, "Why didn't he ask someone closer?" There is a certain awkwardness built into such necessarily purposive encounters which can be avoided by restricting one's interaction to people who are immediately adjacent. It may be for this reason that friendships are particularly likely to arise among roommates, even when they do not seem to be well matched. As Priest and Sawyer note, it is easy for roommates to interact without making each encounter an occasion. The importance of this easy accessibility in the formation of friendships is surprisingly great.

Further evidence for Homans's point of view comes from an experimental failure. In 1954 and 1955, Theodore Newcomb rented a boarding house and provided free room and board to students transferring to the University of Michigan in exchange for their participation in his study of acquaintance formation.[18] In the first year of the project, roommate assignments were drawn from a hat. In the second year Newcomb adopted a bolder strategy, combining half of the new students in rooming combinations in a way that he thought would insure *minimal* compatibility. He did this by pairing men whose attitudes on a wide range of topics (as indicated on questionnaires that they mailed in before arriving in Ann Arbor) were widely discrepant from one another's. The other half of the rooming assignments paired students who had highly similar attitudes, in an attempt to produce maximal attraction. The experiment did not turn out as Newcomb had expected. In all cases, regardless of whether low or high attraction had been predicted, roommates came to be highly attracted to one another. Since at least some of these pairs were known to have rather little in common, these results provide a strong testament to the power of repeated contact. As Homans wryly suggests, "You can get to like some pretty queer customers if you go around with them long enough."[19]

Getting the Boys Together

Popular versions of the principle of mere exposure are sometimes expressed by mothers who are concerned about finding friends for their children. "If we can only get Bill and Bob together," the reasoning goes, "the boys are sure to like one another." The same argument is also advanced as a means of reducing prejudice and increasing friendship between members of traditionally hostile racial or ethnic groups. If "getting to know you" leads to "getting to like you," as the principle of mere exposure suggests, then all social planners should have to do to eliminate intergroup hostility is to make sure that people from different backgrounds live, work, and play in close proximity, so they can hardly escape frequent exposure to one another. Unfortunately, the case is not nearly so simple.

In many instances enforced contact between members of antagonistic groups has indeed led to demonstrably improved intergroup relations. In the late 1940s social psychologists Morton Deutsch and Mary Evans Collins interviewed white housewives in four municipal housing projects in New York City and Newark, New Jersey.[20] Two of the projects were fully integrated, with black and white families occupying adjoining apartments. The other two projects were biracial but segregated, with blacks and whites being assigned to different areas of the project. The two types of projects were similiar in all respects other than the racial occupancy pattern. Although the families in all cases had consented to live in a biracial project—which in most cases was the best housing available to them—they had no choice about whether it would be an integrated or a segregated one. Deutsch and Collins found, however, that the two types of exposure situations had strikingly different effects on interracial attitudes. In the integrated projects over 60 percent of the white housewives reported having "friendly relations" with Negroes. In the segregated projects less than 10 percent reported such friendly relations, and over 80 percent reported making no contact with blacks at all. Two out of three white women in the integrated projects expressed a desire to be friendly with blacks, while in the segregated projects only one in eleven expressed a similar desire.

But in contrast to these favorable effects of intergroup exposure, other cases have been reported in which such contact had either no effect or even negative effects on intergroup attitudes. The Israeli government experimented with a policy of locating immigrants from various parts of the world in mixed-ethnic communities, on the assumption that exposing Jews of diverse background to one another would help to create a united and homogeneous nation. But Israeli sociologist A. Weingrod noted that the policy rarely succeeded in establishing intergroup friendship: "For example, when questioned regarding their social relations with neighboring villagers, Iraqi settlers responded that they rarely saw the Moroccans, Tunisians, and Hungarians who lived near to them, but that they sometimes visited Iraqi settlers who lived miles away."[21] The official policy of integration also tended to produce conflict between neighboring groups and was subsequently abandoned.

In some cases intergroup exposure gives rise to fears of invasion. A study conducted in the late 1940s focused on the interracial attitudes of whites who lived at the southern edge of the expanding "black belt" in Chicago.[22] The closer the whites lived to the black neighborhood, the more likely they were to spontaneously express anti-black sentiments to the interviewer. The white residents of "Zone 1," the area closest to the black section, expressed concern that, among other things, their children might play with blacks or eventually marry them.

Such negative instances make it clear that the principle of mere exposure provides no panacea for intergroup tension. Where groups of people hold attitudes of deep-seated hostility toward one another even before they are brought into contact, exposure is as likely to intensify the hostility as to reduce it. This state of affairs in fact corresponds to the results of a recent laboratory investigation. Northwestern University psychologists Philip Brickman and Joel Redfield began their experiment by showing students a series of art prints and asking them to indicate which they liked and which they disliked.[23] The students were then shown the slides varying numbers of times. Brickman and Redfield found that the more frequently the subjects were exposed to prints toward which they initially felt positive or neutral, the more they came to appreciate them. But the more frequently they were exposed to prints that they initially disliked, the more *negative* their reactions became.

Professor Homans points to a similar exception to his proposition linking frequency of interaction and liking. If two people find each other's activities punishing rather than rewarding, and yet they are not free to break off the interaction, "then, as we know, frequent interaction will not only not be associated with mutual liking but may even lead to increasing hostility. They are shut up together like two rats in a trap." He cites as an example the case of two rivals for promotion, who are assigned to work together on a problem by their mutual boss. The two will go on interacting frequently, each trying to show the other up, "but they will probably not like, and may even come to despise, each other."[24]

Shattering Our Stereotypes

The discovery that the effects of intergroup contact are sometimes positive and sometimes negative requires us to look beyond the principle of mere exposure toward some of the additional factors that may characterize intergroup contact. One of the most significant potential benefits of intergroup contact is that it can help to eliminate the erroneous beliefs that groups are likely to maintain about one another when they are isolated. Anthropologist Robert LeVine has collected examples of the fantastic images that members of groups have maintained of other groups with which they have had little experience. For example, natives of Romonum in the Caroline Islands reportedly considered the inhabitants of New Guinea to be "unregenerate cannibals whom they group together with sharks and other fearsome and hateful life forms."[25] The Spaniards of the early sixteenth century were not certain that the Indians of Hispaniola were humans rather than animals or creatures of the devil. From the other side of the fence, the Indians of Puerto Rico would drown captured Europeans and then watch them for weeks to see if they would putrefy. LeVine reports that intensive contact between the groups usually tends to eliminate such clearly fictitious images, although in some cases a great deal of information and experience is required before the errors are corrected.

When the images of outsiders are equally erroneous but somewhat more subtle, however, they are less easily corrected as a result of exposure alone. As LeVine notes, powerful groups sometimes encourage the maintenance of unflattering images as a rationale for keeping other groups in subjection. The traditional American white stereotype of the black person as dirty, happy-go-lucky, and incapable of taking care of himself may qualify as such a politically inspired image. Such stereotypes are often maintained tenaciously even in the face of considerable intergroup contact. This is not because the stereotypes have any truth to them. It is rather because people have the remarkable capacity to view the world in such a way as to confirm their preconceived notions about it. Professor Allport provides examples of this unsettling human talent:

From a large number of Negroes in the subway we may select the one who is misbehaving for our attention and disapproval. The dozen or more well-behaved Negroes are overlooked, simply because prejudice screens and interprets our perceptions. Casual contact, therefore, permits our thinking about outgroups to remain on an autistic level. . . .

An Irishman and a Jew encounter each other in casual contact, perhaps in a small business transaction. Neither has, in fact, any initial animosity toward the other. But the Irishman thinks, "Ah, a Jew; perhaps he'll skin me; I'll be careful." The Jew thinks, "Probably a Mick; they hate the Jews; he'd like to insult me." With such an inauspicious start both men are likely to be evasive, distrustful, and cool. The casual contact has left matters worse than before.[26]

The latter instance exemplifies what we have called the self-fulfilling prophecy.

We may interpret an identical piece of behavior on the part of another person in entirely different ways depending on what group we think he belongs to. The point is well made by Robert Merton:

The very same behavior undergoes a complete change of evaluation in its transition from the in-group Abe Lincoln to the out-group Abe Cohen or Abe Kurakawa. . . . Did Lincoln work far into the night? This testifies that he was industrious, resolute, perseverant, and eager to realize his capacities to the full. Do the out-group Jews or Japanese keep these same hours? This only bears witness to their sweatshop mentality, their ruthless undercutting of American standards, their unfair competitive practices. Is the in-group hero frugal, thrifty, and sparing? Then the out-group victim is stingy, miserly, and penny-pinching.[27]

Because of these perceptual mechanisms, intergroup contact may often fortify negative images and stereotypes rather than destroy them. If this is the case, one reasonable recommendation might be to leave bad enough alone and keep the opponents in opposite corners of the ring. Such an argument for racial isolation in the United States has been made by both black and white separatists. And yet, as social psychologist Thomas Pettigrew has forcefully maintained, such an isolationist strategy is not only defeatist but is potentially more dangerous than one of uneasy integration. Whereas isolation may indeed reduce conflict in the short run, it also makes it less likely that the groups involved will ever discover the underlying similarities that exist between them by virtue of their common humanity. Isolation fosters the growth of vested interests in both groups for continued separation. These vested interests may in turn perpetuate stereotypes that become increasingly divorced from reality and that may plant the seeds of further conflict in the long run. "Racial separatism. . . is a cumulative process," Pettigrew writes. "It feeds upon itself and leads its victims to prefer continued separation."[28]

The more promising response to the recognition that exposure may sometimes fortify negative group stereotypes is to attempt to distinguish the conditions under which this occurs from those under which contact is likely to have more positive effects. Contact with others often causes our images of them to become more complex and, as such, more in tune with reality. "I like to think members of the medical profession are mercenary bastards," a friend of mine observed, "but the fact that every doctor I know personally is humane and generous makes it very hard to maintain my stereotype." Even when contact reveals other people's weaknesses, as indeed it is likely to do, it may provide a fuller and more sympathetic view of these weaknesses than that provided by uninformed stereotypes. Such an effect seemed to emerge in Deutsch and Collins's comparison of segregated and integrated housing projects.[29] When asked by the interviewer to describe the chief faults of Negroes, the segregated housewives called them aggressive, rowdy, and dangerous, while the integrated housewives were more likely to mention such personal problems as feelings of inferiority and oversensitivity. In the latter case one senses the emergence of a fuller and more complex picture of what members of "the other group" are like.

The trick, then, is to move from *mere* exposure to the sort of exposure that can shatter prevailing stereotypes. We must discover ways to create opportunities for the sorts of intergroup contacts that lead people to recognize their underlying similarities and to appreciate rather than disdain their differences. The best way to accomplish this, as we shall see, is to provide opportunities for contact in which both parties are placed in the same boat, forced to contend with external forces that affect both of them equally.

The Fraternity of Strangers

Gordon Allport suggests that intergroup contact is most likely to be effective in reducing prejudice "if it is of a sort that leads to the perception of common interests and common humanity" between members of the two groups.[30] As a promising first step he mentions the neighborhood festival technique employed by Rachel DuBois, consisting of reminiscences of childhood experiences on the part of all present. "All who compose the group—Armenians, Mexicans, Jews, Negroes, Yankees—are invited to compare their recollections of autumn days, of fresh bread, of childhood pleasures, hopes, punishments. Almost any topic will bring out the universal (or closely similar) values of all the ethnic groups."[31] A more direct approach to creating a "perception of common interests" is to establish common experiences in the present. We are most likely to view another as a *person* rather than as a Pole or a Piranian if we are forced to undergo stressful experiences together, in which both of us are affected equally by external forces.

During the great Northeastern power failure of 1965, for example, observers were struck by the extent to which good fellowship reigned among urbanites of different colors and nationalities. Passengers on a stalled subway car danced together in the aisles; when night fell on a powerless Long Island railroad train, commuters went to sleep with their arms wrapped around persons who had been complete strangers several hours earlier. One group, trapped for five hours in an Empire State Building elevator, formed a Blackout Club and made plans to meet later on. "All across the Megalopolis," a magazine reporter observed, "the cliff dwellers— who had come to believe in their own folk image as so many encapsulated, private atoms—surprised themselves with their neighborly good spirit at an hour when everyone, at last, had something in common." As Victor Hugo once wrote, "Great perils have this beauty, that they bring to light the fraternity of strangers."[32]

The era of good feeling created by the crisis was short-lived. Once the power was restored and the lights came back on, the cliff dwellers returned to their private spheres, their paths never to cross until the next catastrophe came along. And yet it is possible that at least some of their unflattering stereotypes of those who dwell on different cliffs were permanently put aside that day as a result of a shared experience in a subway car stopped in its tracks or an elevator suspended in midair. Roger Brown provides another graphic example of the way in which the perception of a common fate leads to a feeling of solidarity. When French mountaineers reach a certain critical altitude, they shift their form of address from the more distant *vous* to the more intimate *tu*. "We like to think," Brown writes, "that this is the point where their lives hang by a single thread."[33]

Most reported instances of successful interracial integration resemble the case of the Northeast blackout in that they involve not mere exposure, but a shared experience. In the integrated housing projects studied by Deutsch and Collins, for example, blacks and whites were placed on an equal footing in a new environment, where they had to cope with common problems of physical and psychological adjustment. In such a setting stereotypes broke down, and new perceptions of basic similarity took their place. "I've really come to like it," one white housewife told her interviewer, "I see they're just as human as we." Her view was echoed by a black officer on an interracial ship off Korea: "After a while you begin thinking of whites as people."[34]

Fritz Heider's "balance theory" proposes that people conceive of their ties to others in terms of two kinds of relationships.[35] One kind, the "unit relationship," is the person's perception that he is linked with another person by virtue of being similar to him or of sharing the same fate. As a result, the two are viewed as belonging to the same larger unit. The other kind of relationship is the "sentiment relationship" or, in more common terms, liking. A central proposition of balance theory is that the two types of relationships tend toward consistency with one another: When we perceive ourselves as being in a unit relationship with someone else, there is a strong psychological pressure to like that person as well. The accumulated evidence suggests that mere exposure or proximity to another person is usually not sufficient to establish a unit relationship, but being on an equal footing with another person in a stressful situation is.

Actual face-to-face exposure to another person is not always necessary for the establishment of a unit relationship. In some cases simply anticipating a shared experience is enough to set the psychological balancing processes in motion. This possibility was demonstrated in an experiment conducted by social psychologists John M. Darley and Ellen Berscheid.[36] Coeds at the the University of Minnesota were recruited to take part in two-person discussion groups concerning their dating history and sexual activities. Before the women met their assigned partners, they were asked to look through folders containing "personality data" on two other women, one of whom was to be their partner. The folder for each woman contained rather ambiguous information, including a nondescript "value profile" and a typed paragraph concerning her reasons for wanting to go to college. The experimenter stressed that the pairings had already been made on a random basis and that no one would be able to select her own partner. After looking through the folders, the subjects were asked to indicate how much they thought they would like each of the other women. Darley and Berscheid found that a significant majority of the subjects indicated greater liking for the girl with whom they understood they would be paired. Since the information presented to the subjects was counterbalanced in such a way that half thought they would be paired with "Girl A" and half thought they would be paired with "Girl B," this preference cannot be ascribed to any objective differences between the two profiles. Rather, the anticipation that they would be sharing an emotional experience with another person gave rise to the perception of a unit relationship—the feeling of being in the same boat—which in turn led to increased liking for her even before they met.

The Call of the JubJub

But whereas the anticipation of a shared experience can set the stage for attraction, direct exposure in such a situation is necessary to create more durable bonds. Whether it is the experience of coping with the vicissitudes of everyday life in the same housing project or of facing a common enemy on the battlefield, such contact provides opportunities for communication that, in Allport's terms, "leads to the perception of common interests and common humanity." It may be suggested, in fact, that the greater the shared stress—assuming it is successfully overcome—the more capable it is of reducing hostility. In a well-known poem of Lewis Carroll, the Butcher and the Beaver, mortal enemies, set out on a snark hunt and accidentally find themselves pursuing the same trail through the valley:

> But the valley grew narrow and narrower still,
>   And the evening got darker and colder,
> · Till (merely from nervousness, not from goodwill)
>   They marched along shoulder to shoulder.
> Then a scream, shrill and high, rent the shuddering sky,
>   And they knew that some danger was near;
> The Beaver turned pale to the tip of its tail
>   And even the Butcher felt queer.
> " 'Tis the voice of the JubJub," he suddenly cried,
>   " 'Tis the call of the JubJub we hear."
>
> .   .   .   .
>
> Such friends as the Beaver and Butcher became
>   Have seldom if ever been known.
> In winter or summer 'twas always the same—
>   You could never meet either alone.
> And when quarrels arise—as one frequently finds
>   Quarrels will, spite of every endeavor—
> The song of the JubJub recurred to their minds
>   And cemented their friendship forever![37]

People's underlying commonality of purpose becomes emphasized by a common enemy like the JubJub. A well-worn science fiction theme has the nations of the world uniting in order to fend off an invader from outer space. An analogous uniting role is played by any common goal that can be achieved only when members of both groups pull together. In one of social psychology's classic field experiments a group of researchers headed by Muzafer Sherif was able first to create and then to eliminate hostility among two groups of youngsters at a summer camp.[38] The hostility was created by dividing the boys into two groups and pitting them against one another in athletic contests until all goodwill evaporated and tension mounted. Merely exposing the groups to one another at this point in variants of the "goodwill dinners" periodically held in American communities did not help the situation in the least. The contact was simply taken as an opportunity for creative new expressions of hostility such as pushing in line and food-throwing.

Once the goodwill-dinner approach had failed, however, Sherif introduced a series of events that created a commonality of purpose between the groups. During a hike one day the boys discovered that the truck that was to go into town to pick up lunch would not start. Only when all of the boys worked together, pulling on a rope, was it possible to get the truck started. Another morning the water pipeline to the camp was surreptitiously broken, and the boys were told that unless they worked together to solve the problem they would all have to leave the camp. In another instance the two groups were told that they would have to pool their resources if the camp was to be able to procure a desired movie. These cooperative activities succeeded where the goodwill dinners had failed. By the end of camp, friendships had developed between the two groups. They held joint campfires and even treated one another to refreshments.

In Sherif's terms, the key to reducing intergroup hostility is to establish "superordinate goals" whose attainment requires joint action: "Only when erstwhile rivals come into contact in the pursuit of a vital purpose that grips all participants can contact situations provide opportunities for creative moves toward reducing intergroup hostility. The participants must feel a common steadfast pull in the same direction if not toward the same actions." He adds, in keeping with our earlier discussion of selective perception, that when hostile groups are exposed to one another without superordinate goals, "favorable information . . . tends to be ignored, rejected, or reinterpreted to fit prevailing stereotypes. But when groups are pulling together toward superordinate goals, . . . information about the outgroup is seen in a new light. The probability of information being effective in eliminating unfavorable stereotypes is enormously enhanced."

Exposure is indeed a vital ingredient in the elimination of hostility. As Thomas Pettigrew has concluded, "The attainment of a viable, democratic nation, free from personal and institutional racism, requires extensive racial integration in all realms of life. To prescribe more separation because of discomfort, racism, conflict or the need for autonomy is like getting drunk again to cure hangover."[39] But reducing deeply ingrained hostility between groups turns out to be harder to accomplish than teaching unbiased newborn rats to prefer Schoenberg to Mozart. It requires not mere exposure, but exposure combined with the perception of a common threat or purpose.

If Lewis Carroll were around to survey the recent research on the topic, he would have been able to summarize it infinitely more gracefully—but perhaps not too differently in basic substance—than the following bit of doggerel:

> When you see a strange cat in a weird-looking hat
>   There is no need to lose your composure;
> Just keep him in view—he will soon grow on you,
>   All you need is a bit more exposure.
> But if you can tell from his nose or his skin
>   That he's rotten (though he may have rhythm),
> Then it's sad but it's true Mere exposure won't do—
>   You must manage to share something with him.
>
> You must search for a cause you can both get behind
>   Like fishing or bottle-collection;
> You must look for a JubJub to blow both your minds
>   And drive you from hate to affection!

Chapter 7
BIRDS OF A FEATHER
The Attraction of Like to Like

And they are friends who have come to regard the same things as good and the same things as evil, they who are friends of the same people, and they who are enemies of the same people. . . . We like those who resemble us, and are engaged in the same pursuits. . . . We like those who desire the same things as we, if the case is such that we and they can share the things together.

—ARISTOTLE, *Rhetoric*

Back in those awkward, in-between years after John V. Lindsay had been rejected by the Republicans but before he became a Democrat, he ran as a Liberal for mayor of New York against a Democratic candidate named Mario A. Procaccino. Lindsay and Procaccino differed in many ways. The former was a well-bred, highly polished, Yale-educated, politically liberal WASP from Manhattan. The latter was a relatively conservative Roman Catholic from the Bronx with, Jimmy Breslin reported, "his mustache from Arthur Avenue, his suit from the garment center, his language from all the years of all the neighborhoods of New York."[1] All of these differences undoubtedly made it easy for many New York voters to decide between the two candidates. But to all these differences add one more: Lindsay was tall, measuring in at six-foot-three. Procaccino was a full nine inches shorter, standing only five-foot-six. This final difference is the one that attracted the attention of an alert young social psychologist named William Berkowitz, himself an impartial five-foot-eleven.

Berkowitz and a group of his students trooped into the city from Lafayette College in Pennsylvania during the week of the election.[2] They cornered 300 male pedestrians in midtown and downtown Manhattan and asked them who they were voting for and how tall they themselves were. The result: Lindsay's partisans averaged over an inch taller than Procaccino supporters. The average heights of the two groups were 69.68 and 68.31 inches respectively, a difference that would come about by chance fewer than once in a thousand times. Berkowitz's study was not a shot in the dark. He had already asked male students in his introductory psychology class at Lafayette to report their own heights and those of their closest male friends and found that pairs of friends were more similar in height than would be expected by chance.[3]

How does this tendency for friends to be of similar height come about? Novelist Sol Stein pointed to one sort of possibility in *The Magician*:

> Cantor's size [six-foot-four], an advantage in crowds, made men avoid him in private. At twenty-nine, he did not have a single close friend. Once, just out of Harvard Law, he and a journalist named Henry Siller had seen a lot of each other, but Siller, then working as a desk man at *The New York Times*, had stopped his vertical ascent into manhood at five-foot-seven, and the two of them together looked ridiculous. It was not only the occasional cliché remarks of rude people; even when they talked alone, Cantor was conscious of looking down at Siller, just as he was certain that Siller was aware of looking up. Despite an easy rapport, the silly difference in height ultimately proved an insuperable obstacle, and they drifted apart.[4]

Of course this explanation is not quite so readily applied to the case of a man's preference for the mayoral candidate who is closer to his own size. But regardless of what the reasons for it may be, the observed association between attraction and similarity of stature provides one illustration of a more general principle, already documented by hundreds of investigations, that people tend to be attracted to others who resemble themselves.

A Gallery of Resemblances

In Detroit several years ago, University of Michigan researchers asked a sample of some 1,000 men to name and describe the characteristics of their three best friends.[5] One of the survey's clearest findings was an overwhelming tendency for respondents to name others who were socially and economically similar to themselves. Jews, for example, comprised less than 3 percent of the Detroit sample, but almost 80 percent of the friends named by Jewish men were Jewish. Whereas Catholics comprised 42 percent of the sample, 62 percent of their friends were Catholic. Congrega-tionalists comprised only 1 percent of the sample, but fully one-third of their friends belonged to the same denomination. Friends were also highly similar to one another—and, in statistical terms, much *more* similar than randomly paired men would be—with respect to their age, occupational status, educational level, and political allegiances.

In his well-known investigation of "Elmtown's" youth, con-ducted in the 1940s, sociologist August Hollingshead reported that cliques of high school students were largely made up of boys and girls from the same or adjacent socioeconomic classes.[6] Friend-ships and cliques were also based to a large degree on similarities in the experimental boarding house established at the University of Michigan by Theodore Newcomb. One clique, for example, con-sisted of five men who were all enrolled in the liberal arts college and who had liberal political views and strong intellectual and aesthetic interests. Another clique comprised three veterans, all in the college of engineering, politically conservative, and with inter-ests more "practical" than "theoretical."[7]

Another sort of evidence of the impact of similarity comes from Donn Byrne's "phantom-other" experiments.[8] Subjects are shown a questionnaire supposedly filled out by another person, with the responses fabricated in such a way as to indicate that the other person is either similar or dissimilar to the subject with re-spect to a variety of opinions and beliefs. The subjects are then asked to indicate how much they think they would like the other person. The consistent result of many such experiments is a close fit between the proportion of items on which the phantom other agrees with the subject and the subject's liking for him. Byrne and his colleagues have obtained the same finding not only from Amer-ican college students, but also from elementary and high school students, elderly people, surgical patients, alcoholics, schizo-phrenics, Job Corps trainees, and college students in India, Japan, and Mexico. In a recent paper Byrne calls the link between attitude similarity and attraction "the ubiquitous relationship."

If similarity dictates our choice of friends, it even more cer-tainly dictates our choice of spouses as well.[9] Hundreds of statisti-cal studies, dating back to Francis Galton's study of heriditary genius in 1870, have found husbands and wives to be significantly similar to one another not only with respect to such biographical and social characteristics as age, race, religion, education, and social status, but also with respect to physical features like height and eye color, and psychological characteristics like intelligence.

It is still possible that there are times when opposites attract, as when a dominant person hits it off with a submissive one, or an outgoing person is drawn toward a more contemplative sort. But the operation of such an "opposites attract" principle in mate selection has never been conclusively demonstrated, whereas the impact of physical, social, and attitudinal similarities has been demonstrated repeatedly. We will return to the case of mate selection in Chapter 9.

If we are willing to stretch our definitions a bit, similarity leads to attraction even among rhesus monkeys. Psychologists Charles Pratt and Gene Sackett created three different "kinds" of monkeys by raising newborns under three conditions.[10] The monkeys in Condition A lived in isolated individual cages and had no contact with other monkeys and virtually none with humans until they were nine months old, and only visual contact with other isolated monkeys between the ages of nine and eighteen months. The monkeys in Condition B had visual contact, but no physical contact, with other monkeys from birth until eighteen months. Condition C monkeys lived normally in groups throughout. At eighteen months each of the monkeys was tested for his attraction to his peers wih an apparatus called the "Sackett Self-Selection Circus." The Sackett Self-Selection Circus resembles a cross between an automat and a college mixer. The monkey being tested is placed in the center chamber of the apparatus, and three other monkeys whom he has not previously met—one each from Groups A, B, and C—are placed at the ends of each of three arms that radiate from the center. The amount of time that the subject spends in each of the three chambers adjacent to the "target" monkeys provides a quite reasonable measure of his relative preferences. Drs. Pratt and Sackett obtained extremely clear-cut results: Monkeys from each of the three groups overwhelmingly preferred others of "their own kind."*

Given the wide variety of contexts in which similarity has been shown to influence attraction, one might be tempted to put

---

* To account for this finding, Pratt and Sackett suggest that the different rearing conditions create a status hierarchy among the monkeys. The normally reared, socially adept monkeys of Group A are at the top of the hierarchy, the semi-isolated monkeys of Group B are in the middle, and the isolated, socially retarded monkeys of Group C are at the bottom. As in human status hierarchies, there is a tendency for the individual animal to gravitate toward his own level, either because he is most comfortable with others whose behavior patterns resemble his own or, as in the case of the lower-caste monkeys, because he fears rejection or attack by the higher-status animals.

forth a "law of similarity," which would state that people are attracted to one another to the extent that they are similar. For those social scientists who wish to reduce their accumulated knowledge to the smallest possible set of basic principles, such a law would have a great deal of appeal. Unfortunately, it would also be deceptive. Hidden behind its simplicity is a vast array of complexities. Not all similarities are associated with attraction, even though surprisingly many are. We must ask, "Similarity with respect to what—and in what sort of relationship?" It seems likely, for example, that the sorts of "things in common" that are crucial in the early stages of courtship are quite different from the sorts of similarities that become central later on. We must also ask, "Similarity for whom?" For which sorts of people are particular similarities crucial in the selection of friends, and for which people are they inconsequential? And, finally, we must ask the more basic question, "*Why* similarity?" What psychological needs are gratified by associating with others who remind us of ourselves, and what does our characteristic attraction to similar others tell us about the nature of man?

The Importance of Being Agreed With

Whereas virtually all imaginable similarities, from eye color to family size, have been shown to be related to attraction in one instance or another, some similarities weigh more heavily than others. A complicating factor is that any given similarity of significance may bring other insignificant similarites in tow. For example, I would not be much surprised if liking proved to be related to having a similar number of letters in one's last name. But this would not necessarily be due to an inherent tendency to feel a bond toward one's monosyllabically or polysyllabically surnamed brethren. It would more likely stem from the fact that the length of surnames may be correlated with one's ethnic background, which in turn directly or indirectly affects attraction. Similarly, one may have a special fondness for others who like the same brand of coffee not so much because one Maxwell Housewife loves another, as the commercial implies, but because coffee preferences may in turn say something about one's ethnic background or social class. An important research question then becomes to distinguish between those similarities that are significant determinants of attraction and those that are merely hangers-on.

The consensus of recent research is that the basic sort of similarity involves people's attitudes and values. We are less drawn

"GEE, DAD, JUST BECAUSE I HAVE CONTEMPT FOR YOUR POLITICS, SOCIAL STANDARDS, RELIGIOUS BELIEFS, AND MORAL CODE DOESN'T MEAN I DON'T *LIKE* YOU. I REALLY LIKE YOU A LOT."

Drawing by Whitney Darrow, Jr.; © 1970 The New Yorker Magazine, Inc.

toward people who look like us, sound like us, or share our mannerisms than we are toward people who *agree with us.* It is psychologically rewarding to be agreed with, theorists contend, for at least four reasons:

First, agreement often provides a basis for engaging in pleasurable activities with one another, whether it be attending a prayer meeting or taking over a university hall.

Second, as Samuel Johnson observed, "Every man who attacks my belief diminishes in some degree my confidence in it, and therefore makes me uneasy." There is a strong human predisposition to translate such uneasiness into hostility toward the person who produced it. Agreement, on the other hand, bolsters self-confidence and thus breeds attraction.

Third, even when their confidence in their own beliefs is unshakable, people have the egocentric habit of assuming that anyone who shares their views must be a sensible and praiseworthy individual, while anyone who differs with them must be doing so because of some basic incapacity or perversity. It is "cognitively imbalanced," in Fritz Heider's terminology,[11] to conclude that one well-liked person (oneself) can believe X and that another (someone else) can believe X's opposite. To restore balance to the situation, we see to it that the other person is not liked at all.

And fourth, agreement has the advantage, at least for the faint-hearted among us, of keeping bickering, argument, and other such unpleasantries to a minimum.

Hugo Bohun (in Disraeli's *Lothair*) may have had any or all of these reasons in mind when he declared, "My idea of an agreeable person is a person who agrees with me." A confident, open-minded person who enjoys diversity and relishes controversy might disagree with Hugo Bohun—and like him anyway—but precious few of us fall into this category.

The extent to which we experience agreement as pleasant and disagreement as unpleasant will of course depend on the importance of the opinion or belief in question. Although advertisers would have us believe otherwise, the discovery that another person does or does not like the same brand of toothpaste we do will probably have little impact on our feelings toward him. On the other hand, college roommates who were in basic disagreement about American military policy in the late 1960s and early 1970s were unlikely to have had a fully amicable relationship. Being a "hawk" or a "dove" at that time was more than an isolated opinion. It was an important element of one's approach to life. Being agreed with on such a fundamental issue may amount to confirmation of one's very identity, and disagreement may be equated with disconfirmation. As we noted in Chapter 3, one of the most important reasons for people's desires to affiliate with others is to obtain just this sort of self-confirmation.

In 1969 sociologist Michael Useem interviewed about one hundred young men in the Boston area who had resisted the draft, in most cases by returning or burning their draft cards at a rally.[12] The act of resistance played a central role in these men's lives and self-conceptions. It often represented the culmination of a process in which men whose political philosophies had previously been moderate or liberal became radicalized. Useem found that this process of radicalization was also accompanied by a shift in the men's networks of friends. As the resisters' political attitudes changed, they tended to abandon (or be abandoned by) old friends who did not share their political views and to make new friends who did. The new friends provided social support for what was in many cases a difficult and tension-filled shift of attitudes. As one resister remarked, "To know a man I wanted to know his politics."

Another demonstration of the importance of being agreed with comes from a study of friendships in suburbia. Sociologist Herbert Gans lived in the mass-produced suburb of Levittown, New Jersey, during the first two years of its existence. He reported that similarities of values and attitudes—or more generally, in his terms, of "life style"—were central determinants of friendship:

> Cosmopolitans are impatient with locals, and vice versa; women who want to talk about cultural and civic matters are bored with conversations of home and family—and, again, vice versa; working class women who are used to the informal flow of talk with relatives need to find substitutes among neighbors with similar experience.[13]

Of course, we may not immediately know whether a prospective friend shares the attitudes and values we consider important. This is why so much of the initial dialogue among people who are getting to know one another is devoted to attempts to "feel out" one another's views. In the meantime, however, we are likely to apply Heider's balance principle by assuming that anyone who seems congenial must share our beliefs, while anyone who seems uncongenial must not. This perceptual tendency was documented in Dr. Newcomb's boarding house.[14] Before the start of the term, incoming boarders were shown standard descriptions of six basic values—the "theoretical," "economic," "aesthetic," "social," "political," and "religious"—and asked to rank them in order of their importance to themselves. Subsequently, at various intervals during the term, the students were asked to estimate how each of the sixteen other house members would rank the six values. In the early weeks the students tended to guess, often quite incorrectly, that the value hierarchies of fellow boarders whom they liked resembled their own rankings, while the outlooks of the housemates whom they disliked were quite different from their own. As the term progressed, estimates of other students' values became increasingly accurate. At the same time, the students reshuffled their feelings of liking and disliking in such a way as to keep their sentiments in balance with their perceptions of agreement and disagreement. By the end of the term there was a strong correlation between actual value similarity and friendship.

Documenting the impact of agreement upon attraction is sometimes a ticklish methodological problem—more ticklish than many researchers have realized. The simple observation that friends or spouses tend to have similar attitudes leaves us in the dark about the causal process involved: Is it the agreement that leads to the attraction, or is it the attraction that leads to the agreement? Indeed, both causal sequences are likely to be operating.* Michael Useem writes, for example, "The formation of ideological and interpersonal links into the movement appears to have been an interactive one, with new companions and new politics mutually reinforcing one another." It is possible for the careful researcher to focus most squarely on these causal processes by extending his observations over time, as in the case of Newcomb's study. A more recent longitudinal study of friendship formation in a University of Washington dormitory made use of the statistical technique of cross-lagged correlation to confirm Newcomb's analysis: *Actual* value similarity caused *perceived* value similarity, and both types of similarity predicted future attraction.

In the University of Washington study, students provided measures of their own values, their liking for their dormitory "cluster-mates" (all initial strangers), and their perception of the cluster-mates' values at five points during the course of a term.[15] At each testing, they also completed a short version of a standard personality test (the Edwards Personal Preference Schedule) and estimated how each cluster-mate would complete this test. The investigators found that whereas both perceived and actual value similarity predicted attraction, neither perceived nor actual *personality* similarity predicted attraction at all. Their finding jibes with a more general failure of researchers to find a relationship between personality similarity and attraction. As Theodore Newcomb has suggested, there is indeed no strong reason to expect people to be attracted to others who have the same constellation of inner needs, motives, and dispositions as themselves. In such primarily internal matters people may well be content with a wide range of "types." It is only when people confront one another's values and attitudes about mutually relevant issues, that bear directly on the establishment and maintenance of a shared sense of reality, that similarity becomes a central determinant of attraction.

It follows from this argument that the variety of resemblances that may in one instance or another be related to liking and loving derive their impact from the fact that they *imply* the sharing of a

---

* It is also possible that some third factor, such as a common ethnic background may underlie both the agreement and the attraction, with neither of the latter factors having a direct impact on the other.

common outlook or perspective. Herbert Gans suggests that this
was the case in Levittown. He writes that when friendships were
formed within lines of age and social class, as was often the case,
the binding factor was not similarity of age or social class per se,
but rather similarity of underlying concerns and attitudes. For
example, mothers who had children of the same age and who
agreed on how they should be brought up—which might in turn
reflect their own similar age and social backgrounds—were particularly likely to become friends. One woman explained her friendship with her next-door neighbor in the following terms: "We see
eye to eye on things, about raising kids, doing things together with
your husband, living the same way; we have practically the same
identical background."[16] My reading of her explanation is that
"the same identical background" was important only insofar as it
was associated with the two women's shared attitudes. The implication of likemindedness may even explain the impact of such
frivolous similarities as that of height. A tall man's preference for
John Lindsay or a short man's for Mario Procaccino may go beyond
the narcissistic desire to see a man who resembles oneself physically in City Hall. When another person is about as tall as we are
we may assume—correctly or not—that we indeed "see eye to
eye on things," that we share a common view of the world.*

Like Skins or Like Minds?

For all of this emphasis on shared beliefs, it is painfully obvious
that people frequently hold deep antipathy toward other people
whose beliefs may be quite similar to their own, but who differ
with respect to such other items as race, religion, or nationality.
Ethnic differences have surely given rise to considerably more
conflict, animosity, and bloodshed than differences of opinion ever
have. Nevertheless, to ascribe such hostility to differences of race
or religion alone may obscure our understanding of the roots of intergroup conflict and prejudice. Social psychologist Milton Rokeach

* Roger Brown observes that similarity with respect to a physical characteristic such as height is especially likely to constitute a social category, and
thus create a perception of likemindedness, when people are at an extreme
of the physical dimension. Thus, "similarity of height among dwarfs and
similarity of weight among circus 'fat ladies' should be grounds for solidarity."[17] The fact that dwarfs are not only short but are also categorized by
others as deviant is likely to increase the probability that they will have certain similar interests and concerns. In other cases, of course, similarity of
height may provide the basis of joint activities, such as those involved in
being a jockey or playing basketball.

has made a persuasive case for the proposition that assumed dissimilarities of belief and value are more important than ethnic or racial differences as determinants of social discrimination.[18]

Children are not born prejudiced. They must *learn* to hate members of out-groups—from their parents, peers, and surrounding culture. But what is learned, Dr. Rokeach contends, is not simply that blacks or Jews or Italians are undesirable, but that they are undesirable because their values differ from those the child is taught to adopt. Rokeach suggests, for example, that among middle-class whites, "Indoctrination about race takes place within a yet broader context aimed at indoctrinating beliefs about the virtues of cleanliness, hard work, monogamous sexual behavior, middle-class values. . . ." Thus, the white child learns to reject the Negro not simply because his skin is black, but because his beliefs are presumably at odds with those espoused by white middle-class culture.

In Rokeach's view, the founding of prejudice on assumed disagreement rather than on differences of race or religion persists into adulthood. One group's stereotypes of another may at heart be attributions of particular beliefs to that other group:

> When a non-Jew says of the Jew that he is *exclusive*, he apparently attributes to the Jew the belief: "Jews should stick together to prevent gentiles from entering into competition with them." What he may also be saying is that he, a non-Jew, believes that Jews should not stick together for such a purpose. When the same person says that Jews are *intrusive*, what he apparently believes is that Jews believe, and act on the belief, that they should be permitted social entrance to places that exclude Jews. What he may also be saying is that he, a non-Jew, believes the opposite.

If "belief congruence," as Rokeach terms it, indeed underlies "racial" or "religious" prejudice, then the prejudice will surely be reduced if and when a person discovers that members of the out-group are in basic agreement with him after all. As we noted in Chapter 6, there are at least some instances in which such discoveries apparently have the impact that Rokeach would predict. For example, "When a non-Jew says 'Some of my best friends are Jews' he may be trying to say that he knows and likes some Jews because they hold to the same beliefs he does. . . . It may also mean that his homogeneous complex image, the Jew, has broken down upon contact with certain Jews who believe as he does."

But although Rokeach's theory has intuitive appeal, its validity is difficult to assess in real-life situations. Whether a particular white person reacts negatively to a particular black because of his race, his assumed beliefs, or both must usually remain a matter of conjecture. But laboratory experimentation is well suited to unraveling this sort of theoretical knot. The general approach, which has been employed with variations in several experiments, is to present a subject with information about other people who belong to either the same or a different group from his own (most of the studies have exposed white subjects to white and black "targets") and who at the same time either agree or disagree with certain of his central beliefs. It is thus possible to assess the subject's reactions to others with different combinations of characteristics. For example, how much does the subject think he would like a person who is white and who agrees with his political views? How about a person who is black and agrees with his political views? And how does he feel about whites and blacks who are at odds with him politically? The subject's pattern of reactions can be analyzed so as to reveal which factor—race or belief—is given greater weight. Although the "other people" being reacted to are fictional, the experiment is made more realistic by inducing the subject to think they are real.

One of the most careful studies along these lines was conducted by social psychologists David Stein, Jane Allyn Piliavin, and M. Brewster Smith.[19] Their subjects were white teen-agers living in a working-class California community. Two months prior to the study these students had completed a value scale that called for them to indicate how strongly they felt teen-agers "ought" (or ought not) to do a variety of things like "have school spirit," "treat other students as equals," and "live up to strict moral standards." At the experimental session two months later, the researchers explained, "We would like to know how you would feel about some teen-agers who took the same questionnaires as you did, but in other parts of the country. Therefore, we have taken some of their answers and presented them on the following pages." Each subject was now shown the questionnaires that had supposedly been filled out by four other students. As in Dr. Byrne's procedure, the experimenters had prefabricated the questionnaires in such a way that two of the "students" expressed values that were quite similar to the subject's own previously expressed "oughts," while the other two expressed quite different views on a number of the items. In addition, each questionnaire was accompanied by an information sheet (see sample) that had supposedly been filled in by the other student. All four of the "students" were presented as being of the same sex as the subject, in the ninth grade (like the subjects), in a college preparatory course, and with "about B" grades. But one of the agreeing and one of the disagreeing students were "white," and the other agreeing and disagreeing students were "Negro."

Teenager I

1. Sex _*M*_   Grade _*9*_
2. What program are you taking in school? (If undecided, mark the program you think you will take.)
   0 _____ Vocational
   1 _____ Commercial
   2 _X_ College preparatory
   3 _____ General
   4 _____ Other _____ (write in)
3. Last year, what kind of grades did you get?
   0 _____ about an A average   4 _____ about a C average
   1 _____ between an A & B   5 _____ between a C & D
              average   average
   2 _X_ about a B average   6 _____ about a D average
   3 _____ between a B & C   7 _____ below a D average
              average
4. What is your race?
   0 _X_ White   1 _____ Negro   2 _____ Oriental
   3 _____ other (What? _____)

After looking over each of the questionnaires and accompanying information sheets, the subjects were asked to indicate how friendly they thought they would feel toward the other teen-ager. Their responses fit the pattern suggested by Rokeach's theory. When the other student's values were similar to the subject's own, the average response was between "quite friendly" and "a little friendly," regardless of whether the target was presented as being black or white. When the other student disagreed with the student's own values, the ratings were closest to "nothing either way," once again regardless of the race of the target. There was a slight tendency for the students to have more friendly reactions to white than to black targets, but this tendency was dwarfed by the much larger impact of belief congruence.

But these results do not present the total picture. Other studies using the same general procedure have found strong "race effects" as well as "belief effects." One variable factor is regional.

In a study of white college students in Wisconsin, Missouri, and Louisiana, "belief effects" were found in all three samples, but an even stronger "race effect" was found in Louisiana.[20] Regardless of where the study is conducted, the obtained reactions also depend to a large extent on the specific questions that the subject is asked about the target. In the Stein study, for example, the target teen-ager's race was weighted more heavily than his beliefs when the questions concerned willingness to invite him home for dinner and to have him date the subject's sister (or, for girls, her brother).

Other experiments have painted a similarly complex picture: Subjects are influenced considerably more by another person's beliefs than by his race when they are asked how much they think they would like him, or how good, valuable, or pleasant a person he is. When it comes to willingness to accept the other person in ways that are specifically governed by cultural taboos, however, belief congruence becomes less important and race becomes more im-portant. Race seems to have its greatest impact in contexts of institutionalized intimacy, such as dating and marriage. In a study of white teen-agers in North Carolina conducted in the mid-1960s, race also had a larger impact than belief when the question in-volved willingness to eat together. "Traditional Southern culture tolerates friendship between Negroes and whites, as long as the Negroes stay in 'their place,' " the North Carolina investigators ob-served, "but does not tolerate eating with Negroes."[21]

As long as certain forms of interracial association, whether it is intermarriage or eating together, are taboos, the discovery of shared beliefs may not do much to overcome the taboos. There may in fact be relatively few explicit taboos about interracial liking and friendship, however. As a result, the discovery of common beliefs and values may indeed be able to change negative reactions to positive ones. Unfortunately, members of different groups often have no opportunity to discover the extent to which their basic values in fact coincide. As long as they have no information to the contrary, people tend to make the dubious assumption that others who are "different" in some respects—such as the obvious differ-ences of race and religion—have different basic values and beliefs as well.[22]

When Similarity Is Threatening

The Jewish population of the State of Israel can broadly be cate-gorized into two groups, the "Europeans" (Jews of European de-scent, as well as a smattering of North and South Americans) and the "Orientals" (Jews of Asian and African descent). There are enormous economic and cultural differences between the two groups. The Europeans come from modern middle-class backgrounds, are well educated, technologically advanced, and have a virtual monopoly of the nation's positions of power and leadership. The Orientals lag behind in all of these respects, coming from backgrounds which provided little preparation for modern ways of life. When they arrived in the Promised Land, moreover, they found the most prestigious jobs already filled, the most desirable neighborhoods taken, and the opportunities for advancement limited.

There is considerable conflict between Israel's European and Oriental Jews, but the two groups are united in their animosity toward Israel's third major ethnic group, the Arabs. Because of their identification in the public mind with Israel's external enemies, Israeli Arabs are widely scorned, oppressed, and mistrusted. This attitude extends to a certain contempt for everything that symbolizes the Arab world: "Arab music is never broadcast on the radio; Arab art is not displayed, and most people would feel uneasy if they spoke Arabic in public places."[23] Since the Oriental Jews come from Arab-speaking backgrounds, where they adopted many elements of Arab culture and behavior, these attitudes are indirectly extended to them as well. But the cultural similarity between Oriental Jews and Arabs has not softened anti-Arab sentiment on the part of the Oriental Jews. In apparent defiance of the principle of similarity, Oriental Jews feel even greater hostility toward Israeli Arabs than European Jews do.

The point has been documented by surveys taken in Israel by sociologist Yochanan Peres in 1967 and 1968.[24] Oriental teenagers and adults, in comparison with Europeans, said they were less willing to marry, be friends with, or live in the same neighborhood as Arabs. Orientals were also more likely to agree with such ethnocentric statements as "Arabs will not reach the level of progress of Jews." "At first, this discovery seems astonishing," Peres writes. "It might have been assumed that the Orientals, with close ties to the Arab culture, could serve as mediators between European Israelis and Arabs. However, this is clearly not the case." But Peres also proposes an explanation for the seeming paradox. He suggests that "the Orientals feel that they must reject the remaining traces of their Middle Eastern origin to attain the status of the dominant European group. By expressing hostility to Arabs, an Oriental attempts to rid himself of the 'inferior' Arab elements in his own identity. . . ." Oriental Jews despise the Arabs, it seems, not in spite of their similarities but in part because of them. To bolster this analysis, Peres has found that among the Oriental Jews, those who most resemble Arabs in appearance and accent tend to be the most anti-Arab of all.

Similarity, in the general case, fosters attraction because of the rewards a similar person can provide, such as joint activities, easy communication, and support for one's own view of the world. But there are instances in which similarity is more threatening than it is rewarding. Much as an extremely myopic person may resent a blind man, or one who is hard of hearing may despise the deaf, the Oriental Jew rejects the Arab, who reminds him of the origins he hopes to renounce and the fate he hopes to avoid.

Even similarity of attitudes may be threatening if it suggests the possibility of an undesirable fate. Social psychologists David Novak and Melvin Lerner employed the "phantom other" technique to make Kentucky college students think that their partners in an experiment (who were unseen, but ostensibly waiting in an adjacent room) had attitudes that were either very similar to or quite different from their own.[25] In addition, half of the similar and half of the dissimilar partners were presented as being emotionally disturbed. The "partner" had completed a "Personal Data Sheet" which included the heading, "*Any other information which might be relevant to your participation in the experiment.*" In the "normal partner" conditions the word "none" was written in this space. To create "emotionally disturbed partners," the experimenters had scrawled on behalf of the "partner," "I don't know if this is relevant or not, but last fall I had kind of a nervous breakdown and I had to be hospitalized for a while. I've been seeing a psychiatrist ever since. As you probably noticed, I'm pretty shaky right now." This sheet was delivered to the subject together with the attitude questionnaire purportedly completed by the partner. The experimenter created the impression that the Personal Data Sheet had been left inadvertently, noticing it and removing it with apparent surprise in the course of checking on the subject's progress.

After the subject had had a chance to digest this information, he was asked to indicate whether he preferred to work with the partner or by himself in the next part of the experiment, and how strongly he felt about this preference. When the partner was "normal," the subjects were more eager to meet him if he had been presented as sharing their beliefs. When the partner was "emotionally disturbed," however, the subjects were considerably more anxious to *avoid* him if his beliefs were similar to their own than if they were dissimilar. The experimenters had predicted this reversal of preferences, because of the potentially threatening nature of similarity:

> It is more difficult for someone to believe that he can avoid becoming emotionally handicapped (i.e., can control his own fate) if he is confronted with the fact that this highly unpleasant fate has occurred to someone quite like himself. On the other hand, it is relatively comforting, or at least not particularly threatening, to believe that only people who are different from oneself in essential respects are likely to become emotionally disturbed.

Similarity can sometimes be a dangerous thing, and we react to the danger by rejecting the person who gave rise to it, in effect dissociating ourselves from him and his kind. Such a reaction is psychologically understandable—but we should not fail to note that it comes frighteningly close to rejecting ourselves.

The Lure of Diversity

Association with similar others gratifies some of our needs, but frustrates others. While we seek the security and self-confirmation that comes from others who share our attitudes and outlooks, we humans are also curious animals, desirous of the excitement and stimulation that can best be provided by others whose backgrounds and experiences are different from our own. Herbert Gans noted the value of diversity in Levittown:

> Most Levittowners were pleased with the diversity they found among their neighbors, primarily because regional, ethnic and religious differences are today almost innocuous and provide variety to spice the flow of conversation and the exchange of ideas. For example, my Southern neighbor discovered pizza at the home of the Italian–American neighbor and developed a passion for it, and I learned much about the personal rewards of Catholicism from my Catholic convert neighbors.[26]

Some community planners would like to go far beyond Levittown in encouraging friendships among diverse people. After examining the budding middle-class suburbs of the 1950s and finding them to be "natural breeding places of conformity," Frederick Lewis Allen, the late editor of *Harper's*, advocated the establishment of neighborhoods that crosscut not only racial and religious lines, but also lines of age and economic status. Allen wrote:

We all enjoy, naturally, having the bulk of our intimate day-to-day contacts with those who look at things with eyes like our own, but the tendency, today, to group together large numbers of people of the same economic status in housing projects, housing developments, and urban areas may tend to insulate them from the problems and preferences of those in other sections of the population, and thus hinder that approach to the classless civilization which is such a source of American strength. . . . A community which includes a diversity of people, with different kinds and degrees of fortune, may be livelier and more productive than a standardized one.[27]

Allen's proposal is a provocative one. But would it work?

There is experimental evidence that people are indeed eager to associate with others of unfamiliar backgrounds, especially when they feel reasonably certain that these other people will not reject them. Elaine and Bill Walster gave Stanford undergraduates the choice between joining a discussion group consisting of people similar to themselves (fellow introductory psychology students) and joining a group of dissimilar others (either married night-school students, graduate students, professional psychologists, or factory workers.)[28] A clear majority of the students opted for one of the dissimilar groups. This was especially true when the students were assured that they would be introduced to whichever group they chose in a way that would encourage the other members to like them.

In another experimental condition, however, the students were warned that they should consider in advance how members of each of the five groups would react to them personally, and that it was best to choose a group that would respond to them in a friendly way. When the students were sensitized in this way to issues of popularity, their desire to meet diverse others was tempered by the fear of rejection. Over half of the subjects in this condition elected to have their discussion in a "safe" group of fellow psychology students. Many of us go through life behaving like the subjects in this sensitized condition. Uncertain as to whether or not dissimilar others will like us, we stick with the similar and the predictable.

In keeping with this analysis, one recent study found that people who were identified by a personality test as being emotionally insecure were more likely to confine their associations to similar others than were more secure people.[29] Abraham Maslow took the security argument even further, contending (albeit without much evidence) that truly healthy people—those who, in his terms, have gratified their basic physical and emotional needs and have moved on to a stage of "self-actualization"—are not concerned about similarity when they choose friends or lovers. "Self-actualizing people are not threatened by differences nor by strangeness," Maslow wrote. "Indeed, they are rather intrigued than otherwise. They need familiar accents, clothes, food, customs, and ceremonies far less than do average people."[30]

Most of us, alas, are "average people" rather than "self-actualizers." Nevertheless, even we ordinary mortals are often enticed by diversity, especially when we feel reasonably sure of ourselves. Social psychologist Howard Fromkin has argued that we are especially likely to be attracted to dissimilar others when we feel that we have become "one of the crowd," with little distinguishing us as unique individuals. Fromkin and his colleagues conducted another "phantom other" experiment, in which one group of subjects first received "computer feedback" indicating that their own expressed attitudes about a variety of issues corresponded closely to the answers given by a large majority of students in a national survey.[31] When these students later reacted to a "phantom other," they indicated only a small and nonsignificant preference for a person who agreed with them over one who disagreed. Fromkin contends that the computer feedback robbed these students of their feelings of distinctiveness. As a result, they came to value a disagreeing other—from whom they could easily distinguish themselves—more than they otherwise would have.

Because of the apparent lure of diversity, one is tempted to conclude that Frederick Allen's proposal *would* work—that establishing more diverse communities would lay the groundwork for wider-ranging and more rewarding friendships. But we must bear in mind that diversity is rewarding only within limits. Most of us welcome a great deal of diversity occasionally, and a modicum of diversity most of the time. But a great deal of diversity most of the time is more than we can reasonably be expected to tolerate. As Gans writes, "People so different from each other in age or class that they cannot agree on anything are unlikely to derive much enrichment from heterogeneity."[32] Gans strongly opposes racial or religious segregation of any sort. He suggests, however, that individual blocks or subblocks that are relatively homogeneous with respect to age and economic status be embedded within more heterogeneous larger neighborhoods. This plan would maximize contact among those of similar age and social class, and would provide an opportunity for more diverse contacts in schools and other neighborhood facilities.

Such a prescription clearly might have to be modified in one way or another to fit the needs of any particular community. But its underlying principle accords well with the implications of social–psychological research. Diversity is valuable and enriching, and there is evidence that under certain conditions people actively seek it. But we also need to recognize without embarrassment that people with fundamentally different approaches to life are unlikely to become fast friends. For a human being to adapt to a rapidly changing world, he needs the companionship and support of others with whom he may sometimes disagree, but nevertheless feels a fundamental bond of likemindedness.

Chapter 8

BECOMING COMMITTED
The Long Road to Intimacy

The die is cast.
     —Julius Caesar

As we enter the last quarter of the twentieth century, men and women in industrialized societies throughout the world may expect to have more acquaintances, more casual friendships, more fleeting romances, and fewer enduring relationships than ever before in history. People are moving from job to job, from neighborhood to neighborhood, and from city to city at heretofore unparalleled rates. By the time a person begins to get to know his co-workers or neighbors at a new location, he finds that they are already packing for their next move. By the time their replacements move in, he himself may be contemplating new horizons. As a result, the making of social contacts must often be a hurry-up affair. "The knowledge that no move is final," Alvin Toffler writes in *Future Shock*, "that somewhere along the road the nomads will once more gather up their belongings and migrate, works against the development of relationships that are more than modular, and it means that if relationships are to be struck up at all, they had better be whipped into life quickly."[1]

The increasing turnover of friendships results not only from the increasing changeability of people's places of work and residence, but also from the increasing diversity and changeability of people's interests and life-styles. No longer is there a single well-trodden path to follow, along which a person might lead his life with a sense of certainty and acquire a stable complement of like-minded friends. Instead, the process of making basic choices of interest and life-style often continues far into life. The college graduate today may be a religious monastic tomorrow, a political activist the day after next. Among my own small circle of college friends, one has quit his law firm to study philosophy, a second has left divinity school to become a management consultant, a third has left a career in journalism to live in the woods, and a fourth has already been an art teacher, then a carpenter, then a premedical student, and is currently farming seaweed. And all of this in the first seven years since graduation. To the extent that friends are bound together by a commonality of interests and values, it is no wonder that people's friendships are becoming increasingly short-lived.

Few social scientists would deny the trend toward less enduring interpersonal relationships. But they differ among themselves in their reactions to it. Some of the prognoses are strongly pessimistic. They suggest that because of the increasing number and turnover of interpersonal contacts, people's interpersonal relationships will become increasingly superficial. Psychoanalyst Leopold Bellak has gone furthest in his pessimism, warning that the trend toward short-term relationships will be accompanied by the development of "a character structure . . . which we used to consider a character disorder, one characterized by shallow, transitory object relations with little subjective feelings. . . ."[2]

Others accept the trend toward shorter-lived interpersonal relationships with greater equanimity, however. They predict that people will adapt to the situation resourcefully, by developing new interpersonal skills. In a paper entitled "Friendships in the Future," psychologist Courtney Tall predicted that "individuals will develop the ability to form close, 'buddy-type' relationships on the basis of common interests or subgroup affiliations, and to easily leave these friendships, moving either to another location and joining a similar interest group or to another interest group within the same location."[3] Some social scientists advocate educational programs to help people develop such capacities. Social psychologist Warren Bennis writes that people need help in "learning how to develop intense and deep human relationships quickly—and . . . how to 'let go.' In other words, learning how to get love, to love, and to lose love."[4] The recent proliferation of sensitivity training groups, encounter groups, and other variants of the "human potential movement" is in part an attempt by psychologists and others to provide this sort of training. At some such group enterprises participants are encouraged to communicate intimate feelings and experiences to people they have barely met and whom they will probably never again encounter. Verbal disclosures are supplemented by hugging, stroking, and other forms of nonverbal contact, which are intended to accelerate further the process of becoming intimate.

Such enterprises may often be useful in helping people to develop their skills of self-expression and communication. They may help shy people to gain self-confidence, overly aggressive people to tone themselves down, people who are too constrained by particular roles to break loose from them. To the extent that many people in modern society in fact have a need for "instant intimacy," such groups may help them to achieve it. I also believe, however, that the development of the capacity to form and drop close interpersonal bonds quickly is likely to fall far short of satisfying basic human needs for involvement with others. More than "instant intimacy," we need to develop close and enduring interpersonal relationships. We need to learn not only how to become intimate, but also how to become committed.

Bennis, an early and important figure in the sensitivity training movement, stresses this persisting need. He writes:

> Somehow with all the mobility, chronic churning and unconnectedness we envisage, it will become more and more important to develop some permanent or abiding commitment. If our libidinal attachments . . . become more diffused, it will be essential that we focus commitment on a person or an institution or an idea. This means that as general commitments become diffuse or modified, a greater *fidelity* to something or someone will be necessary to make us more fully human.

And, as Bennis notes, the capacity to develop such commitments in a turbulent world may be one "which . . . our educational system cannot provide, nor can we hope to acquire it easily."[5]

Even if we are persuaded that interpersonal commitments are required, there is room for considerable debate about what form they should take. The debate comes to a head with reference to marriage. As Nelson Foote has observed, "To expect marriage to last indefinitely under modern conditions is to expect a lot."[6] As a result, many social observers have predicted that fewer people in the future will marry at all, and that when they do, it will be under less binding arrangements than those which currently prevail. Temporary marriages are already much more readily accepted in America than they were a decade ago. Whereas it used to be the case, for example, that getting divorced was the political death-knell of an elected official, within the past few years many politicians have proved that it is possible to get divorced without any perceptible effects on their careers.

Yet the vast majority of young people today do plan to get

married. Of some 2,500 college students in the Boston area who responded to a mail survey that I conducted in 1972, 97.8 percent indicated that they would probably get married, and 93.7 percent ventured that they would do so within the next ten years. Although only time will tell whether or not they are correct, the vast majority of the students expect that their marriages will be lasting ones. Yet the question remains as to whether these students are in fact developing relationships that will withstand the strains that will undoubtedly be placed upon them.

In this chapter I will be concerned with the general case of the establishment of relationships that are both intimate and enduring, whether they be marriages, non-marital sexual relationships, or nonsexual friendships. A key word in the following discussion is *commitment*, which may be defined as the pledging of oneself to a line of action, whether it be the fight for a political ideology or the struggle for intimacy with another person. The creation of commitment is a painstaking process that is fraught with dangers, including one of the most dangerous of all—the need to make choices. As such, the process of becoming committed is the long road to intimacy. As I have already suggested, intimacy of sorts can be achieved more rapidly in other ways. But as most motorists know, there are times when the long road is also the better.

Disclosing Oneself to Others

The most literal meaning of "intimate" is to get into another person —to really know another. Yet there often is considerable reluctance among people to be known. Self-disclosure invariably entails a risk, and the greater the disclosure, the greater the risk. When we reveal to another person something of our "true self," we must be prepared for the possibility that he will examine what we have revealed and find it wanting. Or he may use the information to take advantage of us. In courtship, for example, one partner's revelation of some blemish in his background may prompt the other to abandon him. Or one partner's disclosure of the depth of his affection for the other may enable the other to exploit him by making large and unreasonable demands. In light of these risks, it is no wonder that many of us learn early in life to be wary of revealing ourselves. "We conceal and camouflage our true being before others," psychologist Sidney Jourard writes, "to foster a sense of safety, to protect ourselves against unwanted but expected criticism, hurt, or rejection." But this protection, Jourard goes on to argue, is purchased at a steep price: "When we are not truly known by other people in our lives, we are misunderstood. . . . Worse, when we succeed too well in hiding our being from others, we tend to lose touch with our real selves, and this loss of self contributes to illness in its myriad forms." Thus, disclosing ourselves to others may be necessary not only for the establishment of close relationships, but also to permit us to keep in touch with ourselves. "A friend is a person with whom I may be sincere," Emerson wrote. "Before him, I may think aloud."

Although self-disclosure is often difficult for men and women alike, it seems to be especially difficult for men in our society. Women surveyed by Jourard typically report that they have revealed more information about their feelings and experiences to family members, friends, and lovers than men do. As Jourard suggests, "The male role, as personally and socially defined, requires men to appear tough, objective, striving, achieving, unsentimental, and emotionally unexpressive. . . . If a man *is* tender . . ., if he weeps, if he shows weakness, he will likely be viewed as unmanly by others, and he will probably regard himself as inferior to other men."[7] During the first of the 1972 Democratic Presidential primaries, Senator Edmund Muskie, at that time the leading candidate for the nomination, expressed his displeasure with a New Hampshire newspaper publisher in an outburst that was simultaneously indignant and tearful. The incident was widely reported to have seriously weakened his drive for the nomination. It was not his indignation that hurt the senator, for this is an expression that men are generally permitted, but rather his tears. Muskie's genuine expression of feelings was considered a sign of unmanliness and weakness.

The rise of women's consciousness-raising groups has served to emphasize the relative inability of men to reveal themselves—especially to other men. Marc Fasteau writes:

Can you imagine men talking to each other saying: "Are you sure you're not angry at me?" . . . "I'm not as assertive as I would like to be." . . . "I feel so competitive that I can't get close to anyone." . . . "I just learned something important about myself that I've got to tell you." . . . "I don't have the self-confidence to do what I really want to do." . . . "I feel nervous talking to you like this."

It just doesn't happen. . . .

As a man, my conditioning and problems are not only different, but virtually the inverse of those of most women. We've been taught that 'real men' are never passive or dependent, always dominant in relationships with women or other men, and don't talk about or directly express feelings; especially feelings that don't contribute to dominance.[8]

In Jourard's view, men's inability to disclose themselves to others is a literally lethal aspect of the male role, contributing to the shorter life expectancy of males. "Men keep their selves to themselves and impose an added burden of stress beyond that imposed by the exigencies of everyday life. . . . The time is not far off when it will be possible to demonstrate with adequately controlled experiments the nature and degree of correlation between level and amounts of self-disclosure, proneness to illness and/or death at an early stage."[9] I frankly cannot imagine what sort of "controlled experiments" Jourard has in mind—all of the possibilities that occur to me are rather macabre. Nevertheless, the point that openness is likely to be related to psychological and perhaps even physical health is well taken. People of either sex who are totally unable to reveal their feelings to others are likely to be labeled as poorly functioning or, in extreme cases, as autistic or schizophrenic. One recent study of Peace Corps trainees documented the link between self-disclosure and psychological adjustment by showing that those trainees who were most willing to reveal personal information about themselves to others also tended to be the most cognitively complex, adaptable, flexible, and popular.[10]

It would be highly misleading to equate the ability to disclose oneself with positive mental health, however. People who disclose *too much* are apt to be considered as sick or sicker than those who disclose too little. To be a hallmark of psychological health or interpersonal competence, a person's disclosure must be appropriate to the particular situation and relationship in which it occurs. The appropriateness of disclosures is important in fleeting encounters between strangers as well as in the development of intimate relationships over longer periods of time. In the next section I will describe one of my own studies of encounters among strangers. The study will hopefully be of interest in its own right. But my main reason for introducing it at this point is my belief that these fleeting encounters illustrate certain mechanisms that are central to the development of intimate relationships.

Notes from the Departure Lounge

Several recent laboratory experiments have been concerned with the exchange of self-disclosure among unacquainted pairs of subjects. Their general finding is that, as one would expect, self-disclosure tends to be reciprocal. The more Person A reveals about himself to Person B, the more Person B is likely to reveal to Person A in return. My own experiment also concerned the exchange of self-disclosure among pairs of strangers, but it was conducted in a real-life setting—departure lounges at Boston's Logan Airport—rather than in the laboratory.[11] Its central goal was to go beyond another demonstration of the "reciprocity effect" toward a better understanding of the mechanisms that underlie it.

The reciprocity effect may in fact be ascribed to at least two different mechanisms. One mechanism is that of *modeling*. Especially when norms of appropriate behavior are not completely clear, people look to one another for cues as to what sort of response is called for. If a person sitting next to you on a train talks about the weather, you are likely to respond in kind. If he proceeds to discuss his recent illness—and at the same time seems to be in command of the situation—then you may well infer that disclosing personal matters is the proper thing to do under the circumstances. Such modeling phenomena can also be observed in the initiation of new recruits to sensitivity training or encounter groups. At first unsure about how they should behave, the new members observe their fellows disclosing themselves intimately and as a result conclude that they too are expected to reveal personal information.

A second mechanism that may underlie the reciprocity effect goes beyond modeling, however, and may be called *trust*. When another person reveals himself to you, you are likely to conclude that he likes and trusts you. He has, after all, made himself vulnerable to you, entrusting you with personal information that he would not ordinarily reveal to others. A common motivation in such a situation is to demonstrate to the other person that his affection and trust are well placed. One effective way to do this is to disclose yourself to him in return. It is by means of such reciprocal displays of trust and affection that people are most likely to move from acquaintanceship to friendship.

In many instances the two mechanisms operate simultaneously and lead to essentially the same end-state. In the encounter group, for example, members not only model one another's levels of disclosure, but also demonstrate their increasing trust for one another by means of reciprocal disclosure. There are instances, however, in which the two mechanisms should lead to rather different results. These are the cases in which the first person reveals *too* much, going beyond the level of intimacy with which the second person feels comfortable. To the extent that reciprocal disclosure is dictated by modeling, even extremely intimate revelations may lead to intimate disclosures in return.* But excessively intimate disclosures will often breed suspicion rather than trust. If, for example, a person reveals the details of his sex life to a co-worker on their first day at the job, the second person may have reason to suspect the first's motives or discretion. Instead of being motivated to reveal the details of his own sex life in return, he will be likely to clam up.

In the experiment that I conducted at the airport, the experimenter, either a male or a female college student, began by approaching a prospective subject, an adult man or woman sitting alone in the departure lounge, and asking him if he would write a sentence or two about himself to be used as part of a class project on "handwriting analysis." There is, to be sure, a deception involved here that I wish we could avoid. In a previous experiment my students and I found, however, that when we asked people to write something about themselves as part of a study of "the way people describe themselves"—which is of course the true purpose —several problems emerge. Foremost among these was that over half of the male subjects approached by male experimenters refused to take part. As we have already noted, men find it particularly difficult to express themselves to other men. In the all-male context, "self-description" seemed to be a threatening word. When we represented the study as concerned with handwriting analysis, on the other hand, we were able to reduce male refusal rates substantially. In addition, by obtaining "handwriting samples" rather than "self-descriptions" I hoped to minimize the subjects' self-consciousness about the content of their messages. As far as the subjects knew, only their handwriting, and not their personal disclosures, would later be evaluated for research purposes.

After the subject had agreed to participate, the experimenter explained that the class would be comparing the class members' own handwriting with the handwriting of other people. Therefore, the experimenter would write a few sentences about himself or

---

* This modeling effect may explain in large measure why laboratory experiments have failed to find withdrawal as a common response to excessively intimate disclosures. In the laboratory context, the subject typically experiences considerable pressure to determine and accede to the "demand characteristics" of the experiment, those subtle cues that define the experimental situation for the subject and suggest to him how a "good subject" should behave. Thus, he utilizes his partner's disclosure as a cue to what sort of behavior is appropriate to the situation and responds in kind. As a result, laboratory studies of disclosure tend to overemphasize those aspects of encounters that evoke modeling and to underemphasize those that are relevant to trust.[12]

herself in the top box of the response form, labeled "Class Member's Sample." The subject was invited to look at the experimenter's sample and then to write a sentence or two about himself or herself in the bottom box. The "Class Member's Sample" was the device by which I was able to vary the intimacy of the experimenter's self-disclosure to the subject. The "sample" provided by the experimenter was either a non-intimate, moderately intimate, or extremely intimate statement about himself. In all cases the experimenter began by writing his or her name and the fact that he was a junior or senior in college. In the "low intimacy" condition, he proceeded to write:

> . . . right now I'm in the process of collecting handwriting samples for a school project. I think I will stay here for a while longer, and then call it a day.

In the "medium intimacy" condition he wrote:

> . . . Lately I've been thinking about my relationships with other people. I've made several good friends during the past couple of years, but I still feel lonely a lot of the time.

And in the "high intimacy"—or, if you will, "excessively high intimacy"—condition the experimenter wrote:

> . . . Lately I've been thinking about how I really feel about myself. I think that I'm pretty well adjusted, but I occasionally have some questions about my sexual adequacy.

The experiment included a further variation. In half the cases within each of the intimacy conditions, the experimenter simply *copied* the message from a card in front of him. It was obvious to the subject that the experimenter was not directing the message to him personally, but rather was working from a prepared script. In the other half of the cases the experimenter pretended to *create* the message especially for the subject. He did not have a cue card in front of him, and he occasionally glanced up at the subject thoughtfully as he wrote. My purpose in setting up this variation was to establish conditions in which the two mechanisms of modeling and of trust would be differentially salient.

When the experimenter copied his message, it presumably furnished the subject with a cue as to what sort of statement would be appropriate to the situation. Since the experimenter was not singling the subject out for his revelation, however, there was little reason for the subject to interpret the experimenter's disclosure as a demonstration of any particular affection or trust. Under these circumstances the subject was relatively unlikely to react suspiciously or defensively to the "extremely high" message. The experimenter was not being excessively forward or indiscreet; he was merely doing his job. Following this reasoning, I predicted that as the intimacy of the experimenter's message varied from "low" to "medium" to "high," the intimacy and length of the subject's own message would correspondingly increase.

When the experimenter seemed to create a unique message for the subject, on the other hand, considerations of trust inevitably entered the picture, supplementing the modeling mechanism. Up to a point the subject might be expected to respond positively to the experimenter's apparent demonstration of affection and trust and, as a result, to disclose himself in return. Thus the reciprocity effect, considering only the low-intimacy and medium-intimacy messages, was expected to be stronger in the "create" than in the "copy" condition. But the high-intimacy message, when delivered in a personal way, might indeed be going too far and consequently should arouse sentiments of mistrust and defensiveness. "After all," a typical subject might think, "it's nice to have a young person confide in you, but this bit on 'sexual adequacy' is really going too far. I wonder what his *real* problem is. I had better write something short and be done with it."

Before revealing the results of the study, let me present a few of the "handwriting samples" provided by subjects, to give you a sense of the ways in which airport passengers responded to the request to write a sentence or two about themselves. Some of the responses were not intimate at all. They were personally uninformative or even evasive:

005*   Today is the 29th of October and this is Logan Airport. It is very warm for this time of year especially when waiting for a late airplane.
031   This is the start of a trip to Atlanta and other states in the adjacent area.
047   I've got to go.

Other subjects provided factual information about themselves but did not get into highly intimate revelations:

028   My name is Frank Peterson and I'm a retired police officer. I served for 30 years on the Boston Police department.
133   My name is Bertha Schwartz. I am a housewife and very happy.

* Numbers are the subjects' identification numbers. Names and other potentially identifying information provided by the subjects have been altered.

236   My name is Ronnie, live in Boston—like art, studied at B.U., think handwriting analysis is a great hobby.

Still other subjects did reveal what seemed to be much more personal and private thoughts and feelings:

144   My name is Gloria Baker. I'm a grandmother but I too have been thinking of myself—where I've been—what to do—I too question my identity.

089   I've just been attending Alumna Council at Cooper College.—looking ahead to my 40th Reunion. I still feel sexually adequate —never felt otherwise.

197   My name is Thomas O'Day. I'm a 3rd year medical student. Recently I haven't been getting much sleep and have been under extreme pressure; Thus, my handwriting is terrible. Generally I am well-adjusted, but 3rd year students have many adjustments to make, and I often question my ability to function under pressure.

It is possible to have raters code the intimacy of these samples with quite good reliability. In some cases, however, interesting patterns emerge quite as clearly, or even more so, simply by using the number of words in the subject's sample as a measure of his or her self-disclosure. This is the measure employed in Figure 8.1.

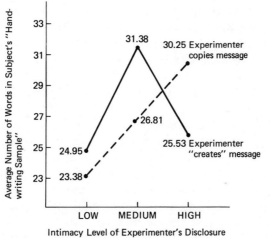

FIGURE 8.1   Length of subjects' messages in departure lounge experiment. Each point represents about 40 subjects. The statistical interaction between the two experimental factors is significant at the .014 level.

As the graph indicates, the predictions outlined ‘above were very neatly confirmed. In the impersonal, "copy" condition, the length of the subject's statement increased steadily as the intimacy level of the experimenter's statement increased from low to medium to high. The modeling mechanism apparently operated across the entire range of the experimenter's disclosures. In the personal, "create" condition, on the other hand, the length of the subject's statement increased sharply as intimacy of the experimenter's message increased from low to medium, but it dropped off just as sharply as the intimacy of the experimenter's message increased from medium to high.

Lovers and Other Strangers

Although the airport study involved encounters between strangers, I believe that the results contain several lessons about the development of intimate relationships. In every sort of interpersonal relationship, from business partnerships to love affairs, the exchange of self-disclosure plays an important role. In some respects this exchange closely resembles other transactions on the interpersonal marketplace that we examined in Chapter 4. Just as people may exchange such commodities as approval, assistance, and status, they also exchange information about their experiences and feelings. But the exchange of self-disclosure is governed by several additional motives and mechanisms. In some cases, it is not really an exchange at all, even though the two people are sequentially emitting similar behaviors to one another. In fact they are not exchanging anything, but instead are imitating or modeling one another's behavior. Such modeling is an important aspect of the development of relationships, especially in their early stages. At such times, when people are tentatively exploring each other's potential as a friend or lover, they are especially concerned about responding in ways that are appropriate to the situation, and they frequently do so by picking up and modeling one another's cues.

At a deeper level, the exchange of personal disclosures is in fact an exchange of trust. The discloser shows that he likes and trusts the person to whom he discloses, thereby implying that he might value the establishment of a relationship with him. The person disclosed to must decide how to respond to this "move" on the part of the discloser. If he is disposed to keep relations cool, and at the same time to retain a position of relative power, he may disclose little in return.[13] Knowing more about another person than he knows about you is a way to remain "one-up" in interpersonal relationships.

It seems to be a general rule of social behavior for powerful people to receive more personal information from the less powerful than they are willing to disclose about themselves in return. Erving Goffman writes, for example:

> In American business organizations the boss may thoughtfully ask the elevator man how his children are, but this entrance into another's life may be blocked to the elevator man, who can appreciate the concern but not return it. Perhaps the clearest form of this is found in the psychiatrist-patient relations, where the psychiatrist has a right to touch on aspects of the patient's life that the patient might not even allow himself to touch upon, while of course this privilege is not reciprocated.[14]*

Sociologist Gerald Suttles suggests that societies make a point of according especially high status to the recipients of such unilateral disclosures, such as psychiatrists, as a way of assuring all those concerned that even though he does not reveal himself in return, the recipient is a trustworthy person.[15]

If, on the other hand, the recipient of an intimate disclosure is predisposed to keep alive the possibility of a more symmetrical relationship, then he will demonstrate his trustworthiness and good intentions by disclosing something about himself in return. He thus equalizes the vulnerability of the two parties, implicitly telling the other, "I am as willing to let you know me as you are to let me know you." And he may go on to take further initiatives in disclosing himself, thus facilitating a gradually spiraling build-up of intimacy.

To the extent that a personal revelation is to be significant, however, it cannot be a standard tape that one plays to all listeners, like the experimenter's handwriting sample in the "copy" condition. For a disclosure to serve as a demonstration of trust and affection, it must single out the recipient as a confidant. People who are willing to tell anyone and everyone all about their personal strengths or weaknesses do not find it easy to establish intimate relationships. Because their feelings and experiences are available to all, they cannot serve as a basis for an intimate and unique bond. As Georg Simmel suggests, the emotional tone of an intimate relationship is based in large measure on "what each of the two participants gives or shows only to the one other person and to nobody else."[16]

---

* Note that this hierarchy of who discloses to whom parallels the hierarchy of touch that we discussed in Chapter 2. In both cases, the higher-status person has more ready access to the lower-status person than vice-versa.

For this reason, it is difficult to create intimate relationships under conditions that allow for little privacy and require people to conduct all their dealings in public view. Friendships formed in such "open" contexts as mental hospitals, prisons, army barracks, and even college dormitories often involve a sense of duress, a sense that private experiences and feelings were shared out of necessity rather than out of choice. As a result,

> Friendships begun under these confined circumstances seem to have a rather short half life once they are removed to more spacious quarters. Despite their own protests to the contrary, army buddies seldom see each other after they are discharged. Cell mates in prison ("cellies") make a concerted effort to avoid one another on release despite the general absence of alternative associations.

Gerald Suttles concludes that "it is easy to dismiss such past friendships because they do not rest on the sure coin of spontaneity, which is assumed necessary to a completed friendship."[17] The sort of self-revelation that is conducive to the establishment of friendship is more like the experimenter's statement in the "create" condition. In this condition the subject had reason to believe that the disclosure was free and uncoerced, and that he had been singled out for the purpose of receiving it.

Paradoxically, this limitation of hospital wards and army barracks may be shared by some of the institutions that have been specifically designed to facilitate intimacy, such as encounter groups. When interpersonal openness becomes the normative pattern—the "expected thing to do"—any act of self-disclosure may involve less risk and, simultaneously, represent less of an investment in the future of a relationship than the same act would represent if it were made under less officially sanctioned circumstances. Instead of being attributed to the discloser's trust and affection for a particular other person, it may be written off as an act of conformity. "The commercial programming of self-disclosure," Suttles observes, "tends to provide only another social scenario that can be studied, practiced, and performed. Thus, no matter how spontaneous and crude a person's expressed self, there is a shade of doubt about his reality."[18]

But even if self-disclosure is spontaneous and personal, it by no means guarantees the development of intimacy. As psychologist Joseph Luft observes,

> Disclosing too much creates at least as many problems as disclosing too little. . . . The overdiscloser appears to trust everyone because he has not yet learned to discriminate the qualities of differ-

ent relationships. It is the other person who must take the responsibility for defining the nature of the relationship. . . . In appropriate disclosure, [in contrast], behavior is reciprocal or mutual, and both persons take their proper share of responsibility in defining what the relationship is and what it is becoming.[19]

We have seen that even in fleeting encounters, people respond to personal disclosures that are too intimate by withdrawing rather than by reciprocating.

In encounters between strangers some of the usual constraints upon interaction between acquaintances or potential friends are short-circuited. In his classic essay on "The Stranger," Simmel observed that "the stranger who moves on . . . often receives the most surprising openness—confidences which sometimes have the character of a confessional and which would be carefully withheld from a more closely related person."[20] When one is with a passing stranger, a person with whom one has only a present, but no past and no future, there is a feeling of unaccountability which can have the effect of increasing openness. As one college coed remarked about the annual spring pilgrimage to Fort Lauderdale, "You're not worried about what you do or say here because, frankly, you'll never see these people again."[21]

An additional finding of my airport study pointed up the short-circuiting mechanism. After the subjects had provided their "handwriting samples," they were asked to complete a short background form that included a question about whether they lived in the Boston area or elsewhere. There was a striking tendency for people who were not from Boston to write longer messages than people from Boston. In addition, when the experimenter had revealed a great deal about himself, people from outside Boston responded with much more intimate disclosures of their own than did the Bostonians. The results may reflect the "Fort Lauderdale phenomenon." Although all of the subjects were strangers to the experimenters, the non-Bostonians were strangers *par eminence*. Whereas a Bostonian subject might conceivably expect to run into the experimenter again at some time, the non-Bostonian could be virtually certain that their paths would never cross again. As a result, he could take the opportunity to unburden himself of private thoughts and feelings with impunity. The most striking example of such a disclosure from a person "passing through town" was obtained in an earlier study:

I'm supposed to be a respectable housewife, but guess what? I am at the Logan Airport now going back to Cleveland to my impotent husband. I just left my lover in Boston.

It is likely that if the woman had been a Boston housewife on her way to her lover in Cleveland, her statement would have been more guarded.

The relative invulnerability of the stranger may sometimes prevail at encounter weekends and other transient enterprises in "instant intimacy." More usually, however, intimacy is more slowly and painfully won. In this process, many of the same factors as those affecting disclosure among strangers are in force, including sex-role constraints, modeling, and the creation of trust by means of personal but prudent disclosures. Such disclosures, as we will see, not only serve to communicate information and to establish trust, but also to create commitment.

Dissonance Reduction in Utopia

I suggested at the start of this chapter that commitment may be defined as a person's pledging of himself to a line of action. It is a generic concept, equally applicable to a person's ties to an ideology, a religion, a group, or a relationship. A study of group commitment will help to illustrate the process of becoming committed. Rosabeth Moss Kanter, a sociologist at Brandeis University, has employed archival materials to explore the social arrangements of nineteenth-century utopian communities in the United States. She selected the case of the utopias for her analysis precisely because they highlight the problems involved in creating commitment:

> Since the community represents an attempt to establish an ideal social order within the larger society, it must vie with the outside for members' loyalties. It must insure high member involvement despite external competition without sacrificing its distinctiveness or ideals. It must often contravene the earlier socialization of its members in securing obedience to new demands. It must calm internal dissension in order to present a united front to the world. The problem of securing total and complete commitment is central.[22]

Kanter assumed that the degree to which the social arrangements of the commune facilitated commitment would be directly reflected in the commune's success, as measured by its longevity. By comparing relatively successful communities (those that lasted at least thirty years) with relatively unsuccessful ones (those that lasted no more than fifteen years), she was able to obtain useful leads on the mechanisms that induce commitment.

Of greatest relevance to our current concerns, Kanter found that the successful communes were more likely than the unsuccessful ones to make use of mechanisms of *sacrifice* and *invest-ment*. The successful communities were more likely to require abstention from such worldly pleasures as sex, tobacco, alcohol, meat, personal adornment, dancing, and even reading. Few if any of the communes required all of these sacrifices, but the successful communes required more of them than did the unsuccessful ones. The investments required by the more successful communes included the signing over of all property at admission, often accompanied by a policy of not reimbursing defectors for their property or labor. Thus, these investments were not only substantial but also irreversible. Another sort of investment, which Kanter calls "mortification," was extensive self-disclosure to other members of the commune. The more successful groups were more likely to make use of practices of confession, mutual criticism sessions, and surveillance of members' activities.

One explanation of the effects of sacrifice and investment upon commitment is provided by a more general social–psychological formulation, Leon Festinger's theory of cognitive dissonance.[23] The basic premise of the theory is that much of human behavior is motivated by the need to avoid inconsistencies among one's attitudes and actions. It is "dissonant," for example, for a person simultaneously to have the knowledge (or "cognitions") that (a) cigarette smoking is harmful to his health, and (b) he smokes a pack a day. Some people live with such dissonance, often at the price of considerable anxiety. More often, according to Festinger's theory, the person will attempt to change one or both of the cognitive elements in order to bring them into line. The most rational solution in this case would be to stop smoking, but not everyone chooses the rational path. Instead, the smoker may decide that regardless of what the Surgeon General says, smoking really is not harmful to him. After all, he can list at least a dozen people who smoked heavily and lived long lives. Or the smoker may underestimate the amount that he actually smokes, fooling himself into believing that it is not enough to be harmful. These cognitive contortions restore consistency and thereby serve to reduce the smoker's inner tension.

An analogous logic may underlie commitment to utopian communities. It is dissonant to believe that (a) I have deprived myself of meat, sex, and adornments for the sake of the commune and have given it my worldly goods; and (b) the commune doesn't amount to much, and I will leave it as soon as I get bored or find something better. Assuming that the sacrifices and investments cannot be undone, the main way that a member can reduce his dissonance is by intensifying his attachment to the community. As Kanter writes, "The more it 'costs' a person to do something, the more 'valuable' he will consider it, in order to justify the psychic 'expense' and remain internally consistent. . . . In the eyes of the group and in the mind of the individual, sacrifice for a cause makes it sacred and inviolable."[24]

In applying dissonance theory to the establishment of commitment, however, we must deal with the difficult question of cause and effect. Most people entering the utopias presumably anticipated the hardships that would be imposed on them. Thus it is at best uncertain to argue that the deprivations led to their commitment. It seems at least as likely that their initial attraction or commitment led to their willingness to undergo the deprivations. But this causal ambiguity can be removed by resorting to the laboratory experiment. Using such a procedure, two of Festinger's students, Elliot Aronson and Judson Mills, succeeded in demonstrating that severe initiations into a group can directly strengthen commitment.[25]

Aronson and Mills's subjects were college women who had volunteered to take part in discussion groups on sex. The experimenter first explained to the subjects that since some people are shy or embarrassed about sex and might therefore dampen the discussion, they would have to pass an "embarrassment test" before being allowed to join the group. One-third of the subjects were given a "mild" test. It required them to read aloud five words that were related to sex but not obscene, such as *prostitute, virgin,* and *petting.* One-third of the subjects were instead given a more severe initiation. They had to read aloud to the male experimenter twelve obscene words, followed by "two vivid descriptions of sexual activity from contemporary novels." Following the mild or severe initiation, each of the women was told that she had performed satisfactorily and could join the group meeting then in progress. The final one-third of the subjects served as a control group. They gained admission to the group without undergoing any initiation rite.

In order to present a standardized group to all of the subjects, Aronson and Mills then had the subjects listen through headphones (on the pretext that "it's easier to talk about embarrassing things if other people aren't staring at you") to what was represented as an ongoing group discussion, but was actually a tape recording. The subject was told that at the first session she should simply listen without talking herself. The subjects were then tuned into the dullest discussion of "sex" that Aronson and Mills could create:

The participants spoke dryly and haltingly on secondary sex behavior in the lower animals, "inadvertently" contradicted themselves
and one another, mumbled several *non sequiturs*, started sentences
that they never finished, hemmed, hawed, and in general conducted
one of the most worthless and uninteresting discussions imaginable.

At the conclusion of the "meeting," the subjects were asked to evaluate the discussion and the group members on a variety of dimensions, such as "dull–interesting" and "intelligent–unintelligent."
As predicted, the women who went through the severe initiation
rated both the session and the participants more positively than
did the women who went through the mild initiation or no initiation at all.

The dissonance-theory interpretation of these results is
straightforward. If one goes through a mild initiation (or no initiation at all) to gain admission to a boring group, the experienced
dissonance should be relatively slight. The experience may be
disappointing, but there is no basic inconsistency. And so there
is no compelling reason to deny the group's banality. When admission to the boring group is gained only after a painful initiation,
however, the dissonance is considerable. There is a basic inconsistency in paying high costs for a commodity that is essentially
worthless. Aronson and Mills suggested that "subjects in this
[severe initiation] condition could reduce their dissonance either
by denying the severity of the initiation or by distorting their cognitions concerning the group discussion in a positive direction. The
initiation . . . was apparently too painful to deny—hence they reduced their dissonance by overestimating the attractiveness of the
group."

Thus the theory of cognitive dissonance interprets the facilitating effects of sacrifice and investment upon group commitment
in terms of the motivational pressure toward consistency. The
same analysis is equally applicable to the development of commitment to a single other person or relationship. If, for example, a
young woman believes that (a) sleeping with a person whom one
does not love is immoral, and (b) she has been sleeping with a boyfriend whom she does not love, she may experience considerable
dissonance. One likely way to reduce the dissonance would be to
decide that she loves him after all. There is an alternative and,
perhaps, more useful way to conceptualize this effect, however.
Rather than postulate that the young woman is motivated to avoid
inconsistency, we may explain her behavior in terms of a process
of *self-attribution*: She notes that she has been sleeping with her

boyfriend, tries to determine why she has engaged in this behavior, and arrives at the conclusion that it must be because she loves him. In the next section we will explore the self-attributional approach in greater detail.

Commitment as Self-Attribution

In Chapter 5 we examined the attributional processes involved when one person forms an impression of another person. We noted that a central consideration in inferring another person's inner dispositions from his visible behavior is the extent to which his actions are ascribed to him personally, as opposed to the extent to which they are attributed to situational constraints. If we believe that a person's action was coerced by external circumstances, whether it be the tight discipline of an army camp or the enforced openness of an encounter group, then the action tells us little about his inner nature. If, on the other hand, we believe the other's action was free and unconstrained, it can serve as the basis for inferences about his personality. The self-attributional approach, growing in large measure from the work of social psychologist Daryl Bem, goes on to make the radical assumption that we determine our own attitudes and self-conceptions in precisely the same way as we determine the attitudes and dispositions of others—by drawing inferences about the causes of our own behavior.[26]

A usual assumption of social psychologists is that people's actions are shaped in large measure by their underlying attitudes. Bem's "self-perception theory" maintains just the opposite, that people's attitudes are often shaped by their perception of their own actions. Bem writes:

> Most people agree that the question, "Why do you eat brown bread?" can properly be answered with "Because I like it." I should like to convince you, however, that the question, "Why do like brown bread?" frequently ought to be answered with "Because I eat it."[27]

In fact, Bem's contention is not so radical as it may seem at first glance. From infancy on, people characteristically devote more time to acting than they do to considering the underlying reasons for their actions. We decide what to eat, whom to approach or avoid, and how to spend our money on the basis of a variety of unexamined internal inclinations and external pressures, without pausing to determine that "I like hamburgers," "Betty is an interesting person," or "There is a sale at Macy's." It is typically only after we have a file of data about our own behavior that we begin to pigeonhole ourselves as Republicans or Democrats (by looking back at our voting record), as active or passive (by reflecting on the tempo of our daily activities), as liking or disliking rhubarb (by recalling how frequently we have eaten it). But these self-attributions, once we have made them, play a central role in determining our future actions. One defines oneself, on the basis of past behavior, as the sort of person who may be expected to engage in certain comparable behaviors in the future. This self-definition may often constitute the "pledging of a person to a line of action" that defines commitment.

An experimental study of the creation of commitment to a social cause illustrates the process.[28] Two different students called on California housewives at their homes. The first student made a small request, which most of the housewives were glad to comply with. Depending on the experimental condition to which the housewife had been assigned, the request was to sign a petition or to put a small sign in her window, advocating either safe driving or keeping California beautiful. The second request, made about two weeks later by a second student who had no ostensible connection with the first, was a larger one. The student represented himself as being from the Citizens for Safe Driving, and he asked the housewife whether she would allow a large sign reading "Drive Carefully" to be placed in front of her house for about a week. (To maximize the extent of the request the subject was shown a sample picture of a huge "Drive Carefully" sign in front of an attractive house, obscuring the front of the house and completely concealing the doorway.)

In a control condition in which the first contact was never made, only 17 percent of the subjects were willing to have the sign erected. In the condition in which the housewife had previously been asked to put a small safe-driving sign in her window, however, fully 76 percent of the subjects acceded to the request. (In each of the other experimental conditions, involving either petition-signing or a small keep-California-beautiful sign, slightly less than half of the housewives complied with the larger request.) Social psychologists Jonathan Freedman and Scott Fraser, who conducted the study, interpreted the striking difference in compliance rates as a testament to the "foot-in-the-door technique" commonly used by salesmen, advertisers, and other persuaders. The assumption is that once the persuader has gotten his foot in the door—that is, gotten his audience to accede to a small request —it will be easier for him to induce compliance to larger demands. The underlying mechanism seems to be a self-attributional one:

> What may occur is a change in the person's feelings about getting involved or about taking action. Once he has agreed to a request, his attitude may change. He may become, in his own eyes, the kind of person who does this sort of thing, who agrees to requests made by strangers, who takes action on things he believes in, who cooperates with good causes.

In other words, he begins to become committed.

Analogous mechanisms operate in the development of a two-person relationship. As one person spends time with another, discloses himself, and goes out of his way for the other's benefit, he may also reflect on his own actions and attempt to infer its causes. One likely conclusion is that he trusts and cares for the other person. Declarations of love may have the same effect. "The fact that I had been able to tell him that I love him," a college student named Deborah recalled, "had assured me that I truly did love him and that he was the man for me."[29]

In Chapter 3 we observed that people may often look to others in their attempt to label their own reactions and emotions. Similarly, in our attempt to infer the causes of our own behavior, we may look to others for additional information. A person's perception of how others see him often has a direct impact upon how he sees himself, a phenomenon that sociologist Charles Horton Cooley once dubbed the "looking-glass self."[30] Such an influence of others' ascriptions upon one's own self-definition plays an important role in courtship:

> The commitment stage is distinguished by . . . confirming activities: other people more consistently treat the couple as a couple. Invitations and communications are usually sent to the couple instead of to an individual. . . . Even individual activities without the future spouse may have a joining effect in the commitment period. Showers and bachelor parties are official rituals which a person would betray should he subsequently decide not to marry. Even more casual social activities may have a "last fling" quality. They are farewell parties, and they communicate to the individual that he or she is now expected to get married.[31]

Similar confirming activities are built into those social institutions that have the function of facilitating dyadic commitment, such as the college sorority:

> Sorority ritual reinforces the progression from dating to marriage. At the vital point in the process, where dating must be turned into engagement, the sorority shores up the structure by the pinning ritual, performed after dinner in the presence of all the sorority sisters (who are required to stay for the ceremony) and attended, in its classic form, by a choir of fraternity boys singing outside. The commitment is so public that it is difficult for either partner to withdraw.[32]

These rituals work in part simply by making it embarrassing for the couple to abandon their relationship. In terms of our self-attributional analysis, however, they also work by providing the individual with additional leads at to how he must be feeling. "If everyone else thinks I am in love," the inner reasoning goes, "then the chances are that I am." Oscar Hammerstein, one of the most psychologically astute of songwriters, alluded to such reasoning in *Oklahoma*:

> Don't throw bouquets at me,
> Don't please my folks too much,
> Don't laugh at my jokes too much—
> People will say we're in love.

The implied point is that if we behave in such a way as to make other people think that we are in love, then inevitably we will be.

Other people may also encourage such self-attributions in subtler ways, by providing models of the emotion to be inferred. "We did not see each other until exam period a few weeks later," Deborah wrote, "when Peter and I studied music with two of my girlfriends and their boyfriends. Somehow being with these two couples put a pressure on Peter and me. There was a sense of warmth, of my belonging to him and him to me that had not been present before."[33] But such social structuring of intimacy may sometimes have a diametrically opposite effect. As suggested earlier, if everyone else in the vicinity is also disclosing himself, holding hands, or making love, then it suggests that we should attribute our similar actions not to our own distinctive feelings but rather to the constraints of the situation. The young woman who finally agrees to sleep with her boyfriend at a party when "everyone else was doing it" is more likely to decide that she was swayed by the party atmosphere than that she really loves him. Thus, a key element in the attribution of personal dispositions to oneself, as to others, is the perception of freedom. Actions that a person believes to have been externally coerced will not foster commitment, but actions for which a person accepts personal responsibility will.

There is a circularity built into our analysis. On the one hand we have been viewing the establishment of commitment as a road to intimacy. On the other hand we have suggested that intimacy, as approached by disclosing oneself to others, is a basic ingredient in the development of commitment. But this circularity does not really bespeak flawed logic. Rather, the development of intimacy and of commitment are closely linked, spiralling processes. When one person reveals himself to another, it has subtle effects on the way each of them defines the relationship. Bit by bit the partners open themselves to one another, and step by step they construct their mutual bond. The process only rarely moves ahead in great leaps. It is often so gradual, in fact, that it is not noticed. "It is hard for both of us to say when we privately got engaged," a recently married man told an interviewer. "The subject would come up time after time, and each time we would be more seriously attached afterward, until it was just 'there.' "[34]

Sometimes the process takes on a momentum of its own, leading to a seemingly inevitable movement toward increasing commitment. One team of researchers interviewed newlywed couples about their courtships and came to the following conclusion:

> We expected description of emotional excitement and found flatness. We expected to learn of deliberation and reflection, alternating perhaps with impulsivity—what was described was drifting. The experience of listening was like watching an automated production line, with life proceeding at a regulated pace. Such things as dating, going steady, engagement, and marriage seemed to be imposed from the outside with our subjects caught in the system.[35]

To some extent the development of commitment is indeed imposed from the outside by the system. The more time, effort, and emotion one invests in a cause, group, or relationship, the harder it will be for him to extricate himself from it. As Rosabeth Kanter writes, "When individuals invest their resources in one system rather than in other potential paths, they tie their rewards and the future usefulness of their resources, in effect, to the success of the system, burning other bridges, cutting themselves off from other ways to allocate resources."[36] The same sort of irreversibility characterizes interpersonal relationships, sometimes to their detriment. "Inevitably," Gerald Suttles observes, "one finds friends, marital partners, and lovers who are regretful of having advanced so far that they have reached 'the point of no return.' "[37]

Without denying this external component of commitment, our self-attributional analysis implies that commitment will be strongest when it is embedded in a context of continuing choice. One is committed to a relationship not because he has invested more than he can afford to lose, but rather because he continually defines and redefines himself as opting for that relationship rather than any possible alternatives. And inasmuch as no one can ever disclose himself totally to another person, continuing acts of self-revelation remain an important part of the developmental process.

It must be admitted, finally, that much of the analysis presented in this chapter relies heavily on speculation. In their investigations of interpersonal attraction, social psychologists have devoted a disproportionate amount of attention to isolated encounters among strangers in the laboratory. Far less systematic attention has been paid to the development of relationships over longer periods of time. In the final two chapters of this book, however, we shall pursue our exploration in this direction, focusing on relationships between men and women. The next chapter will be devoted to an examination of courtship and mate selection in contemporary America. The final chapter is a report of my own initial endeavor to conceptualize and measure romantic love.

Chapter 9

DATING AND MATING
The Americanization
of the Romantic Ideal

Americans are firmly of two minds about it all, simultaneously hardheaded and idealistic, uncouth and tender, libidinous and puritanical; they believe implicitly in every tenet of romantic love, and yet they know perfectly well that things don't really work that way.

—MORTON HUNT, *The Natural History of Love*

Celtic mythology is not one of today's more popular forms of light reading, but the opera buffs among us may be acquainted with the romance of Tristan and Iseult, which provides the plot for one of Wagner's works. Although the precise origins of the Tristan myth are unknown, it was first committed to writing by several poets in twelfth-century France. The essentials of the plot are as follows:

Tristan, as his name suggests, is born in sorrow. His father has just died, and his mother dies in childbirth. He is brought up by his uncle, King Mark of Cornwall, in his castle at Tintagel. As a youth, Tristan demonstrates his virility by slaying the Morholt, an Irish version of the Minotaur, who had come for his tribute of young Cornish maidens. In the process, unfortunately, Tristan is wounded by a poisoned barb. With no hope of recovery, he begs to be put on board a boat with his sword and harp and is cast adrift without sails or oars. The suffering voyager lands in Ireland and is nursed back to good health by Princess Iseult, who, as luck would have it, knows of a secret remedy. Tristan is tactful enough not to reveal how he received his wound since the Morholt happens to have been Iseult's uncle. As far as the reader is given to know, the convalescent period passes uneventfully, and when our hero is healed, he returns home.

Several years later King Mark dispatches Tristan to find him a queen. Once again he is cast ashore in Ireland, where he pauses to kill a dragon that is threatening the capital. Once again he is wounded, and once again he is treated by Iseult. This time, however, she learns that Tristan is the man who killed her monster of an uncle. She seizes his sword and threatens to transfix him in the bathtub. But when Tristan tells her of his noble mission, she spares him because she would like to be a queen and, according to some sources, because she notices that he is irresistibly handsome. On the way back to Cornwall a significant event takes place. Iseult's maid gives the pair a drink, but—in an innocent mistake of the sort that the discerning reader knows will inevitably prove to be tragic—she picks up the wrong bottle and serves the love potion that Iseult's mother had prepared for her daughter and King Mark to drink after their wedding. Tristan and Iseult drink the potion and fall madly in love.

In spite of his drug-induced passion, Tristan feels duty-bound to fulfill his mission and, concealing his agony as best he can, delivers Iseult to King Mark. He cheers up after Iseult and the king are married because he is offered a position as Iseult's "guard." This post demands that the guard share the lady's bedroom, a requirement that the lovers manage to put to their advantage. All is well for a few days or weeks until Frocin the Dwarf sets a trap to establish the lovers' guilt. He cunningly scatters flour on the floor between Tristan's bed and the queen's and persuades King Mark to send Tristan on a mission to King Arthur the next morning. As Frocin has anticipated, Tristan is determined to embrace his mistress in the morning before setting off. To avoid leaving footprints in the flour, he fearlessly leaps from his own bed to that of the queen. This strategy is clever, but it backfires. The effort reopens a leg wound inflicted the day before by a boar. Led by Frocin, the king and his barons burst into the bedroom and find the blood-stained flour. (If they also found Tristan and Iseult in the same bed, the poets do not mention it.) Persuaded by this proof of adultery, King Mark hands Iseult over to a party of a hundred lepers and sentences Tristan to the stake. But on the way to his cremation Tristan performs like a Celtic James Bond. First he escapes from his executioners by jumping off a cliff; then he snatches Iseult from the decaying hands of the lepers. Finally, they manage to elude the king's posse and hide in the forest.

After three years have gone by, the love potion apparently

wears off, at least temporarily. Tristan decides that he has done wrong, and Iseult begins to wish that she were a queen again. So they return to the king, who promises forgiveness, and they sorrowfully prepare to part. But now the fire of love flares up again, and the pair has several secret meetings. The barons get wind of this and accuse Iseult of infidelity. She eventually clears herself by means of a brazenly sacrilegious trick. She submits to a "judgment of God" that requires her to hold a red-hot iron, which, it is well known, will not harm one who has spoken the truth. Before grasping the iron, Iseult swears that no man has ever held her in his arms except for the king and a poor pilgrim who has just carried her ashore from a boat. The pilgrim, of course, was Tristan in disguise.

Now the lovers' situation seems to be safe and secure. As we have already seen, however, Tristan and Iseult do not thrive on safety and security. And so, before long, new adventures take Tristan far away from Iseult, and, mail service being what it was in those days, he comes to believe that she no longer loves him. He ends up marrying another Iseult, "Iseult of the White Hand," but remains obsessed and tormented by his love for "Iseult the Fair." At last, wounded by a poisoned spear and about to die, Tristan sends for Iseult from Cornwall since she alone can save his life. As her ship draws near, she hoists a white flag as a sign of hope. Upon seeing the flag, Iseult of the White Hand vindictively runs to Tristan and tells him that the sail is black. His remaining hopes crushed, Tristan dies. When Iseult the Fair arrives, she lies down beside her dead lover, holds him close, and then, with all the weight of their passion upon her, she dies too.[1]

The Romantic Ideal

The Tristan myth typifies a conception of love that first arose in the games of "courtly love" played by members of the European nobility in the twelfth century. It is a conception known as the "romantic ideal," and its distinguishing features include the beliefs that love is fated and uncontrollable, that it strikes at first sight, transcends all social boundaries, and manifests itself in turbulent mixtures of agony and ecstasy. The definition provided by Andreas Capellanus, the scribe of Eleanor of Aquitaine's mock-legal "Court of Love," conveys the passionate nature of the ideal: "Love is a certain inborn suffering derived from the sight of and excessive meditation upon the beauty of the opposite sex, which causes each one to wish above all things the embraces of the other and by common desire to carry out all of love's precepts in the other's embrace."[2]

Courtly love in its traditional, extramarital form was epitomized by the *Frauendienst* (or "service of woman") of Ulrich von Lichtenstein, an Austrian knight of the thirteenth century.[3] When he was a boy of five, Ulrich later reported in his autobiography, he first heard older boys saying that true honor and happiness could come only from serving a noble woman, and when he was twelve, he first saw and fell in love with the princess, already married, to whom he was to devote the next fifteen years of his life. After years of silent devotion as a page in her court, he finally dared to send her news of the many tourneys he had won for her sake. She sent back news that he was presumptuous and ugly. Undaunted, Ulrich had his harelip fixed, and the princess graciously responded by accepting his service. When the princess once pouted that Ulrich had falsely spoken of losing a finger in battle for her, he pulled out his knife, hacked off the finger, and sent it to her in a green velvet case with a gold clasp, together with an appropriate song.

This must have made an impression, for it was only a few months later that Ulrich, after an unprecedented jousting expedition from Venice to Bohemia during which he was dressed up as the goddess Venus, was allowed to visit the princess and, ultimately, granted her love. What this entailed was probably the right to embrace and kiss her, to fondle her naked body, and possibly—here the authorities are in some doubt—to engage in sexual relations. Regardless of what the prize may have been, as Morton Hunt notes, "sexual outlet was not really the point of all of this. Ulrich had not been laboring nearly fifteen years for so ordinary a commodity; his real reward had always been in his suffering, striving, and yearning." After two years, in fact, he tired of court life and moved on to new conquests.

Although the romantic ideal has undergone certain important changes over the centuries, it is still with us today. It is most clearly recognizable in a large and popular genre of novels, movies, magazines, soap operas, and comic books in which passionate love is exalted. In one recent literary example, Samantha, a waitress at the "exclusive Carleton Colony Club," is considering marriage to a wealthy lawyer named Mr. Coles. She agrees to give him a chance to make her fall in love with him and is sitting under a tree thinking about all of the beautiful things he has promised to buy for her. But then, just as when Iseult was contemplating her prospective marriage to King Mark, fate takes a momentous turn. In Samantha's case no love potion is required. All it takes is a single word, uttered by a handsome young man named Sandy who happens to pass by. The word is "Hi," and it is love at first sight. ("*It had struck like a flash of lightning*," Samantha later recalls, "*blinding us to everything else in the world . . . shocking us and stunning our senses so that we were conscious only of one sensation of bittersweet pain. . . .*") Sandy and Samantha spend the afternoon together until he tells her that he is beginning work at the restaurant as a busboy. This is tragic news indeed, for Samantha's sole ambition in life is to marry a wealthy man. She runs off in tears, crying, "Love is not enough!" and visits Mr. Coles again. But she soon realizes her mistake: She does not love Mr. Coles, and she cannot marry a man she does not love. And so Samantha rushes back to Sandy, who is waiting for her with open arms. They walk off hand in hand, headed for a life of unending happiness.[4]

Like the authors of the Tristan myth, the creator of the Samantha tale (entitled "A Price on My Love") must remain nameless. We know only that he is on the creative staff of *Young Romance* comics. Whoever he is, he has remained faithful to the essentials of the romantic ideal.

Countess Marie's Verdict

There is, however, one immense difference between the romantic ideal in its original twelfth-century form and its manifestation in "A Price on My Love" and other modern sources. The contemporary reader can safely assume that Samantha and Sandy, having found one another and fallen in love, will soon be married. One can be certain, on the other hand, that the thought of marriage never even occurred to Tristan and Iseult. Through most of the long history during which the romantic ideal has held sway over popular conceptions of love it has been applied only to extramarital relationships.

During his *Frauendienst*, for example, Ulrich had a perfectly good wife and children back home in the castle at Steiermark. He regarded his wife with affection and even stopped to visit her and the kids while still in his Venus get-up. But whereas Ulrich was fond of his wife, as one might be fond of a congenial business partner, love for her was unthinkable. Only love for another man's wife could have the ennobling effect that was the goal of the practitioners of courtly love. Marie, Countess of Champagne (and the daughter of Eleanor of Aquitaine) made this norm quite official in one of her verdicts in the Court of Love.[5] "We declare and hold as firmly established," Marie decreed in 1174, "that love cannot exert its powers between two people who are married to each other. For lovers give each other everything freely, under no compulsion of necessity, but married people are in duty bound to give in to each other's desires and deny themselves to each other nothing."*

The game of courtly love became a consuming passion for some individuals like Ulrich, just as football or chess is for many present-day Americans. But it was not an institution of fundamental economic or social importance. Marriages, on the other hand, have throughout history been arranged on sober economic and social grounds. As sociologist John Finley Scott has observed, "The nuclear family—surprisingly invariant among societies in its basic features—has evolved not because it satisfies individual preferences, but because it is socially useful, combining the functions of reproduction, child care, sexual gratification, and economic cooperation with an overall efficiency that no alternate arrangement has been able to match."[6] Because of their acknowledged importance for the fabric of society, marriages in most societies of the world have typically been contracted by parents and matchmakers instead of being left to the prospective mates themselves.

Several twentieth-century cases are illustrative. A Kwakiutl Indian of Vancouver Island reported the following events leading to his marriage:

> When I was old enough to get a wife—I was about twenty-five—my brother looked for a girl in the same position that I and my brothers had. Without my consent, they picked a wife for me—Lagius' daughter. The one I wanted was prettier than the one they chose for me, but she was in a lower position than me, so they wouldn't let me marry her. I argued about it and was very angry with my brother, but I couldn't do anything. . . . Anyway, my older brother made arrangements for my marriage. He gave Lagius, the head chief of the Nimkis, two hundred blankets to keep Lagius from letting others have his daughter.

A Baiga woman in India gave an anthropologist the following account:

> In Dadaragon I was forcibly married to Marru. None of us wanted the marriage. I was too young, only ten years old, and my

---

* Marie's explanation follows the attributional logic discussed in Chapter 5: If service is necessitated by marital vows and roles, then it reveals little about the spouse's underlying disposition of love. Only when such service is given outside marriage can it be attributed unambiguously to the lovers' personal dispositions rather than to situational constraints.

father didn't like Marru. But my brother Chaitu had run away with Marru's wife, and Marru said he must have a girl in return.

And a recent survey in Japan, where arranged marriages (known as *miai*) are only gradually giving way to the Western-style "love match," obtained the following report:

> I was the youngest among my brothers and sisters. They were all married and I was left alone as a single woman. My mother got high blood pressure from worry about my being unmarried. My family were anxious to arrange a marriage as soon as possible and showed my mother the picture of my prospective husband. I was thus in haste to marry. After the *miai*, I did not love my partner but I married him. It was not for my sake but because I wanted to relieve my mother and my family of their anxiety that I decided to marry.[7]

Even in societies where marriages are controlled by the parental generation, prospective spouses are usually given at least some say in the matter, such as the power to veto a prospective partner whom they find to be totally unacceptable. And affection is almost universally acknowledged to be an important element of marriage. But it typically is the sort of affection that grows out of companionship and domestic felicity. "Most societies are less keen on romance than on congeniality," the anthropologist Ralph Linton has observed. "They train their young people to believe that any well-bred boy and girl, once married, will be able to live together contentedly and will in time develop a real fondness for one another. In most cases this seems to be correct."[8] The point was nicely made in *Fiddler on the Roof*, the Broadway musical set in the nineteenth-century Jewish *shtetl*, where marriages were arranged by the ubiquitous matchmaker. "Do you love me?" Tevye asks Golde after twenty-five years of contented marriage. "I'm your wife," Golde first answers, not really understanding the question. Only after reflecting on their years of life together, the joys and sorrows they have shared, the children they have raised, does she come to the inevitable self-attributional conclusion, "I suppose I do."

This sort of companionate love is a far cry from the passionate attraction of Tristan and Iseult, or of Samantha and Sandy. And whereas the romantic ideal, as typified by Tristan and Iseult, has a long historical tradition, the transposition of the ideal to the context of marriage is a relatively recent innovation. "All societies recognize that there are occasional violent emotional attachments between persons of the opposite sex," Linton wrote in 1936, "but our present American culture is practically the only one which has attempted to capitalize on these and make them the basis for marriage."[9] Although the incorporation of the romantic ideal into marriage was first advocated in eighteenth-century Europe, it seems to have thrived particularly in America. The breakdown of an inherited aristocracy made the strict parental control of mate selection somewhat less necessary than it had been in Europe, and the pioneering spirit that stressed individuality was extended to mate selection as well. Thus, a system of free choice developed in America that frequently surprised—and sometimes horrified— visitors from overseas. "A very remarkable custom in the United States," a Frenchman observed in 1842, "gives girls the freedom to choose a husband according to their fancy; practice does not permit either the mother or the father to interfere in this important matter."[10]

With the rise of industrialization the purely economic importance of marriage became further reduced. A man's farming skills and a woman's domestic aptitude became less essential criteria for the selection of a spouse, and the possibility that love might freely take its course became even greater. The psychological potential for love was already present among young Americans, as it presumably is among young people of all cultures. All that remained to complete the transformation, therefore, was to export some of the trappings of the romantic ideal—the heart throbs ("*When a lover suddenly catches sight of his beloved, his heart palpitates*"); the torment ("*He whom the thought of love vexes eats and sleeps very little*"); the all-consuming passion ("*A true lover is constantly and without intermission possessed by the thought of his beloved*"); the overcoming of obstacles ("*The easy attainment of love makes it of little value; difficulty of attainment makes it prized*")—and to make them a part of the popular mythology of courtship.[11]

And so, Countess Marie's verdict was overruled. Today the socialization of young Americans for love begins even before they are old enough to read love comics like *Young Romance*:

> The telling of the myth is begun in the nursery with fairy tales: Cinderella, Sleeping Beauty, Snow White, Frog Prince, and half a hundred less famous stories. Hardly a child *believes* the tales, but they all have the same message: A handsome prince overcomes obstacles to marry the poor maid with whom he has fallen in love; they are married and live in bliss. Alternately, the handsome but poor peasant boy overcomes obstacles to marry the princess, with whom he has fallen in love; they are married and live in bliss. Always beauty,

always obstacles, always love, always a class barrier (presumably changing from frog to human leaps an ethnic barrier), always married bliss. The unsaid last line of each story is "some day this may happen to you." Parents set the proper example for their children by relating to the child their own prince-and-beauty story. "Why did you marry Daddy?" "Because we fell in love."[12]

"A Pathological Experiment"

What has been the impact of the adoption of the romantic ideal on Western marriage? In the view of many social observers it has been a colossal mistake and a key factor in precipitating the sharp rise in divorces that took place during the first half of the twentieth century. The most scathing attack was mounted by the European social critic Denis de Rougemont. "We are in the act of trying out —and failing miserably at it," de Rougemont wrote in 1949, "one of the most pathological experiments that a civilized society has ever imagined, namely, the basing of marriage, which is lasting, upon romance which is a passing fancy."[13] De Rougemont argues that the modern man, especially in America, is seduced by the romantic ideal to ignore all of the practical considerations that in the past helped to insure successful marriages: "To him all considerations of social level or education, of suitability of temperament, background, age, material resources, outlooks on the future, family, career, religious preference, theories of upbringing, and intellectual and spiritual communion have become secondary; the prime mover is romance. 'If they're in love,' thinks he, 'if they possess *that* kind of love, let them get married.' "

But "*that* kind of love," in de Rougemont's view, is not the sort of love that is likely to endure. Rather, it is "a fever, generally light and considered infinitely interesting to contract." Such love can be sustained only in a mythical world like that of Tristan and Iseult, whose numerous separations, adventures, and obstacles have the purpose of sustaining the excitement and thereby keeping their love alive. De Rougemont contends that Tristan and Iseult are not in love with one another, but rather with the idea of love itself. "Their need of one another is in order to be aflame, and they do not need one another as they are. What they need is not one another's presence, but one another's absence." Their frequent separations make it possible for the lovers to retain their idealized images of one another, images that would inevitably be destroyed in the face of prolonged contact. But whereas courtly love thrived on separation, excitement, and idealization, marriage requires companionship, routine, and objectivity. And so, de Rougemont concludes, "The logical and normal outcome of marriage founded only on romance is divorce, for marriage kills romance; if romance reappears, it will kill the marriage by its incompatibility with the very reasons for which the marriage was contracted."

De Rougemont is not alone in taking a dim view of marriages based on romantic love. Psychoanalyst Lawrence Kubie has used a somewhat different vocabulary to express a similar point of view: "It is obvious that the state of being in love is no guide [for the advisability of marriage]. It is an obsessional state which, like all obsessions, is in part driven by unconscious anger."[14] Sociologist Willard Waller gave college students the same sort of advice in his 1938 textbook on marriage:

> It is possibly very unfortunate that people must make one of their most important decisions on the basis of certain delusive emotions of adolescence. There is truth in the ancient proverb, *Amantes amentes,* lovers are mad. And the persons who have the power to excite this madness in others are by no means always the persons with whom it is possible to live happily after the knot is tied.[15]

In recent years, however, writers of such textbooks have toned down their criticisms of romantic love as a basis for marriage. Sociologists seem to have become more aware of the fact that although the romantic ideal has continued to provide much of the basis for modern marriages, it has not been adopted in its unadulterated twelfth-century form. As we shall see, marriages in modern America do not in fact ignore the considerations of social level, temperamental compatibility, and similarity of outlook that de Rougemont accuses them of ignoring. In the following section we will survey some of the factors that have been shown to determine who marries whom in contemporary America. We will then be in a better position to examine the actual impact of the romantic ideal on modern marriage.

Who Marries Whom?

On Monday Cpl. Floyd Johnson, 23, and the then Mary Ellen Skinner, 19, total strangers, boarded a train at San Francisco and sat down across the aisle from each other. Johnson didn't cross the aisle until Wednesday, but his bride said, "I'd already made up my mind to say yes if he asked me to marry him." "We did most of the talking with our eyes," Johnson explained. Thursday the couple got off the train in Omaha with plans to be married. Because they would need the consent of the bride's parents if they were married in Nebraska, they crossed the river to Council Bluffs, Iowa, where they were married Friday.[16]

This report appeared in a reputable newspaper, so we know that "love at first sight" must occasionally occur in life as well as in fiction. There is even a psychological theory to account for the phenomenon, to be found in the writings of the psychoanalyst Carl Jung. Jung proposes that every man is born with an *anima*, an unconscious representation of his feminine nature. Similarly, every woman has an *animus* representing her masculine side. These representations—in Jung's terminology, "archetypes"—come to the fore only when a person encounters someone of the opposite sex who closely matches the representation. "You see that girl, or at least a good imitation of your type," Jung explained[17] several years before his death in 1961, "and instantly you get the seizure; you are caught."*

But there is no systematic evidence for the validity of Jung's theory of love at first sight, and interviews with engaged and married couples suggest that the phenomenon is extremely rare. In the late 1940s sociologists Ernest Burgess and Paul Wallin interviewed 226 engaged couples, primarily college students, as part of a larger survey. Only 8 percent of the men and 5 percent of the women recalled feeling "strong physical attraction" for their partner within one or two days of their first meeting. Presumably even fewer of the cases could be characterized as "love at first sight." Burgess and Wallin present the following account as more typical of their interviewees' experiences:

> I was twenty when I first met my fiancé. We worked in the same office. We had our first date a couple of months after I started working there. In about six months I felt I was falling in love with him. I think our love was about mutual in time. He mentioned it first about the end of six months and I told him I felt practically the same way. About three or four months later I started wearing his fraternity pin.[18]

The Girl Next Door

The office romance illustrates the more general tendency for people to marry partners who are close at hand. In Chapter 6 we considered the strong impact that residential arrangements have

* "And afterward," he added, "you may admit that it was a hell of a mistake."

on people's choice of friends. In the M.I.T. housing project studied by Leon Festinger and his colleagues, for example, the closer one family lived to another—even within the same building—the more likely they were to be good friends. The impact of spatial arrangements—or, in the inimitable jargon of the social scientists who brought you "interpersonal attraction" and "mate selection," *residential propinquity*—is at least as great in the case of the choice of marriage partners. In 1931 a sociologist named James Bossard examined 5,000 marriage license applications in which one or both applicants were residents of Philadelphia. He found that one out of four couples lived within two city blocks of one another at the time of their application, and one-third of the couples lived within five blocks. More generally, the proportion of marriages "decreased steadily and markedly as the distance between contracting parties increased," a generalization that has come to be known as Bossard's Law. More recent studies have found similar patterns in cities throughout America as well as in other countries.[19]

The likelihood that a person will fall in love with and marry "the girl next door" seems to fly in the face of the romantic notion that one's perfect mate may be waiting for one across a crowded room in some far corner of the globe. Nevertheless, the tendency to be attracted to people who are close at hand makes perfect sense in terms of the profit motive of the interpersonal marketplace. If a suitable mate lives next door, there is no need for a man in search of a partner to scour the entire block. If she lives in the neighborhood, there is no need for him to spend time and money on the cross-town bus. In addition, the principle of mere exposure suggests that the more opportunities he has to bump into a prospective partner, the more likely he is to come to like her. Once a close relationship has been established, it is indeed possible that absence will make the heart grow fonder, as it seems to have done for Tristan and Iseult. But until that stage is reached, as Bossard suggested, the wings of Cupid are best adapted for short flights. In all of this the romantic ideal is not renounced; it is merely amended in a way that better corresponds to practical considerations. "When I'm not near the girl I love," as the song goes, "I love the girl I'm near."

A "Suitable" Background

When marriages are based on "a fever, generally light and . . . infinitely interesting to contract," de Rougemont argues, another set of practical considerations—those concerning the suitability of a prospective mate's ethnic, religious, and social background—will inevitably fall by the wayside. A "suitable" background, of course, tends to be a background that is similar to one's own. Interracial marriage is viewed with particular distaste in America, and until recently many states outlawed it. Interreligious marriage has consistently been condemned by clergy and laymen alike. In the Jewish tradition, for example, the Jew who married a gentile was considered dead and officially mourned by his parents. Marriages that cross socioeconomic lines are similarly frowned upon. Unless the lower-status partner has some striking and visible compensating quality, such as rare beauty or acknowledged brilliance, the match is likely to be feared by the parents of the higher-status partner as a threat to their own social position. The family of the lower-status partner may often be just as opposed to the match, for fear of being disowned or ridiculed by their own friends.

Norms of within-class marriage—technically termed "endogamy"—are seen as necessary for group survival (as in the case of the Jews) and for the perpetuation of social-class distinctions. As sociologist William Goode has noted, "To permit random mating would mean radical change in the existing social structure."[20] Such radical change is strongly resisted, particularly by those who want to retain their position at the top of the structure. Endogamy indeed seems sorely threatened by the demise of arranged marriage and the rise of romantic love, which according to the ideal can easily overcome bars of race, religion, and social class. If the romantic ideal were to prevail fully, we should quickly see a breakdown in the prevailing system of ethnic, religious, and class stratification in America: Whites would be as likely to marry blacks as other whites; Jews would as easily fall in love with Catholics or Protestants as other Jews; and sons of bankers like Oliver Barrett IV would as routinely marry daughters of bakers like Jennifer Cavilleri in real life as they do in fiction.

In this respect too, however, the romantic ideal has not in fact been adopted in its unadulterated form. According to 1960 Census data, whites in the United States surpass Ivory Snow by being 99.8 percent pure, with only one-fifth of 1 percent marrying non-whites. Similarly, 99 percent of black Americans marry fellow blacks. There have been small increases in the proportion of interracial marriages over the past several decades, but the phenomenon remains very rare. American marriages also remain strongly ingrown with respect to religion. According to 1957 data, husbands and wives belong to the same major religious grouping (Protestant, Catholic, or Jewish) in 93.6 percent of American marriages,* whereas only 56 percent of the couples would share the same religion if the marriages had taken place without regard to the religious factor. And the Oliver Barretts notwithstanding, marriages still respect distinctions of social class. When the socioeconomic status of American husbands and wives is categorized on the basis of their respective fathers' occupations, a strong positive correlation between the partners' social origins is found.

When marriages do cross ethnic or class lines, moreover, they seem to be characterized by compensating factors. Black men who marry white women, for example, tend to be more highly educated than black men who marry black women, whereas white women who marry black men tend to be *less* highly educated than white women who marry white men.[21] These interracial marriages can be seen as exchanges on the interpersonal marketplace, in which the higher educational status of the black husband (and the earning power that may go along with it) is exchanged for the higher social status of the white wife (which accrues to her simply by virtue of her skin color).

Such exchanges take place in interclass marriages as well. My own analysis of data collected by the Bureau of the Census in 1962 revealed that contrary to the impression conveyed in previous sociological writings, there is no general tendency for American women to marry men whose social origins are higher than their own.[22] There is such a tendency, however, if we restrict our attention to marriages linking members of the two highest class levels. It is significantly more likely that the daughter of a white-collar worker will marry the son of a higher-status professional or manager than it is that the white-collar worker's son will marry the professional's daughter. It may well be that the lower-status wife in such marriages tends to be characterized by personal qualities that make the marriage bargain a "fair" one. For example, in a study that was cited in Chapter 4, Glen Elder found that girls who were rated as better looking when they were in high school were more likely to end up marrying higher-status men than were their less attractive classmates. If love is a fever, we must conclude that it is the sort of fever that closely adheres to the trading rules of the interpersonal marketplace.

---

* This figure refers to the *present* religions of husbands and wives, however, rather than to their religious backgrounds. Inasmuch as in some interfaith marriages one spouse will convert to his or her partner's religion, the figure somewhat underestimates the proportion of marriages that cross religious lines.

The Sharing of Values

Another of de Rougemont's contentions is that couples smitten by love will ignore such crucial factors as "outlooks on the future, family, career, . . . theories of upbringing, and intellectual and spiritual communion" when they plan to get married. Once again, there is abundant evidence to indicate that he is wrong. The engaged couples surveyed by Burgess and Wallin tended to agree with one another to a striking degree when they were individually asked for their views on matters ranging from smoking and drinking habits to opinions about whether the woman should work, how many children they should have, and what sort of dwelling they should live in. The rewards of agreement seem in fact to be as relevant to loving as they are to liking. "We have so many interests that are the same," one woman explained when she was asked why she loved her fiancé. "Our ideas and beliefs and ambitions are identical in all major respects."[23]

The fact that people are most likely to begin dating others who live nearby (or attend the same school) and who share their social background makes it likely that a large proportion of their attitudes and values will be in basic agreement from the start. And once a relationship becomes established, the couple's gradual discovery of just how much agreement there is becomes crucial in determining whether or not they will move in the direction of marriage. This process was illustrated in a study conducted by social psychologists Alan Kerckhoff and Keith E. Davis.[24] They began by asking members of dating couples at Duke University to rank a list of family values in order of their importance to them. The list included such values as "healthy and happy children," "economic security," and "moral and religious unity." Seven months later the investigators recontacted the students and asked them whether or not their relationship had moved closer toward permanence. They found that those couples who agreed highly in their rankings of what was important in marriage were significantly more likely to progress toward a permanent relationship than those who were in less close agreement.

Kerckhoff and Davis suggest that the mate selection process can be described as a series of successive filters. Proximity and "suitability" of background are the initial filters in the series. They determine to a large extent the likelihood that a man and woman will meet—and, if they do, the probability that they will consider one another to be potentially eligible partners. The dating couples in the Kerckhoff–Davis study were all attending the same school and were already homogenized to a large extent with respect to race, religion, and social status. At this point the discovery of the extent to which they share attitudes and values comes into the picture. Those couples who discover that their views are widely discrepant will break up, while those who find that they have similar values stay together.

It is only after a couple has successfully survived the test of value consensus, Kerckhoff and Davis go on to speculate, that more subtle processes of personality matching come into play to determine the further course of the relationship. In support of this speculation, they report that value consensus was most predictive of progress in courtship among "short-term" couples—those who had been going together for less than eighteen months at the time of the original testing. Among "long-term" couples—those who had been dating for at least eighteen months—the measure of value consensus was less strongly related to further progress, and instead a measure of "need complementarity" was successful in predicting progress. This measure, developed by psychologist William Schutz,[25] attempted to assess the extent to which each person's expressed needs to be affectionate, controlling, and "inclusive" jibed with his or her partner's needs to receive affection, to be controlled, and to be included. Need complementarity, in other words, may be the final quality-control filter on the assembly line that leads from first meeting to marriage.

The Meshing of Needs

The idea that people should be drawn to others whose personal attributes complement or fill out their own has long been a central element in popular conceptions of interpersonal attraction. According to a Greek myth recounted in Plato's *Symposium*, in ancient days the world was inhabited by men, women, and hermaphrodites, all with twice the usual number of arms, legs, heads, and sex organs. Zeus became angry with all of these people and decided to punish them by cutting them in half. This led to a yearning to be whole again, to seek one's complementary part. Those people who were originally double men or double women had homosexual strivings, while those who were originally hermaphroditic were heterosexual. As Ira Reiss notes, the allegory is perhaps the oldest statement of the theory that people seek in love what they themselves are lacking.[26]

The notion of complementarity clearly departs from the more conventional principle that people are attracted to others who resemble themselves. Psychologist Robert W. White writes:

Intimacy requires a large amount of mutual appreciation, but this does not imply that the partners must be just alike. Friendships at all ages can have part of their strength in a complementary relation. Each member can supply the other with something he lacks, at the same time serving as a model from whom the desirable quality can be copied. Thus there may be a relation of leader and follower between a pair of chums, the leader gaining an ally and the follower being bestirred by his friend's initiative; in the meantime the follower learns something about leadership and the leader about followership.

White provides a graphic example of a complementary relationship between two teen-age friends:

Ben, whose school experience had been so unstimulating that he never read a book beyond those assigned, discovered in Jamie a lively spirit of intellectual inquiry and an exciting knowledge of politics and history. Here was a whole world to which his friend opened the door and provided guidance. Jamie discovered in Ben a world previously closed to him, that of confident interaction with other people. Each admired the other, each copied the other, each used the other for practice. In Ben's words: "You see how I was almost consciously expanding my image of myself to include attributes which he already had, so that I felt extended, both of us felt extended by the intimacy."[27]

Such complementarity, in which each partner is well equipped to satisfy the needs of the other, would also seem to be an important basis of mate-selection—perhaps especially, as Kerckhoff and Davis suggest, after the couples have already sorted themselves out on the basis of social and attitudinal similarities. "I do need encouragement and Janette gives it to me," one young man interviewed by Burgess and Wallin reported. "Last year when things looked pretty bad and I didn't know where I was heading . . . she would get me in a different frame of mind. I don't think she needs sympathy and encouragement. I think she is quite self-sufficient."[28] If we assume that the young man is able to fulfill Janette's needs as well as she seems able to fulfill his, then the exchange would be complete. If, for example, Janette has strong needs to be nurturant and encouraging, then she would be rewarded by the very act of helping her fiancé to get out of his depressions.

Can the notion of need complementarity help us to explain who will marry whom? It seems conceivable that it could. If we are able to ascertain, for example, that one member of a couple is an extremely dominant and assertive person whereas his partner is quite meek and submissive, we would expect the couple to have a promising future. Jack will assert and Jill will submit; both will be gratified, and as a result they will keep asserting and submitting themselves all the way to the altar. In an intensive study of twenty-five newlywed couples conducted in the 1950s, sociologist Robert Winch concluded that such complementarity was indeed prevalent. But further studies have made it clear that Winch's "theory of complementary needs" will need considerable refinement before it can serve as a useful predictor in studies of mate selection. With the exception of the Kerckhoff–Davis study, no studies of the mating process have successfully employed measures of need complementarity to predict progress in courtship. And even the Kerckhoff–Davis conclusion has been challenged by subsequent researchers who meticulously repeated their procedures but failed to obtain the same results.[29]

The multiplicity of human needs and aspirations, the variety of ways in which they may be satisfied, and the problem of specifying which are more and which are less central to marriage have all presented obstacles that researchers have not yet succeeded in surmounting. It may well be asked, for example, if a "dominant" woman will be more satisfied with a submissive husband or with a husband who is even more dominant than she. Similarly, it may be asked whether a business executive whose needs to dominate others are gratified at work will be particularly concerned with fulfilling these needs at home. For one couple the dominance–submission dimension may be central to permarital and marital interaction; for another couple it may be rather unimportant. For the second couple a different sort of complementarity—in which the husband glories vicariously in his wife's artistic talent, while the wife is broadened by her husband's intellectual interests—may be the glue that keeps them strongly attracted to one another.

As a result, it proves to be much easier to recognize need complementarity among established couples than it is to predict it ahead of time on the basis of the individual characteristics of the prospective partners. Need complementarity is best viewed as a pattern of interaction that emerges gradually in the course of a relationship, rather than as a jigsaw puzzle that is bound to make a complete picture if only the pieces can be brought together. New complementarities frequently arise in a relationship that not even the most insightful observers or personality-testers could have anticipated. The puzzle is a flexible one, and the pieces often shape one another.

The Parents Have Their Say

The romantic ideal portrays love as an eminently personal affair, a feeling (obsession?) that one experiences directly rather than a decision that one arrives at after consultation with others. In accord with the ideal, young people are likely to resist energetically any suggestion of parental pressure of interference with their romantic life. Nevertheless, parents still have a surprisingly large say in determining who marries whom in contemporary America. Some of this influence is quite direct and aboveboard. About 60 percent of the women and half of the men in Burgess and Wallin's sample of engaged couples reported that they had discussed the advisability of their marriage with other persons, and in the large majority of cases these other persons were their parents. (Interestingly, the parent consulted by both sons and daughters was much more likely to be the mother than the father.)

The bulk of parental influence on mate selection is likely to be more subtle, however. Secure in the knowledge that their children cannot marry people whom they never meet, parents often decide where to live, what schools to send their children to, and what sorts of social activities to encourage on the basis of ethnic and social class considerations. The attitudes, values, and even personality traits that parents instill in their children also help to insure that a partner whom the child finds to be "desirable" will be desirable to the parents as well. Direct protestations or financial threats are rarely exercised, in large measure because they are rarely necessary to insure "appropriate" matches. Parents can let the laws of the interpersonal marketplace take their own course and find that they usually serve the function of the professional matchmaker remarkably well.

In the past half-century, however, increasingly large numbers of young people of the upper and middle classes have left home to attend large, heterogeneous universities. In such an environment, many miles removed from parental control, the possibility looms large that a young man or woman will meet a congenial partner who is "inappropriate" on ethnic, religious, or socioeconomic grounds. As John Finley Scott has pointed out, the parental generation did not take this threat lying down. One of the ways in which parents responded was to promote fraternities and, especially, sororities on campus, which serve to stratify students by their religious and social origins and which then proceed to monitor the young people's romantic activities to insure that they do not stray from the proper path.

Scott compares the American college sorority to a variety of schemes that have been used to control marriages in simpler societies. The Bontok people of the Philippines kept their girls in a special house, called the *olag*, where lovers called and marriage was supposed to result. The aborigines of the Canary Islands sent their daughters to "convents," where old women taught them the special skills and mysteries that a young wife needed to know. In the Jewish *shtetl* matchmakers, called *shatchens*, were employed to pair off girls and boys appropriately, and a father who could afford it would offer substantial sums to acquire a scholarly husband for his daughter. All of these devices focused upon the common problem of "making sure that girls are available for marriage with the right man while at the same time guarding against marriage with the wrong man." Similarly, the college sorority is a house, like the *olag*, where lovers call and "like the Canary Island convent, teaches skills that middle-class wives need to know; like the *shtetl*, provides matchmakers; and without going so far as to buy husbands of high rank, manages to dissuade the girls from making alliances with lower-class boys."

How does the sorority achieve all of these functions? Here are some of Scott's observations on the matter:

A membership composed of the "right kind" of girls is produced by the requirement that each pledge must have the recommendation of, in most cases, two or more alumnae of the sorority. Membership is often passed on from mother to daughter—this is the "legacy," whom sorority actives have to invite whether they like her or not. The sort of headstrong, innovative, or "sassy" girl who is likely to organize a compaign inside the sorority against prevailing standards is unlikely to receive alumnae recommendations. . . .

Alumnae dominance extends beyond recruitment, into the daily life of the house. Rules, regulations, and policy explanations come to the house from the national association. . . . The actives in positions of control (house manager, pledge trainer, or captain) are themselves closely supervised by alumnae. . . .

Sororities keep their members, and particularly their flighty pledges, in line primarily by filling up all their time with house activities. Pledges are required to study at the house, and they build papier-mâché floats (in collaboration with selected fraternity boys) that are a traditional display of "Greek Row" for the homecoming game. Time is encompassed completely; activities are planned long in advance, and there is almost no time or energy available for meeting inappropriate men. . . .

The sorority facilitates dating mainly by exchanging parties, picnics, and other frolics with the fraternities in its set. But to augment this the "fixer-uppers" (the American counterpart of the *shatchen*) arrange dates with selected boys; their efforts raise the sorority dating rate above the independent level by removing most of the inconvenience and anxiety from the contracting of dates.

Dating, in itself, is not sufficient to accomplish the sorority's purposes. Dating must lead to pinning, pinning to engagement, engagement to marriage. In sorority culture, all dating is viewed as a movement toward marriage. Casual, spontaneous dating is frowned upon; formal courtship is still encouraged.[30]

And, as we noted in Chapter 8, sorority rituals like the pinning ceremony are specifically geared to shore up this progression from dating to engagement to marriage. Like de Rougemont, sorority elders are acutely concerned about the threat imposed by the romantic ideal to the social status quo. Instead of decrying the romantic ideal, the sorority accomplishes its goal of preserving the status quo in a more devious and more effective way. It embraces the ideal, building its trappings into its culture, as exemplified by the pinning ceremony. With true love on its side, the parental generation cannot lose.

It is admittedly the case, however, that the fraternity and sorority system is on the way out on a large number of campuses. University administrations are increasingly hostile to their brand of social discrimination, and campus values have shifted away from homecoming parades and tea parties. As a result, fewer and fewer girls rush each year, and more and more sorority chapters are disbanding. Whether the elder generation will come up with new techniques for the remote control of their children's romantic inclinations remains to be seen. As the ingenuity of the American *olag* demonstrates, however, one should never underestimate the ability of parents to achieve, however subtly, the ends of arranged marriage in a free-choice, "romantic" society.

The Romantic Ideal Reconsidered

We have seen that marriages in contemporary America are only rarely based on the sort of blind, unreasoning passion that the romantic ideal calls for. Mates are in most cases found close to home and selected from a field of eligibles who typically share one's race, religion, social status, and important values and attitudes. When marriages cross class lines, they often illustrate processes of social exchange that are more reminiscent of the hardheaded calculation of arranged marriage than of the unpredictable viscissitudes of courtly love. And as in the era of arranged marriage, parents continue to play a noticeable—even if sometimes unrecognized—role in directing their children's search for a mate. But we should not underestimate the very real impact that the romantic ideal has had on contemporary courtship. It has resulted in the undisputed recognition that love is a prerequisite to marriage—not unreasoning love of the "head-over-heels" variety (fewer than one-fourth of Burgess and Wallin's engaged subjects accepted this description) and not love that transcends all obstacles and barriers, but love nevertheless. In the following sections we will consider in greater detail some of the ways in which the romantic ideal has been adapted to the case of mate selection in present-day America.

The Stereotypes Reversed

As we have seen, young Americans are not prepared to fall in love with anyone who should come their way. They often have preestablished ideals or requirements, and only those people who meet the requirements (or come sufficiently close to them) are considered eligible partners. When the requirements concern social and economic status, women seem to be more selective than men. Because this fact leads to the reversal of traditional stereotypes about the "romanticism" of the two sexes, we will pause to consider some evidence for it.

If you had been at a particular gymnasium in Ames, Iowa, several years ago, you would have been exposed to the unusual sight of some 365 male and 365 female Iowa State undergraduates doing the Funky Broadway and, more or less simultaneously, filling out questionnaires. They were attending a new breed of social activity, the "computer dance" arranged by social scientists for research purposes. In this instance the social scientists in charge, Robert Coombs and William Kenkel, were particularly interested in comparing the dating attitudes of the two sexes.[31] They obtained their data from two sources: a preliminary questionnaire in which the subjects indicated their requirements and ideals for a date and a postdance questionnaire in which they reported on their satisfaction with the date they received.

When the subjects were asked what they were looking for in a date, the women made more stringent demands than the men on all but one dimension. The figures revealed that 73 percent of the women as compared to 56 percent of the men insisted that their date be of their own race; and 24 percent of the women but only 14 percent of the men required a date of their own religion. Women were also more concerned than men about getting a date who was intelligent, high in campus status, a good dancer, and a good dresser. The men had higher aims only with respect to the partner's physical attractiveness.

Afterward, which of the sexes had more positive reactions? The data were unambiguous on this point. Men were more satisfied with their dates on all criteria, felt more "romantic attraction" toward them, and when asked to speculate about the chances that they and their date could have a happy marriage, were more optimistic. To some extent the postdate data might have been predicted on the basis of the predate data. If women demand and expect more than men, they are bound to be disappointed more often. But even in the area of physical attractiveness, in which the men had higher aspirations, the men were also more satisfied. It seems that men typically are quicker to fall in love than women are.

Other investigations have pointed to the same conclusion. In the Burgess and Wallin survey, many more men than women reported that they had been strongly attracted to their fiancés at their first meeting or shortly thereafter. In William Kephart's more recent survey of over 1,000 college students in Philadelphia, nearly twice as many men as women said that they were "very easily attracted" to members of the opposite sex.[32] Upon reflection, the pattern seems understandable. Since the woman rather than the man typically takes on the social and economic status of her spouse, she has more practical concerns to keep in mind in selecting a mate. In addition, the woman is often in a greater rush to get married than the man because her years of "marriageability" tend to be more limited. Thus, she cannot as easily afford to be strongly attracted to a date who is not also a potentially eligible spouse. It is largely for these reasons that parents in virtually all societies are more concerned with marrying their daughters appropriately than with securing suitable matches for their sons. Willard Waller, writing over thirty years ago, put the matter in its bluntest terms: "There is this difference between the man and the woman in the pattern of bourgeois family life; a man, when he marries, chooses a companion and perhaps a helpmate, but a woman chooses a companion and at the same time a standard of living. It is necessary for a woman to be mercenary."[33]

The popular stereotype has it, of course, that the female of the human species is more romantic than the male. She is the starry-eyed and sentimental one, the one who reads the love magazines and watches the soap operas, while he hides behind the sports section or the financial reports. There may be some truth to all of that, but if we define "romantic" in terms of adherence to the tenets of the romantic ideal—which states, among other things, that love overcomes all social and economic bars—then it becomes clear that the male is the one who rates the larger cluster of hearts and flowers.

In my own study of some 200 dating couples at the University of Michigan, men received higher scores than women on an attitude scale assessing the extent of one's adherence to the romantic ideal.[34] Men were significantly more likely than women to agree with such romantic statements as "A person should marry whomever he loves regardless of social position," and "As long as they at least love one another, two people should have no difficulty getting along together in marriage"; and to *disagree* with such unromantic statements as "Economic security should be carefully considered before selecting a marriage partner," and "One should not marry against the serious advice of one's parents."

The "Right Kind" of Person

The woman's greater need to consider the social and economic implications of marriage may sometimes tempt her to abandon the romantic ideal altogether. Dr. Kephart asked his sample of Philadelphia students the following question: "If a boy (girl) had all the other qualities you desired, would you marry this person even if you were not in love with him (her)?" Few of the students (4 percent of the women and 12 percent of the men) were so unromantic as to say that they would marry such a person. But only 24 percent of the women, as compared to 65 percent of the men, were unambiguously romantic enough to respond with a flat "no." Fully 72 percent of the women (and only 24 percent of the men) said they were "undecided."

The women's greater degree of indecision seems to reflect, as Kephart delicately phrased it, her "greater measure of control over her romantic inclinations." But this "greater measure of control" should not lead us to believe that the modern American woman is in fact very likely to marry someone she does not love. The indecision expressed by so large a proportion of Kephart's female subjects probably reflected something more like bewilderment, for what Kephart had done was to pose a basic contradiction for the new romantic. For a prospective mate to have "all the qualities you desired" directly implies that one should be in love with him— this is, indeed, the definition of love that modern Americans adhere to. As Margaret Mead wrote in 1962, "Ideals of romantic love have . . . been replaced by a hope of marrying the *right kind* of girl or boy, and attaining the right kind of marriage."[35] One of Kephart's respondents saw through the dilemma most clearly, writing in on the questionnaire, "If a boy had all the other qualities I desired, and I was not in love with him—well, I think I could talk myself into falling in love." Whereas women in modern America may be somewhat more selective than men about "the other qualities," both sexes seem to subscribe equally to this Americanized version of the romantic ideal.

Love for the modern American is a strongly felt emotion. It may sometimes even approximate the "fever" or the "obsession" that de Rougemont and Kubie talk about. But it is an emotion that is closely coordinated to the lover's perception that a particular other person is an "appropriate" partner who can fulfill one's needs for personal satisfactions in marriage. The perception is sometimes incorrect, but probably no more often than were parents' perceptions of who would be an "appropriate" partner for their child in the era of arranged marriage. Although it is hard to know for sure, I suspect that de Rougemont was far off the mark when he attributed the rising rate of divorce in the twentieth century to the basing of marriage on romance. It seems likely that in an era of rapid social change and increased individual autonomy, the divorce rate in America would have climbed at least as rapidly without romantic love as with it. Sociologist Hugo Beigel makes a good case for this contention, concluding that romantic love "has not only done no harm as a prerequisite to marriage, but it has mitigated the impact that a too-fast-moving and unorganized conversion to new socio-economic constellations has had upon our whole culture and it has saved monogamous marriage from dissolution."[36]

We still occasionally come across real-life reports of love in modern America that could have been taken right out of the pages of *The Art of Courtly Love.* Not too long ago one of America's now-defunct popular family magazines included an interview with a beautiful twenty-two-year-old movie star and a glamorous fifty-four-year-old director who had recently fallen in love. Here is how it happened:

She: I had tried to run away from the truth and I tried to fall in love with anyone else but him. But even in Africa, every animal I saw had his face.

He: I asked her to the first showing of our picture. We sat side by side. She suddenly leaned over and kissed me. The whole place turned upside down. I realized this little gesture might be purely platonic—from an actress, you know—but I sensed no, it was true. I said to myself, "By God, face it, you love her. She may even love you." It sounds corny, but there's nothing cornier than life.[37]

But even as life occasionally corresponds to the myth, the current versions of romantic mythology are increasingly being adapted to reality. In *Love Story* the romance of Oliver Barrett IV and Jennifer Cavilleri cuts across social and economic lines, but the two lovers are nevertheless both Harvard students who have spent four years in the same intellectual climate and who met in the Radcliffe library. In the movie *Guess Who's Coming to Dinner?* a rich white girl and a black man of humble origins meet in Hawaii, fall in love at first sight, and in the subsequent week manage to break down their parents' opposition and get married; but he is after all a brilliant physician, by far the girl's intellectual superior. In the eyes of all of those parents whose only wish is that their daughter marry a doctor, he is not too bad a bargain. And what of Samantha, who rejects the wealthy Mr. Coles in favor of the lowly busboy who said "Hi"? For Samantha, too, the romantic ideal is Americanized. After she decides to marry Sandy (after?—or might she have sensed it even before?) she discovers that he is the restaurant owner's son and will some day own the business. Samantha, like so many other hardheaded–idealistic American girls and boys, decides to marry for love and ends up marrying the "right kind" of person anyway.

Chapter 10
THE NATURE OF LOVE
A Researcher's Odyssey*

LOVE, *what is it? Answ. 'Tis very much like light, a thing that everybody knows, and yet none can tell what to make of it.*
—LADIES DICTIONARY (1694)

Setting out to devise measures of love is like setting out to prepare a gourmet dish with a thousand different recipes but no pots and pans. The recipes for love abound. Throughout history poets, essayists, novelists, philosophers, theologians, psychologists, sociologists, and other men and women of goodwill have written more about love than about virtually any other topic. The index to my edition of Bartlett's *Familiar Quotations* lists 769 references to "love," second only to "man" with 843. But whereas the nature of love has long been a prime topic of discourse and debate, the number of behavioral scientists who have conducted empirical research on love can be counted on one's fingers. And, until recently, the tools with which such research might have been conducted have not existed.

The state of our knowledge about interpersonal attraction has advanced considerably in the past two decades, but primarily through research on liking rather than research directly concerned with love. And while liking and loving are surely close relatives, they are by no means identical. The bridge between research on liking and the extensive writings on love remains to be built.

* My study of love is reported most completely in my doctoral thesis, *The Social Psychology of Romantic Love*, University of Michigan, 1969 (University Microfilms, Ann Arbor, Michigan, No. 70-4179). Some of the major results are also presented in "Measurement of Romantic Love," *Journal of Personality and Social Psychology*, 1970, 16, 265–273.

In this chapter I will report on my own initial endeavor to help build this bridge. My attempt hearkens back to our discussion of "measuring the unmeasurable" in Chapter 2. My goal was to develop and validate a self-report measure of romantic love. By the adjective "romantic," I do not wish to connote all the trappings of the romantic ideal that we have just examined. I use the word simply to distinguish the sort of love that may exist between unmarried, opposite-sex partners from such other related forms as love between children and their parents, close friends, and men and God. The fact that the same word, *love*, may be applied to all of these sorts of relationships must be more than linguistic accident. There are undoubtedly important common elements among these overtly different manifestations. As a starting point for my research, however, it seemed wiser to restrict my attention to a single context.

Like love itself, the course of research on love—and, indeed, of social–psychological research more generally—seldom runs smooth. There are numerous pitfalls, bumps in the road, sharp turns, and detours. These rough spots are carefully smoothed out in most research reports, presumably to spare editors and readers the shakes and jostles that the investigator had to endure. In this report, though, I should like to share at least some of the bumps with you. I hope that by doing so I will be able to convey some of the flavor of conducting research in a largely uncharted area.

Eros and Agape

To anchor my attempt to measure love at one end with the work of the "liking researchers," I decided from the start to conceptualize love as an attitude that a person holds toward a particular other person. As such, love—like liking—is an invisible package of feelings, thoughts, and behavioral predispositions within an individual. But I also assumed that the content of this attitude is not the same as that of liking, even extremely strong liking, nor could it be equated with the sentiments that we described in Chapter 2 as affection and respect. To determine the content of the attitude to be called love I would have to look elsewhere, to the many prescriptions provided through history.

"How do I love thee? Let me count the ways," declared Elizabeth Barrett Browning, thereby alluding to the most basic form of measurement. My first problem was to decide which ways to count. What Shakespeare defined as "a spirit all compact of fire" has been defined by others, in such diverse ways as a "centrifugal act of the soul" (Ortega y Gassett), "a sickness full of woes" (Samuel Daniel), and "not ever having to say you're sorry" (Erich

Segal). For Freud, love is a push from within, produced by the sublimation of overtly sexual impulses. For Plato it is a pull from ahead, engendered by the search for the ultimate good. "There are so many sorts of love," Voltaire wrote, "that one does not know where to seek a definition of it." In the midst of all of these conceptions and varieties, however, one dimension stands out as central. This is the opposition of love as *needing* and love as *giving*.

The equation of love with a physical or emotional need can be traced back at least as far as Sappho's symptomatology of love-sickness, offered in the sixth century B.C. The defining features of love, in terms of this conception, are powerful desires to be in the other's presence, to make physical contact, to be approved of, to be cared for. In its most extreme form the love-need appears as a passionate desire to possess and to be fulfilled by another person, corresponding to what the Greeks called *eros*. In more contemporary psychological terms, we can identify the need conception of love with *attachment*, as exemplified by the bonds formed between infants and their parents.

In apparent contrast to the conception of love as a cluster of needs is the conception of love as giving to another person. This is the aspect of love emphasized in the New Testament, epitomized by St. John's declaration, "God is love." Contemporary psychological definitions also depict the lover as the ultimate altruist. For Erich Fromm, "Love is the active concern for the life and growth of that which we love."[1] According to Harry Stack Sullivan, "When the satisfaction or the security of another person becomes as significant to one as is one's own satisfaction or security, then the state of love exists."[2] Love as giving corresponds to what the Greeks called *agape* and to what I will call *caring*.

It can be argued that attachment is a less mature form of love than caring. Whereas infants develop strong attachments toward their parents, for example, caring is a phenomenon that typically does not appear until somewhat later in life. (In Sullivan's view, people first learn to care about others in the context of childhood friendships.) Abraham Maslow associates attachment with people's "deficiency needs" for acceptance and approval. He suggests that "love hunger is a deficiency disease exactly as is salt hunger or the avitaminoses," and, as such, is an immature form of love. People who have reached a higher state of "self-actualization," in Maslow's framework, have already satisfied their deficiency need for love. D-love ("D" for "Deficiency") is replaced by B-love ("B" for "Being"), which is less needful and dependent, and more autonomous and giving.[3]

Maslow's analysis of love implies that attachment and caring stand opposed to one another, and that the more there is of one the less there will be of the other. But it is doubtful that such an opposition corresponds to the actual nature of love relationships. It seems more likely that as a couple's relationship becomes increasingly close, it will be associated with both increased attachment and increased caring. Clinical psychologist David Orlinsky suggests, for example, that attachment and caring merge to form a "dual feeling-impulse," which may be equated with love.[4]

The theologian Paul Tillich also discusses love as ideally being a merger of attachment and caring, as expressed by the Greek conceptions of *eros* and *agape*:

> *Eros* is described as the desire for self-fulfillment by the other being, *agape* as the will to self-surrender for the sake of the other being. . . . No love is real without a unity of *eros* and *agape*. *Agape* without *eros* is obedience to moral law, without warmth, without longing, without reunion. *Eros* without *agape* is chaotic desire, denying the validity of the claim of the other one to be acknowledged as an independent self, able to love and to be loved. Love as the union of *eros* and *agape* is an implication of faith.[5]

Rather than equate love with attachment or with caring, therefore, I would consider both to be basic components of love. Both attachment and caring remain essentially *individual* conceptions, however, referring to inclinations within one person's mind or heart. But there is also an aspect of love that can only be attributed to the relationship between two people, rather than to the two parties individually. Martin Buber makes this point when he talks about the "I–Thou" relationship:

> Love does not cling to an I, as if the Thou were merely its "content" or object; it is *between* I and Thou. Whoever does not know this . . . does not know love, even if he should ascribe to it the feelings that he lives through, experiences, enjoys, and expresses.[6]

It seems useful, therefore, to postulate a third component of love, which refers to the bond or link between two people. This component may be manifest most clearly by close and confidential communication between two people, through nonverbal as well as verbal channels. In keeping with our analysis of the development of relationships in Chapter 8, I will call this third component *intimacy*.

Before constructing a measure of love, it was important to have an idea of how it might be distinguished from liking. In most of the existing research the evaluative component of liking is typically given greatest emphasis. A "likable" person is someone who is viewed as good or desirable on a number of dimensions. In our predominantly "task-oriented" society, the critical dimensions often seem to be task-related ones. We like people who are intelligent, competent, and trustworthy—the sorts of people whom we are disposed to work with and to vote for. This aspect of liking corresponds to what we described earlier as "respect."

What would we expect to be the empirical relationships between one person's love and his liking for another person? One would certainly expect at least a moderately positive evaluation of another person to be a prerequisite for the establishment of attachment, caring, and intimacy. Thus, it would be surprising if liking and loving were not at least moderately correlated with one another. But whereas liking and loving may have much in common, we would hesitate to equate the two phenomena. People often express liking for a person whom they would not claim to love in the least. In other instances they may declare their love for someone whom they cannot reasonably be said to like very well.

A starting assumption in my attempt to develop self-report scales of liking and loving, therefore, was that they should represent moderately correlated, but nevertheless distinct, dimensions of one person's attitude toward another person. My study consisted of three stages. First, I constructed parallel self-report scales of liking and loving that met the requirements of the starting assumption. Second, I examined the ways in which the scores of members of dating couples on each of the two scales related to a variety of other things about them, including their plans for marriage. Third, I proceeded to assess the usefulness of the love scale in predicting people's subsequent behavior and the course of their relationships. I will describe each of these steps in the following sections.[7]

Putting Love on a Scale

The first step in scale construction was to make up about eighty items reflecting aspects of one person's attitudes toward a particular other person. The items spanned a wide range of thoughts, feelings, and behavioral predispositions—for example, "How much fun is _____ to be with?" "How much do you trust _____?" "To what extent are you physically attracted to _____?" "How much does _____ get on your nerves?" As a check upon my own initial intuitions, I asked a number of friends and acquaintances of both sexes to sort the items into "liking" and "loving" sets, based on their own understandings of the meaning of the two terms. After making revisions suggested by these raters' judgments, I presented a new pool of seventy items to 198 undergraduates at the University of Michigan and asked them to respond to each in terms of their feelings toward their boyfriend or girlfriend (if they had one), and again in terms of their feelings toward a "platonic friend" of the opposite sex. I then subjected these ratings to a statistical technique called factor analysis, which serves to indicate which sets of items form internally consistent clusters. This procedure led to the specification of two thirteen-item scales, one of love and the other of liking (see Table 10–1).

Some of the scale items may strike you as misplaced because they do not correspond to your own personal definition of love or of

TABLE 10–1   LOVE-SCALE AND LIKING-SCALE ITEMS*

Love Scale

1. If _____ were feeling bad, my first duty would be to cheer him (her) up.
2. I feel that I can confide in _____ about virtually everything.
3. I find it easy to ignore _____'s faults.
4. I would do almost anything for _____.
5. I feel very possessive toward _____.
6. If I could never be with _____, I would feel miserable.
7. If I were lonely, my first thought would be to seek _____ out.
8. One of my primary concerns is _____'s welfare.
9. I would forgive _____ for practically anything.
10. I feel responsible for _____'s well-being.
11. When I am with _____, I spend a good deal of time just looking at him (her).
12. I would greatly enjoy being confided in by _____.
13. It would be hard for me to get along without _____.

Liking Scale

1. When I am with _____, we almost always are in the same mood.
2. I think that _____ is unusually well-adjusted.
3. I would highly recommend _____ for a responsible job.
4. In my opinion, _____ is an exceptionally mature person.
5. I have great confidence in _____'s good judgment.
6. Most people would react favorably to _____ after a brief acquaintance.
7. I think that _____ and I are quite similar to one another.
8. I would vote for _____ in a class or group election.
9. I think that _____ is one of those people who quickly wins respect.
10. I feel that _____ is an extremely intelligent person.
11. _____ is one of the most likable people I know.
12. _____ is the sort of person whom I myself would like to be.
13. It seems to me that it is very easy for _____ to gain admiration.

* In my current research I am making use of condensed nine-item versions of the two scales, omitting love items 1, 3, 5, and 11 and liking items 1, 7, 8, and 10.

liking. In several cases I have been led to the same conclusion. On the whole, however, the content of the two scales corresponds closely to the conceptions of liking and loving outlined in the previous section. The love scale includes items that seem to tap the postulated components of attachment (e.g., "If I were lonely, my first thought would be to seek _____ out"); caring (e.g., "If _____ were feeling bad, my first duty would be to cheer him (her) up"); and intimacy (e.g., "I feel that I can confide in _____ about virtually everything"). The items on the liking scale focus on the favorable evaluation of the other person on such dimensions as adjustment, maturity, good judgment, and intelligence, and on the associated tendency to view the other person as similar to oneself. The close fit between the scales and the preceding conceptual discussion is not accidental. Rather, my own working definitions of liking and loving were to a large extent given focus by the results of the scale-development procedure.

I now had two paper-and-pencil scales with a reasonable degree of what psychological testers call "face validity"; that is, the content of each scale approximated people's understandings of what liking and loving should mean. Such face validity did not necessarily imply that the scales would be of any use, however. If, for example, people tended to respond to the items in ways they thought would "look good," rather than in terms of their real feelings, then the scales might measure social anxiety rather than liking and loving. The next step, therefore, was to test the scales out, in the context of ongoing dating relationships.

"Only Dating Couples Can Do It"

My subjects for this trial run were dating couples at the University of Michigan.* Trying to make use of the lessons I had learned

---

* By 1968–1969, when I conducted the study, it had already become somewhat outmoded for college students to "date." Continuing and casual contacts between the sexes, often facilitated by residential proximity in apartments or dormitories, have to a large extent replaced the traditional pattern in which boy phones girl days or weeks in advance to invite her to a movie, football game, or fraternity party. In spite of the decline of the date, however, exclusive or semi-exclusive relationships between unmarried men and women still thrive on American campuses. One of the major functions of these relationships, although it is not universally subscribed to, continues to be the selection of marriage partners. For lack of a better word ("opposite-sex relationships" is too pedantic; "boy–girl relationships," too patronizing), I continue to refer to these liaisons as "dating relationships" and to the principals as "dating couples."

during my college summer as a Madison Avenue copywriter, I enticed the couples to take part in the study with a saturation campaign of posters and advertisements like the following:

ONLY *DATING COUPLES* CAN DO IT!

—GAIN INSIGHT INTO YOUR RELATIONSHIP
BY PARTICIPATING IN A UNIQUE SOCIAL–PSYCHOLOGICAL STUDY
. . . AND GET PAID FOR IT TOO! !

- *Who can participate?*
  All Michigan student couples (heterosexual only) who are dating regularly, going together, or engaged. (Married couples are not eligible.)

- *What do you have to do?*
  Simply show up with your boyfriend or girlfriend at one of the times and places listed. You will be asked to fill out a confidential questionnaire, and each of you will be paid $1 for the one-hour session.

- *Then what?*
  All those who fill out the questionnaire will have a chance to be selected as subjects for a subsequent experiment, which (if you agree to participate) should be both exciting and lucrative.

BOTH MEMBERS OF A COUPLE MUST TAKE PART

TUESDAY, OCTOBER 29, 7:30 P.M.—AUDITORIUM C
WEDNESDAY, OCTOBER 30, 7:30 P.M.—AUDITORIUM C

The one-dollar inducement proved to be more than enough to attract throngs of couples to my questionnaire sessions. On each of the two evenings, long lines of couples started forming outside Auditorium C by 7:00, and by 7:30 they were winding completely around the ground floor of the auditorium complex, outdoing even the most popular features of the student cinema league. Approximately 400 couples showed up to take part, and they were clearly motivated more by curiosity and the hope of learning something about themselves than by the token payment. I had prepared questionnaires for about 180 couples, thinking that this would be sufficient for the maximum conceivable turnout. As a result, on each of the two successive evenings I had to make profuse apologies and send about 100 couples home.

My sample of 182 couples comprised a wide cross-section of

Michigan student couples. The modal couple consisted of a junior man and a sophomore woman who had been dating for about one year. Some of the couples had been going together for as long as six or seven years, however, while others had been dating for only a few weeks. About 20 percent of the couples reported that they were engaged. Of the total sample, 52 percent of the women and 29 percent of the men lived in dormitories; 31 percent of the women and 60 percent of the men lived in their own apartments; and over 10 percent of each sex lived in fraternities or sororities. The religious background of slightly over 50 percent of the students was Protestant; 17 percent, Catholic; and 25 percent, Jewish. The remainder belonged to other religions or claimed no religious background.

During the sessions, boyfriends and girlfriends were asked not to sit near one another. Each partner filled out the questionnaire individually. They were assured that their responses would be kept confidential, and that their partners would not be given access to their responses. The questionnaire included the love and liking scales, to be completed first with respect to one's partner and later with respect to a close same-sex friend. In each case the respondent indicated how much he agreed or disagreed with each item by placing a check on the continuous scale. For example:

1. When I am with _____, we are almost always in the same mood.

Not at all true; disagree completely	Moderately true; agree to some extent	Definitely true; agree completely

With the help of a clear plastic ruler these responses were later converted to numbers from 1 to 9, to be used in analyzing the data. The questionnaire also called for a variety of other pieces of information about the subjects and their relationships, which I will say more about as I present some results.

Love's Correlates

The statistical analysis of the questionnaire data began with an examination of the internal structure of the liking and love scales. As desired, each of the two scales proved to be internally consistent; that is, in each case its component items were highly intercorrelated. Also in accord with my starting assumption, the correlation between liking and loving scores was only moderate. The correlation between men's love and liking scores for their girlfriends was

.56, and the correlation between women's love and liking scores for their boyfriends was .36.*

Although the general pattern of intrascale versus interscale correlations emerged as I had hoped it would, the finding that love and liking were more highly related to one another among men than among women was unexpected. It is possible that this difference is a consequence of the distinctive specializations of the two sexes. In most societies, men tend to be the task specialists, while women tend to be the social–emotional specialists. By virtue of their specialization in matters involving interpersonal feelings, women may develop a more finely tuned and more discriminating set of interpersonal sentiments than men do. Whereas men may often blur such fine distinctions as the one between liking and loving, women may be more likely to experience and express the two sentiments as being distinct from one another.

Further insight into the nature of liking and loving for the two sexes was derived from a comparison of their average love and liking scores for their dating partners and their same-sex friends. These averages are presented in Table 10–2. Unsurprisingly, the students reported loving their partners much more than their friends, while the gap between liking for partners and liking for friends was narrower. Less obvious and more informative are the comparisons between the scores of men and women. As Table 10–2 reveals, the average love scores of men for their girlfriends and of women for their boyfriends were virtually identical. But women *liked* their boyfriends significantly more than they were liked in return. I alluded to this result in the course of our discussion of sex roles in Chapter 2. The liking scale is "sex-biased" in that it asks the respondent to size up his partner on such stereotypically male characteristics as maturity, intelligence, and good judgment. It asks whether the respondent would vote for his partner in an election, and whether he would recommend the partner for a responsible job. It seems, in other words, to be getting at that task-related sort of liking that we have referred to as respect. It is doubtful that the

---

* The size of the correlation between any two measures indicates how closely people's relative standing on the first measure corresponds to their relative standing on the second. A correlation of 1.00 indicates a perfect correspondence, while a correlation of 0 indicates that the two measures are totally unrelated. Increasing values of a correlation from 0 to 1 indicates increasing degrees of correspondence between the two measures. As a rough rule of thumb we can consider correlations smaller than .30 to be "small," those between .30 and .70 to be "moderate," and those of .70 or greater to be "large."

men in our sample were in fact more responsible, more intelligent, or endowed with better judgment than their girlfriends. Nevertheless, it is generally considered to be more appropriate for men than for women to excel on these dimensions, and the obtained results conform precisely to these cultural expectations.

TABLE 10–2   AVERAGE LOVE AND LIKING SCORES FOR DATING PARTNERS AND SAME-SEX FRIENDS

	Women	Men
Love for partner	90.57	90.44
Liking for partner	89.10	85.30
Love for friend	64.79	54.47
Liking for friend	80.21	78.38

Table 10–2 also shows that when respondents evaluated their same-sex friends, there was no tendency for men to be liked more than women. Thus, the data do not support the conclusion that men are generally more "likable" than women, but only that they are liked more in the context of dating relationships. The pattern of liking scores suggests that the dating relationship, instead of obliterating stereotypical differences between the sexes, may in fact perpetuate them by emphasizing role and status discrepancies. This pattern is in accord with the feminist critique of traditionally structured male–female relationships as fortifying the favored position of the male and reemphasizing the subservient position of the female.

An additional finding shown in Table 10–2 is that women tended to love their same-sex friends more than men did. It is indeed more common for female friends than for male friends to speak of themselves as "loving" one another, a linguistic fact that may reflect substantive differences in the nature of men's and women's same-sex friendships. Evidence from several surveys suggests that while women do not typically have more same-sex friends than men, women's friendships tend to be more intimate, involving more spontaneous joint activities and more exchanging of confidences.[8] Men's special difficulties in establishing intimate relationships with other men, which we discussed in Chapter 8, are underlined by the love-scale results. The male role, for all its task-related "likability," may limit the ability to love. Loving for men may often be channeled into a single opposite-sex relationship, whereas women may be more able to experience and express attachment, caring, and intimacy in other relationships as well.

Another approach toward assessing the validity of the love and liking scales was to examine their correlations with other measures. One of the items included on the questionnaire was "Would you say that you and _____ are in love?" to be answered by circling "yes," "no," or "uncertain." Slightly over two-thirds of both men and women answered affirmatively, with only about 10 percent of each sex reporting that they were not in love and the remaining 22 percent of each sex pleading uncertainty. The correlations between love scores and this "in love" index were reasonably high: .61 for women and .53 for men. The correlations between liking scores and the "in love" index were considerably lower: .29 for women and .36 for men. Thus, the love scale, even though it nowhere includes the word "love" itself, tapped a sentiment that was distinctively related to the students' own categorization of their relationships.

The partners were also asked to estimate the likelihood they would eventually marry one another, on a probability scale ranging from 0 to 100 percent. The average estimate by women was about 50 percent and by men 45 percent. The correlations between love scores and estimates of marriage likelihood were substantial: .60 for women and .59 for men. The correlations between liking scores and marriage likelihood estimates were much lower: .33 for women and .35 for men. Once again the obtained pattern of correlations is reasonable. In societies like our own with a "love pattern" of mate selection, the link between love and marriage is strongly emphasized by parents, mass media, and other socializing agents. The link between liking and marriage, on the other hand, is too often a well-kept secret. In the next phase of my study I proceeded to put the love scale to a more difficult test, going beyond the questionnaire to direct observations of couples' behavior.

The Glance of Eye to Eye

It is well-known folk wisdom that people who are in love spend inordinate amounts of time gazing into each others' eyes. Not all such truisms are in fact true, but there is reason to believe that this one may be. Sociologists and song-writers alike have noted that eye contact plays, as Erving Goffman puts it, "a special role in the communication life of the community."[9] This is because eye contact serves as a mutually understood signal that the communication channel between two people is open. While eye contact is sustained the actions of either party are automatically defined as relevant to both of them. As a result, Goffman notes, people studiously avoid making eye contact with others when they wish to minimize the possibility that any interaction will ensue between them. Strangers who find themselves in the same elevator stare blankly into space, and the harried waitress takes pains to prevent prospective customers from catching her eye. Georg Simmel eloquently described sociological function of eye contact in his *Soziologie*:

> The union and interaction of individuals is based upon mutual glances. This is perhaps the purest and most direct reciprocity that exists anywhere. . . . So tenacious and subtle is this union that it can only be maintained by the shortest and straightest line between the eyes, and the smallest deviation from it, the slightest glance aside, completely destroys the unique character of this union. . . . The totality of social relations of human beings, their self-assertion and self-abnegation, their intimacies and estrangements, would be changed in unpredictable ways if there existed no glance of eye to eye. This mutual glance between persons, in distinction from the simple sight or observation of the other, signifies a wholly new and unique union between them.[10]

Social scientists have speculated about the developmental and evolutionary origins of the social functions of eye contact. One developmental psychologist concluded, for example, that "not physical, but visual contact is at the basis of human sociability."[11] Another reported that "the nature of the eye contact between a mother and her baby seems to cut across all interactional systems and conveys the intimacy or 'distance' characteristic of their relationship as a whole."[12] On the evolutionary level Konrad Lorenz has, in his characteristic analogical style, noted convergences between the functions of eye contact among humans and among lower animals:

> As he makes his proposal, the male [jackdaw] glances continually toward his love but ceases his efforts immediately if she chances to fly away; this however she is not likely to do if she is interested in her admirer. . . . He casts glowing glances straight into his loved one's eyes, while she apparently turns her eyes in all directions other than that of her ardent suitor. In reality, of course, she is watching him all the time, and her quick glances of a fraction of a second are quite long enough to make her realize that all his antics are calculated to inspire her admiration: long enough to let "him" know that "she" knows.[13]

Whatever its origins, eye contact provides a channel through which intimate feelings can be directly expressed. As a result, when two people do not feel close to one another, eye contact is extremely difficult to sustain. This is particularly true when the physical distance between them is small. A pair of British investigators discovered that subjects made much more eye contact in a discussion situation when they were seated at a distance of six feet from one another than when they were separated by only two feet. They also found that subjects asked to approach a seated man as closely as possible were able to come closer when the man's eyes were shut than when they were open.[14] To the extent that two people love one another, on the other hand, we would predict that they would not only tolerate but in fact welcome the opportunities provided by eye contact as a vehicle for intimate communication.

To test the prediction that love and eye contact would be positively related, I invited dating couples who had previously completed the questionnaire to take part in a laboratory experiment. While the two partners sat across a table from one another, waiting for the experiment to begin, they were observed through a one-way mirror by two assistants. Whenever the man looked at the woman's face, one observer, strategically stationed behind the woman, pressed a button that activated a clock recorder. Whenever the woman looked at the man's face, the second observer pushed a button that activated a second clock recorder. Whenever the two observers were pushing their buttons simultaneously, a third clock recorder was activated. The third clock provided the most important of the measures obtained, because it indicated the amount of *simultaneous* looking engaged in by the two partners.

To provide the clearest test of my prediction, I included in the laboratory session only those couples in which both partners were "strong lovers" (both had scored above the median on the love scale) or in which both were "weak lovers" (both had scored below the median). The results indicated that the "strong love" couples indeed made significantly more eye contact than the "weak love" couples did. This finding was certainly not a surprising one. But it added considerably to my confidence that the love scale measured something that went beyond mere questionnaire-checking. Importantly, the difference between "strong love" and "weak love" couples did not emerge with respect to the sheer quantity of looking-at-the-other by the two partners, as recorded on the first and second clocks, but only with respect to mutual eye contact, as recorded on the third clock. "Weak love" boyfriends and girlfriends were as likely as "strong love" partners to look at one another unilaterally, but "strong love" boyfriends and girlfriends were more likely to look at one another simultaneously.

Eye contact was also measured in two additional experimental conditions. These conditions again compared "strong lovers" and "weak lovers," but the subjects were paired with *other people's* boyfriends and girlfriends rather than with their own partners. These conditions were included to take into account the possibility that "strong lovers" are the sort of people who find it easy to maintain eye contact not only with their partners, but with other people in general. Such a possibility is suggested by Erich Fromm's analysis of love. "Love is not primarily a relationship toward a particular person," Fromm maintains. "It is . . . an *orientation of character* which determines the relatedness of a person toward the world as a whole, not toward one 'object' of love. . . . If I truly love one person I love all persons, I love the world, I love life."[15] Thus one might conjecture that when two "strong lovers" encounter one another, even though they have never before met, they still might find it relatively easy to communicate intimately and to sustain considerable eye contact. Two "weak lovers," on the other hand, might find such intimacy much harder to achieve.

The obtained data did not support this suggestion, however. When the dyads consisted of opposite-sex strangers, the "strong lovers" did not make significantly more eye contact than the "weak lovers." Thus, the pattern of results was more congruent with a conception of love as an attitude toward a particular person than as an orientation toward all mankind. There may still be considerable truth in Fromm's analysis. As codified in Eleanor of Aquitaine's Court of Love, "the man in love becomes accustomed to performing many services gracefully for everyone."[16] But the behavioral implications of this conception of love may be offset by the equally compelling truth that when two people are in love with one another, they have fewer emotional resources left for others. Freud wrote, "The more [two people] are in love, the more completely they suffice for one another."[17] Or, as the popular song has it, "I only have eyes for you."

The Researcher Strikes Out

In the experimental session that followed the observation of the couples' and pseudocouples' eye contact, I obtained two other measures that I expected to be related to romantic love. In neither case, unfortunately, were my expectations confirmed. What was obtained in both cases was what researchers call "negative results"—that is, no differences at all between "strong lovers" and "weak lovers," or even between real couples and pairs of strangers. As is typical in such cases, these negative results have never been published (except as part of my doctoral dissertation). Like people in most other walks of life, psychological researchers prefer to advertise their successes and play down their failures. I include them here, nevertheless, because they illustrate a familiar aspect of every researcher's journey.

The first study was an attempt to test the prediction that when lovers are together, time seems to go by more quickly. "And Jacob served seven years for Rachel," the Book of Genesis records, "and they seemed unto him but a few days, for the love he had to her." Perhaps the same distortion occurred when Jacob was in Rachel's presence. Experimental psychologists have found that people tend to overestimate the duration of time when they are bored or passive, and to underestimate it when they are interested or active.[18] To the extent that attachment, caring, and intimacy imply a focusing of interest upon another person, it would follow that the "strong lover" should indeed underestimate the amount of time that elapses when he is with his partner. It also seemed possible that when the "strong lover" is separated from his partner, he will feel especially forlorn and time will seem to drag.

To test these notions, I asked each subject in each of the four experimental conditions to record his estimate of the duration of two time periods: the waiting period during which eye contact was measured and a later discussion period. In making these estimates, the subjects were cautioned not to consult their watches or one another. Each of the two periods was in fact three minutes long, but the subjects' estimates of their duration ranged widely. Unfortunately for my hypothesis, the differences among their estimates had absolutely nothing to do with their scores on the love scale or whether they were paired with their dating partner or a stranger. I discovered that individual differences in time perception—regardless of where the subjects are or whom they are with—tend to be so great that my attempt to check out the Jacob–Rachel effect empirically was probably doomed from the start. A more promising technique would have been to compare the time estimates obtained from the same subject in two different conditions—for example, on one occasion in the presence of his dating partner and on another occasion in the partner's absence.

The second study attempted to demonstrate that love scores, which include items about "caring," are related to actual helping behavior. The problem in this instance was to devise an appropriate behavioral measure of unselfish helping. Most of the measures that researchers have employed to assess helping among strangers would not have been suitable in the context of an ongoing relationship. A commonly employed laboratory measure of helping, for example, is the number of cardboard boxes or paper envelopes a subject constructs in order to help another student win a monetary prize. For members of dating couples, however, helping one's partner win money might not be altruistic at all. Many couples pool their resources, so that helping one's partner win money might have the direct effect of enriching oneself. Other measures involving face-to-face interaction were ruled out because it seemed too difficult to rule out such ulterior motives as the desire to ingratiate one's partner or to avoid incurring his wrath.

The measure I finally hit upon required an elaborate scenario. The two partners were escorted to separate rooms, where they began reading an interesting case report about a troubled married couple. They were told that they would subsequently discuss the case over an intercom system. Before they had a chance to finish the story, however, both partners were asked to switch over to the tedious task of canceling all of the 3's and 5's on an abundant supply of number-filled sheets of paper stacked in front of them. They were left to continue this task for twelve minutes, by which time virtually all subjects were thoroughly fed up with it. At this point the experimenter's voice (to insure standardization a tape recording was used) was piped into each subject's cubicle:

> Now I'm connected only to you in Room Number One. At this point, one of you will keep canceling for a while longer, while the other gets back to the case material. So, since you're in the first room, I'll just let you decide for both of you. If you want to keep canceling, let me know right now by pushing the button on the wall, and if you want to get back to the case, then just don't push the button.

To foster the subject's illusion that he or she was the only one making the choice, a sign labeled "Room One" was prominently displayed in each room. The operational definition of helping was the act of pushing the button, thereby committing oneself to more number-canceling and freeing one's partner from his or her drudgery.

The results were again disappointing. Only one-fifth of all of the subjects "helped," much fewer than what would have been optimal. And the only difference in helping rate between experimental conditions resulted from an interpretation of the situation that I had not anticipated. Women were significantly more likely to help their boyfriends (over a third of them did so) than a male stranger (fewer than 10 percent did so). Whether the woman was a "strong" or "weak" lover made no difference in this regard; and no such differences were found among men. When subsequently asked to explain the reasons for their choice, the majority of the women who elected to "help" their boyfriends made it clear that helping was not on their minds at all. Their motive was, rather, to insure that their boyfriend would have a chance to read more of the case report than they would and thus be able to dominate the expected discussion. One woman wrote, for example, "I felt it would be better if my partner knew more about the case so he could present more of his ideas about the case to think about when discussing it." This finding was an interesting further demonstration of the impact of sex roles, but it indicated that my attempt to obtain a pure measure of helping had been rather wide of the mark.

It is not only because of the vanity of researchers that negative results such as these are rarely reported in psychological journals. An additional reason is that, save for the hints they may provide about how not to do an experiment, negative results are essentially uninformative. They generally do *not* prove that the guiding hypothesis of the research is wrong. It may well be, for example, that love *is* associated with both time perception and helping but that my attempts to measure these potential correlates were inadequate. Leon Festinger, a pioneering experimental methodologist, put the matter bluntly:

> In general a study which yields no differences or no relationships contributes little to our knowledge . . . The way to do research which contributes to our knowledge is to somehow be clever enough to find differences and relationships.[19]

The Romeo and Juliet Effect

By the time I had completed analyzing the results of my foray into the laboratory, I felt that I had been reasonably successful in my attempt to conceptualize and measure romantic love. The love and liking scales related to one another and to other measures in reasonable and occasionally illuminating ways. In spite of my strikeout in attempting to relate love to helping and to the flight of time, the fact that love scores could successfully predict couples' visual behavior had fortified my confidence in the scale's validity. I was confident enough to probe deeper into the questionnaire data to try to provide some initial insights into love's origins.

The question of what factors foster love between two people is an enormously complicated one. Indeed, there are probably as many reasons for loving as there are people who love. In each case there is a different constellation of needs to be gratified, a different set of characteristics that are found to be rewarding, a different ideal to be fulfilled. Moreover, the precipitating events differ from one case to another. Some people may be propelled into love by a loss, such as the death of a parent, or by the breakup of a previous relationship. Others may be most likely to fall in love after a victory, when their self-esteem is at a peak. But in spite of all of these variations, it may be possible for us to advance our understanding of love's antecedents by concentrating on small pieces of the larger puzzle.

On one level the question of what precipitates love concerns the factors that make it likely for a particular man and woman to encounter one another and to consider one another "eligible" for at least a trial period. As we have seen in earlier chapters, physical proximity and attitude similarity are important in determining such eligibility. The fact that all of the couples in my sample were students at the same campus helps to account for the fact that they found one another. I discovered, in addition, that there was a substantial correlation of .51 between boyfriends' and girlfriends' scores on a measure of "authoritarianism," reflecting strong similarity on the dimension of traditional versus liberal attitudes. Thus, attitude similarity seemed to have exerted considerable influence in bringing particular people together.*

But given this sort of "prefiltering," what additional factors can begin to distinguish between those couples who fell deeply in love and those who did not? One relevant variable proved to be the religious composition of the couples. On the whole there was the expected tendency for boyfriends and girlfriends to be of the same religion. In 62 percent of the cases in which both partners listed one of the three major religions as his or her "religious background"

---

* An alternative interpretation of the same data is that the couples were not attracted to one another on the basis of attitudinal similarity, but that their views became more similar *after* they had selected one another, as a result of their interaction. More detailed analysis of the data made this alternative less plausible, however. The correlation between boyfriends' and girlfriends' authoritarianism scores turned out to be just as great among those 40 couples who had been dating less than four months (.58) as among those 60 couples who had been dating for eighteen months or more (.53). The correlations were of the same order of magnitude among the four-to-eleven month and twelve-to-seventeen month groups as well (.47 and .57). If the partners' attitudes had become more similar as a consequence of their interaction, we would have expected the correlation to increase as a function of the length of time the couple had been dating. Since the size of the correlation was extremely stable, it is more reasonable to conclude that attitude similarity on this dimension plays an important role in the initial selection or very early filtering of dating partners.

the two partners were of the same religion. (Only 40 percent would have shared the same religion if the matching were random.) Given that a young man and woman are going together and that they are serious enough to volunteer to fill out a questionnaire about their relationship, how might we expect their religious similarity or dissimilarity to affect their degree of love? My prediction was that members of interfaith couples would love one another more.

There are several rationales for this prediction. There are often strong pressures, especially from parents, against marrying or even dating people of a different religion from one's own. It seemed likely, therefore, that these pressures would be defied only if the partners felt a particularly strong degree of love. Social psychologists Richard Driscoll, Keith E. Davis, and Milton Lipetz propose another reason for making the same prediction, the possibility that parental opposition may directly increase the partners' love for one another. They call this "the Romeo and Juliet effect":

> [In *Romeo and Juliet*,] the short but intense love affair took place against the background of total opposition from the two feuding families. The family conflicts did, in several parts of the play, force the lovers to decide whether their primary allegiance was to each other or to their families, and created difficulties and separations which appear to have intensified the lovers' feelings for each other.[20]

The Roman myth of Pyramus and Thisbe is based on the same theme: "they longed to marry, but their parents forbade it. Love, however, cannot be forbidden. The more the flame is covered up, the hotter it burns."[21] Freud made much the same argument, contending that "an obstacle is required in order to heighten libido."[22]

Driscoll and his colleagues obtained some support for the operation of the Romeo and Juliet effect in a study of dating and married couples in Boulder, Colorado. They found positive correlations between a measure of "parental interference," as perceived by the partners, and a measure of love that was somewhat similar to my love scale. My own results, comparing the same-religion and different-religion couples, yielded further evidence for the effect. But the data suggested that the effect may only be operative among relatively short-term couples. Among those couples in my sample who had been dating up to eighteen months, the love scores of members of different-religion couples were significantly higher than the love scores of same-religion couples. But among those 54 couples who had been dating for longer than eighteen months, including the majority of the engaged couples in the sample, the pattern reversed itself. For these long-term couples love scores were higher if the two partners were of the same religion.

One possible explanation for this reversal is that, as the Colorado researchers suggest, "If such [parental] interference continues without resolution, it is likely to undermine the overall quality of the relationship." The relationships of the long-term interfaith couples may have been subjected to *too much* external pressure to sustain the flames of love. As a result, their relationships may have been in the process of weakening. An alternative explanation is that once the relationship is solidified, differences of religion no longer present a challenge to be overcome and, hence, no longer have a love-heightening effect. These interpretations are speculative, and there is no direct evidence to back either of them up. What seems most clear, however, is that at least under some conditions external obstacles, of the sort that may often prevent or destroy a relationship, can also have the effect of fostering romantic love.* Just as external threats to a group or nation tend to increase ingroup solidarity and morale,[23] parental opposition may help to unify young couples.

Six Months Later

I had begun work on developing the love and liking scales in May of 1968, administered the questionnaire to the sample of dating couples in late October, and conducted the laboratory sessions in November and December. During the first four months of 1969 I devoted myself to analyzing the mass of data that I had collected. But meanwhile, as is typically the case in social–psychological research, I lost touch with the people who had provided the data. Symbolically they were close at hand in the form of identification numbers, love and liking scores, clock readings, and other such relics. But I almost never saw or spoke to any of them.

One exception was the student who appeared in my office early in 1969 and asked to see his girlfriend's questionnaire. He was rather upset when I told him that because of the guarantee of confidentiality that had been made when the couples filled out the

---

* It should be kept in mind, however, that the above data are not based on following couples up over time. Temporal trends can only be cautiously inferred by comparing the scores of couples who have been going together for shorter or longer periods of time. In my current study of couples in the Boston area we are remedying this limitation by obtaining a series of follow-up reports on couples' relationships over a period of several years.

questionnaire, he could not. The student was clearly experiencing some uncertainty about his relationship and had decided that he might reduce it by finding out how his girlfriend had filled out her questionnaire.

It seemed a shame to let my sample of 182 couples pass into research history without any further traces. Although I did not have the time (for I was to complete my dissertation and leave Michigan in early June) nor the resources for an extensive follow-up study, I was able to send a one-page follow-up questionnaire to each of the students in late April, six months after the initial questionnaire sessions. I asked each student to fill out the questionnaire individually and to mail it back to me. My primary interest was in the course their relationships had taken during the half-year interval. Were they still together, or had they broken up? Did they feel closer or less close than they had before? And would the measures of love and liking obtained back in October be able to predict these events?

To answer these questions reliably, it was important that a large proportion of the follow-up reports be returned. Otherwise it would be impossible to derive any firm conclusions. It might be, for example, that those students whose relationships had become closer would be more likely to return the follow-up report than those whose relationships had ended or gone sour. But in the absence of reports from the nonrespondents, there would be no way to know for sure. I therefore made a concerted attempt to obtain as complete a response as possible. I kept the follow-up questionnaire short, provided postpaid envelopes, located new addresses of students who had moved, and persistently phoned students who did not return the report initially to remind them to do so. In the last analysis I had to depend on the students' goodwill. They cooperated remarkably well. I obtained follow-up reports from 162 of the women and 155 of the men, comprising 87 percent of the 364 original respondents. I succeeded in getting a report from at least *one* member of 179 of the 182 couples, fully 98.4 percent of the total.

The follow-up reports indicated that the great majority of the couples' relationships had endured over the six-month period. Of the 179 couples from whom at least one report was obtained, only 29 (one-sixth of the total) had broken up. (In at least two of these cases one of the ex-partners had already married someone else.) Of the 23 initially engaged couples heard from, four had gotten married, sixteen were still engaged, two were no longer engaged but still "going together," and only one had broken up. At least thirteen couples who had not been engaged at the time of the initial questionnaire were now engaged.

The follow-up questionnaire also asked the students to indicate whether their relationship had become more or less "intense" over the six-month period. In general, the reports of the two partners on this matter were in close agreement with one another (the correlation was .88). When they disagreed, I averaged the two reports in order to categorize the couple. These reports also testified to the enduringness of the couples' relationships: 60 percent of the couples reported that their relationships had become more intense; 19 percent, that their intensity was unchanged; and 21 percent, that they had become less intense. Most of the couples in the last category had broken up. As Table 10-3 indicates, the likelihood that a couple's relationship would become less intense or break up was greatest among those who had been dating either for the shortest or for the longest periods of time. The short-term couples were apparently still testing out their relationships and were relatively unstable. And about one-fifth of the long-term relationships (those couples who had been dating for at least a year and a half at the time of the initial questionnaire) had apparently run their course. The "no change" column in the table also suggests that the longer a relationship had lasted, the less changeable it tended to be.

TABLE 10–3   PERCENTAGE OF COUPLES WHO REPORTED ON THE FOL-
LOW-UP QUESTIONNAIRE THAT THEIR RELATIONSHIPS
HAD BECOME LESS OR MORE INTENSE

Duration of relationship as of initial questionnaire	Number of couples	Percentage reporting that relationship had become:			
		Less intense	No change	More intense	Total
0–3 months	39	38%	10%	51%	99%
4–11 months	40	15	15	70	100
12–17 months	40	10	20	70	100
18 months or longer	60	20	27	53	100
All couples	179	21	19	60	100

Progress toward a more "intense" relationship is not necessarily to be equated with progress toward a permanent relationship or toward marriage. But in fact the two sorts of movement did seem to go hand in hand. The index of a couple's reported progress toward a more intense relationship was substantially correlated with the degree to which the students' estimates of the likelihood of marrying their partners were revised upward from October to April. The correlations were .63 for women and .56 for men. A crucial remaining question was what precipitated this progress. Because the follow-up questionnaire had to be quick and easy to complete, it did not include a readministration of the love and liking scales nor any detailed questions about the couple's evolving relationship. On the basis of what was asked, however, it was at least possible to assess the extent to which the students' love and liking scores as measured in October were related to the reported progress of the relationship as of the following April.

The romantic ideal would dictate, of course, that the greater the partners' love for one another, the more likely they should be to progress toward a more intense and permanent relationship. Although some observers have disparaged the founding of marriage upon romance, there is general agreement that this is the modal American pattern. But perhaps the link between love and marriage has been overemphasized. Not all young people wholeheartedly accept the tenets of the romantic ideal. Many are keenly aware of the importance of "nonromantic" factors in mate selection, including considerations of economic and social status that might not have been reflected in the early love scores. Many people also hold the view that love should be enjoyed while it lasts and should not be embedded in a permanent or institutionalized relationship. It should also be noted that the love scores of the two members of a given couple did not always closely correspond. The correlation between boyfriends' and girlfriends' love scores was .43, indicating only a moderate degree of symmetry. This fact of life would necessarily limit the extent to which any individual's love score could predict the outcome of his or her relationship.

The obtained pattern of correlations was illuminating. On the whole there was a positive correlation between love in October and reported progress in April, but it was a relatively small one. The magnitude of this correlation was .19 for men and .20 for women. But the link between love and progress became much clearer when the students were categorized in terms of the degree of their reported agreement with the romantic ideal on the initial questionnaire. The "romanticism scale" employed (see Chapter 9, p. 206) included such items as "A person should marry whomever he loves regardless of social position" and "As long as they at least love one another, two people should have no difficulty getting along together in marriage." Thus, it might be expected that love and progress would be strongly related among the "romantic" students who endorsed these statements and less strongly related—if at all— among the "nonromantic" students.

The follow-up reports confirmed this expectation. Table 10–4 shows that the correlations between love and progress were substantial only among the romantic respondents. When *both* of the partners were romantic, the correlations were even higher: .41 for women and .52 for men. Among the nonromantic students, on the other hand, there was no correlation at all between love and progress. And when both partners were nonromantic, not only did love fail to predict progress, but the correlations became slightly negative: –.16 for women and –.10 for men. The pattern of correlations indicated that love indeed predicts progress in dating relationships, but only for those people who subscribe to the ideology that this is the way things ought to be.

TABLE 10–4 CORRELATIONS BETWEEN INDIVIDUAL LOVE AND LIKING SCORES (OCTOBER) AND COUPLE'S PROGRESS (APRIL) FOR ROMANTIC AND NONROMANTIC STUDENTS

| | Women | | Men | |
	Nonromantic	Romantic	Nonromantic	Romantic
Number of cases:	(95)	(84)	(87)	(92)
Correlation between love and progress	–.02	.41**	–.01	.37**
Correlation between liking and progress	.12	.30*	–.00	.33*

* A correlation this large would occur by chance less than once in a hundred times.
** A correlation this large would occur by chance less than once in a thousand times.

In all of the flurry about love, finally, it is important that liking not be lost in the shuffle. The bottom row of Table 10-4 indicates that liking, too, predicts progress toward a more intense relationship among the romantic students. Liking is not quite so effective a predictor as love is, but it is a reasonably good predictor nevertheless. To some extent this result was predetermined by the fact that love and liking are themselves correlated with one another. It nevertheless appears to be the case that among "simultaneously hardheaded and idealistic" young Americans evaluations of intelligence, maturity, and good judgment and perceptions of similarity play almost as large a role in propelling couples toward more permanent relationships as do the wings of love.

"Love and Peace from Sunny California"

In considering the factors that led to progress in the couples' relationships, there is one additional impetus that must be taken into account. These 182 couples had introduced an extraordinary new input into their relationship by taking part in a study of it. In my recruiting advertisement I had offered the couples a chance to "gain insight" into their relationship, and in many instances this was their primary motive for volunteering. But did the experience live up to its billing? And did the fact that these couples were called upon to scrutinize their relationship have an effect on its subsequent development? Without a matched control group of couples who did not take part in the study, it is impossible to know for sure. But the follow-up questionnaire did ask the students for their own assessment of the impact of the study on the follow-up questionnaire. Many of them had little or nothing to say about this issue, and those who did have opinions were by no means unanimous in their assessment. Nevertheless, their reports helped me to return from the checkmarks and statistics about liking and loving to the people from whom the checkmarks and statistics emanated. I would like to conclude the report of my study by sharing some of their comments with you:

103F*   Mr. Rubin, when we got out of your experiment, we started comparing answers, or those which we could remember. We found out what we felt we knew before, but what you reinforced . . . that we *knew* each other. Good luck, #103.

104M   Study had no effect on relationship (I refused to discuss most of the answers). Found it useful—according to many of my answers, there was little objective reason for liking my girlfriend—as a result, I had to analyze more closely the nature of the relationship.

105F   The only comment I have is that your study raised a lot of questions which Tom and I then discussed and we probably would not have talked about these otherwise. It also raised the question of whether we would marry and we are now talking about getting married at the end of next summer.

111M   You sent this at a fucking inopportune time. We broke it off yesterday, after 3 years.

123F   Effect? Only that we are slightly more aware of how much we look at each other.

135F   Your questionnaire enabled my boyfriend and I to analyze our feelings about marriage. I have a very negative attitude toward

* Numbers are the students' identification numbers. The "M" or "F" identifies the respondent as male or female.

marriage as a suburban, middle-class, split-level, station wagon, 2–3 kid institution and cannot envision myself in such a set-up. So I do not plan to marry unless I can work out a suitable arrangement. The subject of marriage had never come between us before and it was definitely worth discussing, since we have rather disparate views to that question on the original survey. I would say this understanding has made me a little more relaxed—not much, though, I really didn't feel threatened, and I think we understand each other a little better now. Progress.

152M   The test affected our relationship not at all. Although I answered the questions seriously, taking the test was done more for laughs (and the buck) than anything else.

157F   The study made me realize that I love and respect my room-mate more than my boyfriend. Confession!

158F   Very favorable—it is difficult to discuss relationships, this gave us specific grounds for discussion, made each of us realize the depth of our commitment to each other.

159F   My ex-boyfriend took the results of the test in a completely absurd way, as he often took things, so I walked out and never came back. He decided that your test proved that I was too independent and never willing to leave things in his hands. I couldn't understand how he figured that out just from talking to each other about the study, but since things were not going well and he obviously had certain convictions in such absurd deductions, I split. Your study, however, was not the initial cause of the breakup, though!—just a little pusher . . .

173M   Possibly this test had unfavorable effects on our relationship. We both just kept on wondering what each other had put as answers for certain questions. At that time, however, we were not too serious and the unfavorable effect was less intense. If we were to take another one now, things could really explode because of our curiosity as to what each other had put as answers. Certain questions seemed a little ambiguous to me such as "I love___." God knows I love her; but love has to mature just as any other aspect of our personalities. There were other questions that I didn't approve of but this one in particular left me wondering about how I should answer. Good luck in your analysis of this mess.

179M   Nancy and I enjoyed participating in all phases of your experiment, even to the point that it has become part of our everyday conversation. I cannot help but feel that participating brought us closer together in that we participated TOGETHER. Also many of the questions on the numerous questionnaires caused both of us (I believe) to think more about *ourselves* and our feelings and attitudes toward each other. The experience was *at least* beneficial in that it was a *unique* opportunity to do something with each other but, more probably, will be an experience of lasting significance and, well, amusement in that it forced us to, for one of the first times, express our thoughts concerning each other and allowed us, then, to share these thoughts and to make comparisons between each other.

201F   During the experiment my boyfriend became rather upset because he was afraid the experiment would question us about things which would later influence our relationship in a negative way. The results might come out in a "Dear Abby" and "you ought to do . . ." sort of way. Once we had discussed the experiment he was reassured, enough so to complete your last phase of the experiment. After this it had no unfavorable effects and possibly reassured us about our relationship in terms of some of the things you were testing, and your results (which I learned about in the Soc / Psych talk you gave and relayed to him).

222M   Your study had no effect. The breakup could probably be attributed to differing attitudes about sex.

224M   The final phase caused some momentary trouble (about 15 minutes) because it seemed to point up something we already knew: that my girlfriend acts a bit more selfishly because she sees me as being more intelligent and talented, and assumes that I can therefore do with less help.

243M   Though my girlfriend and I have always been close and intimate and honest in our opinions of each other and ideas for the future, the questionnaire did initiate discussion of our relationship and its future. Unfortunately, neither the questionnaire nor our discussions helped to solve the basic problem of our relationship, a difference in religious upbringing. Therefore, while we are now the closest to each other that we have ever been, that problem necessitates my opinion that there is a less than 50% chance of our marriage to each other.

248F   It had some effect in that I realized that he had a very "idealistic" view of couples & marriage—there should be no fighting— & if there are any arguments, this is a sign of weakness in the relationship (I tend to think arguments—if they are conducted partially as discussions, are beneficial to couples because they cure differences that I feel are bound to exist between any two people).

255M   I would like to know exactly what the hell you're studying or trying to find out. Your questions seem very general and not leading to a specific problem or area of study. Are you merely making some type of correlational study, or is there some type of experimental control?

266M   The program has caused the girl to think too much about marriage. This is not healthy, for me.

271F   Probably the test wasn't too *helpful* in our relationship as #271M refused to talk about how he responded while I was ready to talk about it fully. Also for the first time (?)—talking about your idiotic cases—we talked about something without joking—semi-intelligently. This conversation made me feel much more intelligent than #271M and made me feel dominant. After that talk I began to find #271M BORING. Thank you, #271F

271M   If participating in your study had any effect at all, it was favorable, because we both felt that it was sort of fun.

288F   At the time of the first questionnaire my boyfriend and I were surprised to find out from each other the discrepancy on the probability that we would marry. He checked 91% or so & I checked 11% or so. It made for quite a few interesting discussions.

289F   It was good to have to sit down and analyze our relationship—it turned out good for us. This winter term we have continued this by taking marriage (Health Development 345)—it's a great course.

203F   We are living together in Berkeley, California. The experiment really made me *think* about the strength and motivation behind the relationship. Love & peace from sunny California.

EPILOGUE

Meanwhile, back at the party, the late-arriving social psychologist, who had been dashing back and forth between the guests, his questionnaires, and his computer printout, paused for a moment to consider what it all meant. The party had continued for quite a long time after all, and he was fifteen years or so older than he was when he first made his belated appearance. His efforts to determine what led particular guests to approach or avoid, like or dislike, help or hurt particular others had been fun. But it was now time for him to sit back and take stock of what he had accomplished. The guests, who had good-naturedly submitted themselves to his persistent probing, were also beginning to grow impatient about his progress.

As he looked back over his burgeoning file of tables, graphs, and reprints, the social psychologist was able to conclude with considerable satisfaction that he had indeed learned a great deal about liking and loving that had been unknown to the poets and philosophers who had preceded him to the party. Perhaps his central conclusion was that liking and loving have quite as much to do with how people *think* as with how they *feel*. Or, to put it another way, the cognitive aspects of interpersonal attitudes and bonds are closely, perhaps inextricably, bound with their emotional aspects. If there is a single theme that characterizes the thrust of recent social-psychological research, it is that human social behavior is guided by the requisites of efficient information processing. As we have seen, we are motivated to affiliate with others in order to obtain better information about our own attitudes and feelings. In predicting who is most likely to be rewarding to us, we take stock of the bits and pieces of information we have about others and do our best to integrate them into a consistent and meaningful picture. Our friends tend to be those people who help us to confirm our view of "social reality," most often by agreeing with those attitudes about the world that we ourselves hold. Even the processes of becoming committed and of falling in love are to a large extent cognitive ones. Commitment, for example, involves our perception or definition of ourselves, obtained—just as in the case of our perceptions of others—by carefully noting and sifting the available information.

Because of the central role of information-processing in determining patterns of liking and loving, men and women often seem to be much like computers, which can also be taught to integrate bits of information in order to form "images" or "impressions" which, in turn, shape their future decisions. In fact, there have been interesting recent attempts to learn more about human attitudes and relationships by simulating them with computer programs.[1] But the social psychologist had also come to realize, with a mixture of disappointment and relief, that people are *not* computers. Science fiction scenarios notwithstanding, there is an important distinction to be made between the sort of thinking that both people and computers can engage in and the sort of feeling that remains in the exclusive province of people. Clearly this is an area in which more work needs to be done. New approaches to attitude measurement, including psychophysiological techniques, studies of nonverbal communication, and devices like the "bogus pipeline" provide promising lines of attack, but basic conceptual breakthroughs in the ways in which we think and feel about thinking and feeling are still needed.

Another of the social psychologist's central conclusions was that different forms of interpersonal relationships, such as relationships between lovers, friends, acquaintances, and even strangers have much more in common than immediately meets the eye. People's tendency to be attracted to similar others, for example, is of great importance in understanding such diverse phenomena as reactions to residential integration and processes of mate selection. Similarly, the role of external obstacles in building "we-feeling" is as relevant to feelings of romantic love as it is to the morale of soldiers on the battlefield. At a Harvard departmental meeting several years ago someone challenged the coherence of social psychology as a discipline by pointing out that courses on such clearly unrelated topics as race relations and interpersonal attraction were being offered under the catch-all heading of "social psychology." Thomas Pettigrew and I, who were teaching the courses in question and knew better, could only smile.

When the social psychologist reported some of his more specific findings to the party guests, some of them decided that he
had been wasting his time. "Go back to your laboratory," they
snorted. But others were much more enthusiastic, suggesting a
variety of ways in which the social psychologist's new-found knowledge might be put to work. One of them asked the social psychologist to help set up a "scientific" computer dating corporation, which,
he argued, would go a long way toward insuring more successful
marriages; a second offered him a job as a consultant for the design of a housing project; a third invited him to help plan a new
commune. The social psychologist accepted some of these invita-
tions and declined others. In general, however, his assessment of
the contribution he could make was guarded. "What I have been
doing for the past fifteen years is *basic research*," he emphasized.
"Whether it can be successfully applied is quite another question.
And there is so much more that we still need to know."

The question of the applicability of social science research
is a recurring and extremely important one. Some social psychologists, like some scientists in other disciplines, take a determinedly
anti-application view of the matter, as if the possibility that their
work might be put to use would somehow taint the research enterprise. I once asked a social psychologist, whose work at the time
concerned the ways in which people place small humanoid and
geometrical figures on felt-boards, whether his research had any
potential social importance. He looked up from his felt-board and
assured me that it had no social importance whatsoever. "Are you
concerned about that?" I wondered. "I'd be concerned if it had," he
replied.

I do not share this view. I believe that research in the social
sciences must ultimately be justified in terms of its social uses.
With respect to social psychology, however, his belief remains
in large part an article of faith, not yet confirmed by actual results.
It may well be another ten or twenty years before we see much of
the current research on liking and loving being used to help make
our society a more humane and loving one. Nevertheless, when
people ask me, "Then what good is it?" I do have a more immediate
answer. It is that the more we can learn about the processes, biases,
and constraints that shape our social behavior, the more able we
will be to overcome certain of these biases and constraints and to
behave in ways that conform more closely to our real needs and
values. Whereas much of liking and loving is "cognitive," it is not
necessarily rational or maximally enriching. We jump to false conclusions about others on the basis of insufficient information; we

mistakenly shun others who are different from ourselves for fear that they will reject us; we fail to help others who are in need because we erroneously assume "somone else will do it"; we disclose ourselves to others in contexts which inevitably strip the disclosures of much of their significance; we yield to other people's ideas about whom we should date and marry without even realizing that these influences exist. Knowledge may indeed increase freedom, and I hope that the readers of this book, having gained a little bit of additional knowledge about liking and loving, will be a little bit freer as a result.

Yet, as the social psychologist told his fellow guests at the party, there is much to be learned. Although we know considerably more than we used to about liking, the mysteries of love have scarcely been penetrated. As the social psychologist looked back on the party, moreover, he realized that he had been focusing almost exclusively on encounters and feelings occurring at single points in time, and that he had almost never followed up any given pair of individuals over a more extended time period. But precisely such a longitudinal approach is needed if we are to understand liking and loving as developmental processes, rather than as merely static conceptions.

The social psychologist's quest is not without its dangers. In his insightful book, *Love and Will*, the existential psychologist Rollo May has argued that recent statistical studies of sexual behavior have had damaging effects on love relationships:

> It is an old an ironic habit of human beings to run faster when we have lost our way; and we grasp more fiercely at research, statistics, and technical aids in sex when we have lost the values and meaning of love . . . Couples place great emphasis on bookkeeping and timetables in their love-making—a practice standardized and confirmed by Kinsey. If they fall behind schedule, they become anxious and feel impelled to go to bed whether they want to or not. . . . The computer hovers in the stage wings of the drama of love-making the way Freud said one's parents used to.[2]

It is likely that May would have similar reservations about computerized studies of love, and the social psychologist will have to keep such dangers in mind as he continues to conduct them and to publicize their results. And yet he will keep at it, secure in his belief that the values of learning more about love will outweigh its liabilities. As Abraham Maslow has written, "We *must* understand love; we must be able to teach it, to create it, to predict it, or else the world is lost to hostility and to suspicion."[3]

As he pondered all this, the social psychologist suddenly recalled the man and woman who had found one another from across the crowded room much earlier in the party. He resolved to find out what had transpired between them in the interim. Preliminary inquiries revealed that they had gotten married, but things had soured—no one was sure just why—and they were divorced several years later. One of the ex-partners was now living in the Bronx, the other in Brooklyn. Having paused to reflect for quite long enough, the social psychologist hurried to the nearest subway station to pursue his quest. By the time of the next party he will surely have more answers to offer.

NOTES

Chapter 1

[1] Quotes are from Shakespeare, *The Merchant of Venice*; and from Phoebe Cary, "True Love."

[2] Erich Segal, *Love Story* (New York: Harper & Row, 1970).

[3] "Sociograms" were popularized by the maverick psychoanalyst J. L. Moreno, who originated the approach to interpersonal relationships known as "sociometry." See his *Who Shall Survive?* (Washington, D.C.: Nervous and Mental Disease Monograph, No. 58, 1934).

[4] Robert Zajonc, *Social Psychology: An Experimental Approach* (Belmont, Calif.: Wadsworth, 1966), pp. 2–3.

[5] Adolf Horwicz is quoted by Henry T. Finck in *Romantic Love and Personal Beauty: Their Development, Causal Relations, Historic and National Peculiarities* (London: Macmillan, 1887), p. 240.

[6] The possibility of a Schachterian explanation of the Ovid-Horwicz phenomenon is discussed by Elaine Walster in "Passionate Love," in Bernard I. Murstein (Ed.), *Theories of Attraction and Love* (New York: Springer, 1971). Stanley Schachter presents his theory of emotion in "The Interaction of Cognitive and Physiological Determinants of Emotional State," in Leonard Berkowitz (Ed.) *Advances in Experimental Social Psychology*, Vol. 1 (New York: Academic Press, 1964).

[7] Joseph K. Folsom, *The Family: Its Sociology and Social Psychiatry* (New York: John Wiley, 1934), p. 68.

[8] Freud's discussion of the link between love and aggression may be found in "The Instincts and their Vicissitudes" in the *Standard Edition of the Complete Psychological Works of Sigmund Freud*, Vol. 14 (London: Hogarth, 1955).

[9] The Kitty Genovese incident is recounted in A. M. Rosenthal, *Thirty-eight Witnesses* (New York: McGraw–Hill, 1964).

[10] Bibb Latané and John M. Darley, *The Unresponsive Bystander: Why Doesn't He Help?* (New York: Appleton-Century-Crofts, 1970).

[11] The studies yielding the "obvious" findings—in fact running opposite to those cited—are: (1) David W. Novak and Melvin J. Lerner, "Rejection as a Consequence of Perceived Similarity," *Journal of Personality and Social Psychology*, 1968, *9*, 147–152. (2) Jon Jecker and David Landy, "Liking a

Person as a function of Doing Him a Favor," *Human Relations*, 1969, 22, 371-378. (3) Susan Saegert, Walter Swap, and Robert B. Zajonc, "Exposure, Context, and Interpersonal Attraction," *Journal of Personality and Social Psychology*, 1973, 25, 234-242. (4) Zick Rubin, "Measurement of Romantic Love," *Journal of Personality and Social Psychology*, 1970, 16, 265–273. (5) Edward E. Jones, Leslie Rock, Kelly G. Shaver, and Lawrence M. Ward, "Pattern of Performance and Ability Attribution: An Unexpected Primacy Effect," *Journal of Personality and Social Psychology*, 1968, 10, 317–340. (6) Paul C. Rosenblatt, "Marital Residence and the Functions of Romantic Love," *Ethnology*, 1967, 6, 471–480.

[12] Paul Lazarsfeld, "Review of *The American Soldier,* Vols. I and II," *Public Opinion Quarterly*, 1949, 13, 378–380.

[13] Gordon W. Allport, "The Historical Antecedents of Modern Social Psychology," in Gardner Lindzey and Elliot Aronson (Eds.), *Handbook of Social Psychology*, 2d ed. (Reading, Mass.: Addison–Wesley, 1968), Vol. 1, p. 2.

[14] Theodore M. Newcomb, "The Prediction of Interpersonal Attraction," *American Psychologist*, 1956, 11, 575–587.

[15] Harry F. Harlow, "The Nature of Love," *American Psychologist*, 1958, 13, 673–685.

[16] Topeka *Daily Capital*, March 12, 1970.

[17] Louis J. Karmel, "The Case for Love," paper presented at the American Psychological Association convention, Miami Beach, 1970.

[18] Peter L. Berger, *Invitation to Sociology: A Humanistic Perspective* (Garden City, N.Y.: Doubleday Anchor, 1963), p. 17.

[19] A series of studies employing the "phantom-other paradigm" is reported by Donn Byrne in *The Attraction Paradigm* (New York: Academic Press, 1971).

[20] Elaine Walster, "Effects of Self-esteem on Romantic Liking," *Journal of Experimental Social Psychology*, 1965, 1, 184–197; and Sara B. Kiesler and Roberta L. Baral, "The Search for a Romantic Partner: The Effects of Self-Esteem and Physical Attractiveness on Romantic Behavior," in Kenneth J. Bergen and David Marlowe (Eds.), *Personality and Social Behavior* (Reading, Mass.: Addison–Wesley, 1970).

[21] I have discussed some problems and potentials of social-psychological experiments in "Jokers Wild in the Lab," *Psychology Today*, December 1970; and in "Designing Honest Experiments," *American Psychologist*, 1973, 28, 445-448.

[22] Theodore M. Newcomb, *The Acquaintance Process* (New York: Holt, Rinehart and Winston, 1961).

[23] For a "computer dance" study, see Elaine Walster, Vera Aronson, Darcy Abrahams, and Leon Rottman, "Importance of Physical Attractiveness in Dating Behavior," *Journal of Personality and Social Psychology*, 1966, 5, 508–516.

[24] Zick Rubin and Anne Peplau, "Belief in a Just World and Reactions to Another's Lot: A Study of Participants in the National Draft Lottery," *Journal of Social Issues,* 1973 (in press).

[25] Edward O. Laumann, "Friends of Urban Men: An Assessment of Accuracy in Reporting Their Socioeconomic Attributes, Mutual Choice, and Attitude Agreement," *Sociometry*, 1969, 32, 54–69.

[26] Mirra Komarovsky, *Blue-Collar Marriage* (New York: Random House, 1964).

[27] John Morihisa, "An Examination of Interpersonal Interaction in the Swinging Singles Bar," Department of Social Relations, Harvard University, 1971.

[28] Lee Sechrest, "Nonreactive Assessment of Attitudes," in Edwin P. Willems and Harold L. Raush (Eds.), *Naturalistic Viewpoints in Psychological Research* (New York: Holt, Rinehart and Winston, 1969).

[29] James T. Carey, "Changing Courtship Patterns in the Popular Song," *American Journal of Sociology*, 1969, 74, 720–731.

[30] William Griffitt and Donn Byrne, "Procedures in the Paradigmatic Study of Attitude Similarity and Attraction," *Representative Research in Social Psychology*, 1970, 1, 33–48.

Chapter 2

[1] David Riesman, *The Lonely Crowd*, abridged ed. (New Haven: Yale University Press, 1961), p. 22.

[2] Arthur Miller, *Death of a Salesman* (New York: Viking, 1949), p. 86.

[3] H. H. Remmers and D. H. Radler, "Teenage Attitudes," *Scientific American*, June 1958, 198, 25–29.

[4] Angus Campbell, Philip Converse, Warren E. Miller, and Donald Stokes in *The American Voter* (New York: Wiley, 1960).

[5] James Coleman, *The Adolescent Society* (New York: Free Press, 1961), p. 43.

[6] For account of Bales's groups, see Robert F. Bales and Philip E. Slater, "Role Differentiation in Small Decision-making Groups," in Talcott Parsons, Robert F. Bales, and others, *Family, Socialization, and Interaction Process* (Glencoe, Ill.: Free Press, 1955). Bales reports his more recent work on group roles in *Personality and Interpersonal Behavior* (New York: Holt, Rinehart and Winston, 1970).

[7] William Griffitt and Donn Byrne, "Procedures in the Paradigmatic Study of Attitude Similarity and Attraction," *Representative Research in Social Psychology*, 1970, 1, 33–48. An overview of techniques employed to measure liking is provided by Gardner Lindzey and Donn Byrne in "Measurement of Social Choice and Interpersonal Attractiveness," in Gardner Lindzey and Elliot Aronson (Eds.), *The Handbook of Social Psychology*, 2d ed., vol. 2 (Reading, Mass.: Addison-Wesley, 1968).

[8] Zick Rubin, "Measurement of Romantic Love," *Journal of Personality and Social Psychology*, 1970, 16, 265–273.

[9] Fritz Heider, *The Psychology of Interpersonal Relations* (New York: Wiley, 1958), p. 140.

[10] Paul F. Secord and Carl W. Backman, *Social Psychology* (New York: McGraw-Hill, 1964), pp. 97–98.

[11] Theodore Reik, *Listening with the Third Ear* (New York: Farrar, Straus, 1949), pp. 135–136. A recent overview of research on nonverbal communication is provided by Starkey Duncan, "Nonverbal Communication," *Psychological Bulletin*, 1969, 72, 118–137.

[12] Albert Mehrabian, "Communication without Words," *Psychology Today*, September 1968, p. 54.

[13] Shirley Weitz, "Attitude, Voice, and Behavior: A Repressed Affect Model of Interracial Interaction," *Journal of Personality and Social Psychology*, 1972, 24, 14–21.

[14] Mehrabian summarizes his body language studies in "Significance of

Posture and Position in the Communication of Attitude and Status Relationships," *Psychological Bulletin*, 1969, 71, 359–373.

[15] Donn Byrne, Charles R. Ervin, and John Lamberth, "Continuity between the Experimental Study of Attraction and 'Real-life' Computer Dating," *Journal of Personality and Social Psychology*, 1970, 16, 157–165.

[16] Ralph Exline summarizes his own and other investigators' research on eye contact in "Visual Interaction: The Glances of Power and Preference," in James K. Cole (Ed.), *Nebraska Symposium on Motivation, 1971* (Lincoln: University of Nebraska Press, 1971). Also see Jay S. Efran and Andrew Broughton, "Effect of Expectancies for Social Approval on Visual Behavior," *Journal of Personality and Social Psychology*, 1966, 4, 103–107.

[17] See Phoebe C. Ellsworth and J. Merrill Carlsmith, "Effects of Eye Contact and Verbal Content on Affective Response to Dyadic Interaction," *Journal of Personality and Social Psychology*, 1968, 10, 15–20.

[18] Paul Ekman, "Universals and Cultural Differences in Facial Expressions of Emotion," in James K. Cole (Ed.), *Nebraska Symposium on Motivation, 1971* (Lincoln: University of Nebraska Press, 1971), p. 226.

[19] Physiological studies cited are by R. E. Rankin and Donald T. Campbell, "Galvanic Skin Response to Negro and White Experimenters," *Journal of Abnormal and Social Psychology*, 1955, 51, 30–33; Gary Porier and Albert Lott, "Galvanic Skin Responses and Prejudice," *Journal of Personality and Social Psychology*, 1967, 5, 253–259; and Kurt W. Back and M. D. Bogdonoff, "Plasma Lipid Responses to Leadership, Conformity, and Deviation," in P. Leiderman and David Shapiro (Eds.), *Psychobiological Approaches to Social Behavior* (Stanford: Stanford University Press, 1964). An overview of issues related to physiological measurement of attitudes is included in David Shapiro and Andrew Crider, "Psychophysiological Approaches in Social Psychology," in Gardner Lindzey and Elliot Aronson (Eds.), *The Handbook of Social Psychology*, 2d ed., vol. 3 (Reading, Mass.: Addison-Wesley, 1969).

[20] Eckhard H. Hess reports his research in "Attitude and Pupil Size," *Scientific American*, 1965, 212 (4), 46–54; and with Alan A. Seltzer and John M. Shlien, "Pupil Responses of Hetero- and Homosexual Males to Pictures of Men and Women: A Pilot Study," *Journal of Abnormal Psychology*, 1965, 70, 165–168.

[21] Edward E. Jones and Harold Sigall, "The Bogus Pipeline: A New Paradigm for Measuring Affect and Attitude," *Psychological Bulletin*, 1971, 76, 349–364.

[22] Philip Goldberg, "Are Women Prejudiced against Women?," *Transaction*, April 1968, pp. 28–30.

[23] Fred L. Strodtbeck and Richard D. Mann, "Sex Role Differentiation in Jury Deliberations," *Sociometry*, 1956, 19, 3–11.

[24] Sidney M. Jourard, *Self-disclosure: An Experimental Analysis of the Transparent Self* (New York: Wiley-Interscience, 1971).

[25] Theodore White, *The Making of the President 1960* (New York: Atheneum, 1961). It is cited by Edward T. Hall in *The Hidden Dimension*, Anchor ed. (Garden City, N.Y.: Doubleday, 1966), pp. 124–125.

[26] William Schutz, *Joy* (New York: Grove Press, 1967), p. 185.

[27] Data on touching are provided by Sidney M. Jourard in *Self-disclosure*, chap. 11; Susan Goldberg and Michael Lewis in "Play Behavior in the Year Old Infant: Early Sex Differences," *Child Development*, 1969, 40, 21–31; and Nancy M. Henley, "Power, Sex, and Nonverbal Communication:

The Politics of Touch," in Philip Brown (Ed.), *Radical Psychology* (Harper & Row, 1973).

[28] Henley, *op. cit.*

[29] Erving Goffman, "The Nature of Deference and Demeanor," originally published in 1956 and reprinted in Goffman's *Interaction Ritual* (Garden City, N.Y.: Anchor, 1967), p. 74.

[30] Roger Brown, *Social Psychology* (New York: Free Press, 1965), chap. 2.

[31] Goffman, p. 64.

[32] Mehrabian, "Significance of Posture and Position in the Communication of Attitude and Status Relationships."

[33] My analysis of the motives underlying affection and respect draws on ideas presented by Miriam Zellner and George Levinger, "Liking and Self-evaluation: Comfort and Respect as Sources of Attraction," *Representative Research in Social Psychology*, 1971, 2, (1), 58–65.

[34] Riesman, pp. *xx*, 137. The italics are mine.

[35] Mirra Komarovsky's interviews are reported in "Cultural Contradictions and Sex Roles," *American Journal of Sociology*, 1946, 52, 184–189.

[36] Pamela English has pointed up some of the parallels between the roles adopted by women and by slaves in a paper entitled "Behavioral Concomitants of Dependent and Subservient Roles," Department of Social Relations, Harvard University, 1972.

Chapter 3

[1] Konrad Lorenz, *On Aggression*, Bantam Matrix ed. (New York: Harcourt, 1966), pp. 135–138.

[2] Seymour Feshbach and Norma Feshbach, "Influence of the Stimulus object upon the Complementary and Supplementary Projection of Fear," *Journal of Abnormal and Social Psychology*, 1963, 66, 498–502.

[3] Lorenz, p. 135.

[4] Lorenz, p. 137.

[5] Bibb Latané and David C. Glass, "Social and Nonsocial Attraction in Rats," *Journal of Personality and Social Psychology*, 1968, 9, 142–146. Earlier studies of the fear-reducing effects of fellow animals are reviewed by Everett Bovard in "The Effects of Social Stimuli on the Response to Stress," *Psychological Review*, 1959, 66, 267–277.

[6] The reports of the experiences of isolates come from A. Weisberg, *The Accused* (New York: Simon and Schuster, 1951), p. 89; Christopher Burney, *Solitary Confinement* (New York: Clerke and Cockeran, 1952), cited by Frieda Fromm-Reichmann in "Loneliness," *Psychiatry*, 1959, 22, 1–15; Joshua Slocum, *Sailing Alone around the World* (London: Rupert-Hart-Davis, 1948), also cited by Fromm-Reichmann. The McGill experiments are summarized by Woodburn Heron in "The Pathology of Boredom," *Scientific American*, January 1957.

[7] The effects of isolation upon children, soldiers, and drug-takers are reviewed by Bovard, *op. cit.*

[8] Stanley Schachter, *The Psychology of Affiliation* (Stanford: Stanford University Press, 1959).

[9] Lorenz is quoted from *King Solomon's Ring* (New York: Crowell, 1952), p. 152.

[10] Lorenz, *On Aggression*, pp. 210–211.

[11] Illustrative of the criticisms of Lorenz's approach are Leonard Berkowitz, "Simple Views of Aggression," *American Scientist*, 1969, 57, 372–383; and Stuart J. Dimond, *The Social Behavior of Animals* (New York: Harper Colophon Books, 1970), chap. 9.

[12] D. O. Hebb and W. R. Thompson are quoted from "The Social Significance of Animal Studies," in Gardner Lindzey and Elliot Aronson (Eds.), *Handbook of Social Psychology*, 2d ed., vol. 2 (Reading, Mass.: Addison-Wesley, 1968), p. 730.

[13] The analysis of our dependence upon other people to validate our views of reality is based on two classic theoretical papers by Leon Festinger: "Informal Social Communication," *Psychological Review*, 1950, 57, 271–282; and "A Theory of Social Comparison Processes," *Human Relations*, 1954, 7, 117–140.

[14] Stanley Schachter and Harvey Burdick, "A Field Experiment on Rumor Transmission and Distortion," *Journal of Abnormal and Social Psychology*, 1955, 50, 363–371.

[15] Fromm-Reichmann, p. 7.

[16] Schachter, *The Psychology of Affiliation,* chap. 3.

[17] Harold B. Gerard, "Emotional Uncertainty and Social Comparison," *Journal of Abnormal and Social Psychology*, 1963, 66, 568–573.

[18] Stanley Schachter, "The Interaction of Cognitive and Physiological Determinants of Emotional State," in Leonard Berkowitz (Ed.), *Advances in Experimental Social Psychology*, vol. 1 (New York: Academic Press, 1964).

[19] Tom Wolfe, *The Electric Kool-aid Acid Test* (New York: Farrar, Straus, 1968), p. 205.

[20] Lorenz, *On Aggression*, p. 137.

[21] Gustave LeBon, *The Crowd* (London: T. Fisher Unwin, 1896), p. 29. His analysis is reviewed and extended by Roger Brown in *Social Psychology* (New York: Free Press, 1965), chap. 14.

[22] Stanley Milgram, Leonard Bickman, and Lawrence Berkowitz, "Note on the Drawing Power of Crowds of Different Size," *Journal of Personality and Social Psychology*, 1969, 13, 79–82.

[23] Philip G. Zimbardo, "The Human Choice: Individuation, Reason, and Order versus Deindividuation, Impulse, and Chaos," in William J. Arnold and David Levine (Eds.), *Nebraska Symposium on Motivation, 1969* (Lincoln: University of Nebraska Press, 1969).

[24] Terry Southern, "Grooving in Chicago," *Esquire*, November 1968.

[25] Paul B. Sheatsley and Jacob J. Feldman, "The Assassination of President Kennedy: A Preliminary Report on Public Attitudes and Behavior," *Public Opinion Quarterly*, 1964, 28, 189–215.

[26] Irving Sarnoff and Philip G. Zimbardo, "Anxiety, Fear, and Social Affiliation," *Journal of Abnormal and Social Psychology*, 1961, 62, 356–363.

[27] Studies of human spacing are reviewed by Robert Sommer in Part One of *Personal Space: The Behavioral Basis of Design* (Englewood Cliffs, N.J.: Prentice-Hall 1969). The reported findings are drawn from Sommer, "Studies in Personal Space," *Sociometry*, 1959, 22, 247–260; William Leipold, "Psychological Distance in a Dyadic Interview," Ph.D. dissertation, University of North Dakota, 1963; and Howard M. Rosenfeld, "Effect of an Approval-seeking Induction on Interpersonal Proximity," *Psychological Reports*, 1965, 17, 120–122.

[28] Glen McBride, M. G. King, and J. W. James, "Social Proximity Effects on GSR in Adult Humans," *Journal of Psychology*, 1965, *61*, 153–157.

[29] Nancy Felipe and Robert Sommer, "Invasions of Personal Space," *Social Problems*, 1966, *14*, 206–214.

[30] Edward T. Hall, *The Hidden Dimension* (Garden City, N.Y.: Doubleday, 1966), p. 118. Hall's book includes a fascinating treatment of the use of space in different human cultures.

[31] Glenn Lym, "Space in Social Behavior and Experience: A Review," unpublished paper, Department of Social Relations, Harvard University, 1971.

[32] John Dollard and Neal E. Miller present a classic discussion of approach–avoidance conflicts in *Personality and Psychotherapy* (New York: McGraw-Hill, 1950), chap. 22.

[33] Sommer, *Personal Space*, p. 26.

Chapter 4

[1] Thorsten Veblen, *The Theory of the Leisure Class* (New York: Modern Library, 1934), p. 34.

[2] Glen Elder, "Appearance and Education in Marriage Mobility," *American Sociological Review*, 1969, *34*, 519–533.

[3] Gary Van Gorp, John Stempfle, and David Olson in, "Dating Attitudes, Expectations, and Physical Attractiveness," unpublished paper, University of Michigan, 1969.

[4] The medieval Jewish example is suggested by Kingsley Davis, "Intermarriage in Caste Societies," *American Anthropologist*, 1941, *43*, 376–395. The Vanderbilt-Marlborough case is cited by Robert K. Merton, "Intermarriage and the Social Structure; Fact and Theory," in *Psychiatry*, 1941, *4*, 361–374.

[5] For an overview of B. F. Skinner's research, see his collection, *Cumulative Record*, rev. ed. (New York: Appleton-Century-Crofts, 1961).

[6] George Homans' approach to social interaction is set forth in *Social Behavior: Its Elementary Forms* (New York: Harcourt, Brace & World, 1961).

[7] Simmel is quoted from *The Sociology of George Simmel* (translated and edited by Kurt H. Wolff) (Glencoe, Ill.: Free Press, 1950), p. 387.

[8] Peter Blau, *The Dynamics of Bureaucracy* (Chicago: University of Chicago Press, 1955), pp. 108–109.

[9] Homans, *Social Behavior*, p. 365.

[10] Margaret's account is presented in George Goethals and Dennis S. Klos (Eds.), *Experiencing Youth: First-Person Accounts* (Boston: Little, Brown, 1970), p. 283.

[11] Waller, *The Family*, pp. 275–276.

[12] Sara B. Kiesler and Roberta L. Baral, "The Search for a Romantic Partner: The Effects of Self-esteem and Physical Attractiveness on Romantic Behavior," in Kenneth J. Gergen and David Marlowe (Eds.), *Personality and Social Behavior* (Reading, Mass.: Addison-Wesley, 1970).

[13] Erving Goffman, "On Cooling the Mark Out: Some Aspects of Adaptation to Failure," *Psychiatry*, 1952, *15*, 451–463.

[14] Carl Rogers *Client-Centered Therapy* (Boston: Houghton-Mifflin, 1951).

[15] The use of social approval to condition verbal behavior was demonstrated by William S. Verplanck, "The Control of the Content of Conversation: Reinforcement of Statements of Opinion," *Journal of Abnormal and Social Psychology*, 1955, *51*, 668–676.

[16] Homans, *Social Behavior*, p. 55.

[17] For Theodor Reik's observations on love, see *A Psychologist Looks at Love* (New York: Rinehart, 1944).

[18] Elaine Walster, "The Effect of Self-esteem on Romantic Liking," *Journal of Experimental Social Psychology*, 1965, *1*, 184–197.

[19] Elliot Aronson's research is summarized in "Some Antecedents of Interpersonal Attraction," in *Nebraska Symposium on Motivation, 1969* (Lincoln: University of Nebraska Press, 1970).

[20] Peter Blau, *Exchange and Power in Social Life* (New York: John Wiley, 1964), p. 79.

[21] Willard Waller, *The Family: A Dynamic Interpretation* (New York: Dryden, 1938), pp. 232–233.

[22] George Levinger's study is summarized in Levinger and J. Diedrick Snoek, *Attraction in Relationship: A New Look at Interpersonal Attraction* (Morristown, N.J.: General Learning Press, 1972).

[23] Blau, *Exchange and Power in Social Life*, pp. 72–73.

[24] Alvin W. Gouldner, "The Norm of Reciprocity: A Preliminary Statement," *American Sociological Review*, 1960, 25, 161–179.

[25] For reviews of recent research on altruism, see Dennis L. Krebs, "Altruism—an Examination of the Concept and a Review of the Literature," *Psychological Bulletin*, 1970, 73, 258–302; and Jacqueline Macaulay and Leonard Berkowitz (Eds.), *Altruism and Helping Behavior* (New York: Academic Press, 1970).

[26] Dennis L. Krebs, "Empathically Produced Affect and Altruism," unpublished doctoral thesis, Harvard University, 1970. Also see Ezra Stotland, Stanley E. Sherman, and Kelly G. Shaver, *Empathy and Birth Order* (Lincoln, Nebraska: University of Nebraska Press, 1971).

[27] Charles Horton Cooley, *Social Organization* (New York: Scribner, 1909), p. 23. A useful contemporary discussion of the development of mutuality and "we-feeling" is Levinger and Snoek's *Attraction in Relationship*.

[28] Elizabeth Douvan, "Changing Sex Roles: Some Implications and Constraints," paper presented at a symposium on "Women: Resources in a Changing World," The Radcliffe Institute, April 1972. Douvan borrows the terms "integrative" and "heroic" from the economist Kenneth Boulding.

Chapter 5

[1] Vida Blue's statistics were obtained from the *Official Baseball Guide for 1972* (St. Louis: Sporting News, 1972).

[2] *The New York Times*, February 6, 1972.

[3] George J. McCall and J. R. Simmons, *Identities and Interactions* (New York: Free Press, 1966), p. 106.

[4] Harold H. Kelley, "The Warm–Cold Variable in First Impressions of Persons," *Journal of Personality*, 1950, *18*, 431–439.

[5] Theodore M. Newcomb, "Autistic Hostility and Social Reality," *Human Relations*, 1947, *1*, 69–87.

[6] Fritz Heider, "Social Perception and Phenomenal Causality," *Psychological Review*, 1944, *51*, 358–374.

[7] Jim Bouton, *Ball Four* (New York: Dell, 1971), p. 52.

[8] Lyman Strachey's description of Dr. Arnold is from *Eminent Victorians* (New York: Modern Library, 1933), as cited by Albert H. Hastorf, David J.

Schneider, and Judith Polefka in *Person Perception* (Reading, Mass.: Addison-Wesley, 1970), p. 10. Hastorf et al. are quoted from p. 11.

[9] Bouton, p. 13.

[10] The inference of personality traits from physical features is discussed by Paul F. Secord, "Facial Features and Inference Processes in Person Perception," in Renato Tagiuri and Luigi Petrullo (Eds.), *Person Perception and Interpersonal Behavior* (Stanford: Stanford University Press, 1958). A related discussion is provided by Solomon Asch, "The Metaphor: A Psychological Inquiry," in the same book.

[11] Seymour Rosenberg and Russell Jones, "A Method for Investigating and Representing a Person's Implicit Theory of Personality: Theodore Dreiser's View of People," *Journal of Personality and Social Psychology*, 1972, 22, 372–386.

[12] Granville Hicks, "Theodore Dreiser and 'the Bulwark,'" in A. Kazin and C. Shapiro (Eds.), *The Stature of Theodore Dreiser* (Bloomington: Indiana University Press, 1965), p. 229.

[13] Jerry Kramer, *Instant Replay* (New York: Signet, 1969), p. xii.

[14] Heider, "Perceiving the Other Person," in Tagiuri and Petrullo, p. 25.

[15] Albert J. Lott, Bernice E. Lott, Thomas Reed, and Terry Crow, "Personality-trait Descriptions of Differentially Liked Persons," *Journal of Personality and Social Psychology*, 1970, 16, 284–290.

[16] Studies of the effects of the perceiver's needs upon perception include David C. McClelland and John W. Atkinson, "The Effect of Different Intensities of the Hunger Drive on Perception," *Journal of Psychology*, 1948, 25, 205–222; and Jerome S. Bruner and C. C. Goodman, "Value and Need as Organizing Factors in Perception," *Journal of Abnormal and Social Psychology*, 1947, 42, 33–44. These and other studies representing what came to be called the "new look in perception" were analyzed by Bruner in "On Perceptual Readiness," *Psychological Review*, 1957, 64, 123–152.

[17] Harold H. Kassarjian, "Voting Intentions and Political Perception," *Journal of Psychology*, 1963, 56, 85–88.

[18] Saul D. Feldman, "The Presentation of Shortness in Everyday Life—Height and Heightism in American Society: Toward a Sociology of Stature," a paper presented to the American Sociological Association meetings, 1971.

[19] Charles D. Ward, "Own Height, Sex, and Liking in the Judgment of Heights of Others," *Journal of Personality*, 1967, 35, 381–401.

[20] Walter Stephan, Ellen Berscheid, and Elaine Walster, "Sexual Arousal and Heterosexual Perception," *Journal of Personality and Social Psychology*, 1971, 20, 93–101.

[21] McCall and Simmons, *Identities and Interactions*, p. 115.

[22] Stendhal, *On Love* (New York: Grosset & Dunlap University Library, 1967), p. 33.

[23] Fred Davis, "The Cabdriver and His Fare: Facets of a Fleeting Relationship," *American Journal of Sociology*, 1959, 65, 158–165.

[24] McCall and Simmons, p. 116.

[25] Gordon Allport is quoted from *The Nature of Prejudice* (Reading, Mass.: Addison-Wesley, 1954), p. 133. Research on the identifiability of Jews is summarized by Henri Tajfel in "Social and Cultural Factors in Perception," in Gardner Lindzey and Elliot Aronson (Eds.), *Handbook of Social Psychology*, rev. ed., vol. 3 (Reading, Mass.: Addison-Wesley, 1969), pp. 328–331.

[26] Theory and research on attribution processes was spurred by Fritz

Heider's paper on "Social Perception and Phenomenal Causality," cited above, and his larger work, *The Psychology of Interpersonal Relations* (New York: Wiley, 1958). Influential subsequent papers include Edward E. Jones and Keith E. Davis, "From Acts to Dispositions: The Attribution Process in Person Perception," in Leonard Berkowitz (Ed.), *Advances in Experimental Social Psychology*, vol. 2 (New York: Academic Press, 1965); and Harold H. Kelley, "Attribution Theory in Social Psychology," in David Levine (Ed.), *Nebraska Symposium on Motivation, 1967* (Lincoln: University of Nebraska Press, 1967).

[27] Gerald D. Suttles is quoted from "Friendship as a Social Institution," in George J. McCall and others, *Social Relationships* (Chicago: Aldine, 1970), p. 102.

[28] Edward E. Jones, Keith E. Davis, and Kenneth J. Gergen, "Role Playing Variations and Their Informational Value for Person Perception," *Journal of Abnormal and Social Psychology*, 1961, 63, 302–310.

[29] Gustav Ichheiser, "Misunderstandings in Human Relations: A Study in False Social Perception," *American Journal of Sociology*, 1949, 55, Part 2, p. 27.

[30] Heider, "Social Perception and Phenomenal Causality."

[31] Solomon Asch, "Forming Impressions of Personality," *Journal of Abnormal and Social Psychology*, 1946, 41, 258–290.

[32] Abraham S. Luchins, "Primacy–Recency in Impression Formation," in Carl Hovland and others, *The Order of Presentation in Persuasion* (New Haven: Yale University Press, 1957).

[33] Edward E. Jones, Leslie Rock, Kelly G. Shaver, and Lawrence M. Ward, "Pattern of Performance and Ability Attribution: An Unexpected Primacy Effect," *Journal of Personality and Social Psychology*, 1968, 10, 317–340.

[34] Edward E. Jones and George R. Goethals, *Order Effects in Impression Formation: Attribution Context and the Nature of the Entity* (New York: General Learning Press, 1971). I am indebted to that paper for several of the ideas in this chapter.

[35] Erving Goffman, *The Presentation of Self in Everyday Life* (Garden City, N.Y.: Doubleday Anchor Books, 1959), p. 12.

[36] Peter M. Blau, *Exchange and Power in Social Life* (New York: Wiley, 1964), p. 43.

[37] Blau, p. 48.

[38] William Barry Furlong, "Johnny Bench: Supercatcher for the Big Red Machine," *New York Times Magazine*, August 30, 1970.

[39] Elliot Aronson, Ben Willerman, and Joanne Floyd, "The Effect of a Pratfall on Increasing Interpersonal Attractiveness," *Psychonomic Science*, 1966, 4, 227–228.

[40] Bouton, *Ball Four*, p. 77.

[41] Luchins, "Experimental Attempts To Minimize the Impact of First Impressions," in *The Order of Presentation in Persuasion*.

[42] Ichheiser, p. 30.

[43] J. R. Simmons, "On Maintaining Deviant Belief Systems: A Case Study," *Social Problems*, 1964, 11, 250–256.

[44] Robert Rosenthal and Lenore Jacobson, *Pygmalion in the Classroom* (New York: Holt, Rinehart and Winston, 1968).

[45] Robert K. Merton, *Social Theory and Social Structure* (New York: Free Press, 1957), p. 423.

Chapter 6

[1] Mrs. Rose Kennedy's reaction to Bernstein's "Mass" was reported in *Newsweek*, Sept. 20, 1971.

[2] The early studies of the effects of mere exposure are M. Meyer, "Experimental Studies in the Psychology of Music," *American Journal of Psychology*, 1903, *14*, 456–476; J. E. Downey and G. E. Knapp, "The Effect on a Musical Programme of Familiarity and Sequence of Selections," in M. Schoen (Ed.), *The Effects of Music* (New York: Harcourt, Brace, 1927); and Abraham H. Maslow, "The Influence of Familiarization on Preference," *Journal of Experimental Psychology*, 1937, *21*, 162–180. All are cited in Robert B. Zajonc's review, "Attitudinal Effects of Mere Exposure," *Journal of Personality and Social Psychology Monograph Supplement*, 1968, Vol. 9, No. 2, Part 2.

[3] Susan Saegert, Walter Swap, and Robert B. Zajonc, "Exposure, Context, and Interpersonal Attraction," *Journal of Personality and Social Psychology*, 1973, *25*, 234-242.

[4] Henry A. Cross, Charles G. Halcomb, and William W. Matter, "Imprinting or Exposure Learning in Rats Given Early Auditory Stimulation," *Psychonomic Science*, 1967, 7, 233–234.

[5] J. C. Becknell, Jr., W. R. Wilson, and J. C. Baird, "The Effect of Frequency of Presentation on the Choice of Nonsense Syllables," *Journal of Psychology*, 1963, 56, 165–170.

[6] Robert B. Zajonc, "Brainwash: Familiarity Breeds Comfort," *Psychology Today*, February 1970.

[7] Albert A. Harrison, "Exposure and Popularity," *Journal of Personality*, 1969, 37, 359–377.

[8] John W. McDavid and Herbert Harari, "Stereotyping of Names and Popularity in Grade-School Children," *Child Development*, 1966, 37, 453–460.

[9] The case of the Black Bag was reported by the Associated Press and is cited by Zajonc in "Attitudinal Effects of Mere Exposure."

[10] Gordon W. Allport is quoted from *The Nature of Prejudice* (Reading, Mass.: Addison-Wesley, 1954). Quote is on p. 253 of the Doubleday Anchor edition, Garden City, 1958.

[11] Albert A. Harrison, "Response Competition, Frequency, Exploratory Behavior, and Liking," *Journal of Personality and Social Psychology*, 1968, 9, 363–368.

[12] Decrease in galvanic skin response with repeated exposure is reported by Zajonc, "Attitudinal Effects of Mere Exposure."

[13] George C. Homans, *The Human Group* (New York: Harcourt, Brace, 1950), p. 112.

[14] George C. Homans, *Social Behavior: Its Elementary Forms* (New York: Harcourt, Brace and World), 1961, pp. 183–184.

[15] Leon Festinger, Stanley Schachter, and Kurt W. Back, *Social Pressures in Informal Groups: A Study of Human Factors in Housing* (New York: Harper, 1950). Quotes are from pp. 35–36 of Stanford University Press paperback edition.

[16] Leon Festinger, "Architecture and Group Membership," *Journal of Social Issues*, 1951, *1*, 152–163.

[17] Robert F. Priest and Jack Sawyer, "Proximity and Peership: Bases of Balance in Interpersonal Attraction," *American Journal of Sociology*, 1967, 72, 633–649.

[18] Theodore M. Newcomb, *The Acquaintance Process* (New York: Holt, Rinehart and Winston, 1961).

[19] Homans, *The Human Group*, p. 115.

[20] Morton Deutsch and Mary Evans Collins, *Interracial Housing: A Psychological Evaluation of a Social Experiment* (Minneapolis: University of Minnesota Press, 1951).

[21] A. Weingrod, *Israel: Group Relations in a New Society* (New York: Praeger, 1965), p. 33.

[22] B. M. Kramer, "Residential Contact as a Determinant of Attitudes toward Negroes," unpublished doctoral dissertation, Harvard University, 1950.

[23] Brickman and Redfield's study is reported as Experiment III in Philip Brickman, Joel Redfield, Albert A. Harrison, and Rick Crandall, "Drive and Predisposition as Factors in the Attitudinal Effects of Mere Exposure," *Journal of Experimental Social Psychology*, 1972, 8, 31–44.

[24] Homans, *Social Behavior: Its Elementary Forms*, p. 187.

[25] Robert A. LeVine, "Socialization, Social Structure, and Intersocietal Images," in Herbert C. Kelman (Ed.), *International Behavior: A Social-psychological Analysis* (New York: Holt, Rinehart and Winston, 1969).

[26] Allport, *The Nature of Prejudice*, p. 252 in Doubleday Anchor edition.

[27] Robert K. Merton, *Social Theory and Social Structure*, rev. ed. (New York: Free Press, 1957), p. 428.

[28] Thomas F. Pettigrew, *Racially Separate or Together?* (New York: McGraw-Hill, 1971), p. 306.

[29] Allport, *The Nature of Prejudice*, p. 267.

[30] Rachel D. DuBois, *Neighbors in Action* (New York: Harper, 1950).

[31] "The cliff-dwellers" are described in *Newsweek*, November 22, 1965.

[32] Roger Brown, *Social Psychology* (New York: Free Press, 1965), p. 66.

[33] Morton Deutsch and Mary Evans Collins, "The Effect of Public Policy in Housing Projects upon Interracial Attitudes," in Harold Proshansky and Bernard Seidenberg (Eds.), *Basic Studies in Social Psychology* (New York: Holt, Rinehart and Winston, 1965, p. 655.

[34] Cited by Pettigrew, *Racially Separate or Together?*, p. 278.

[35] Fritz Heider, *The Psychology of Interpersonal Relations* (New York: Wiley, 1958), chap. 7.

[36] John M. Darley and Ellen Berscheid, "Increased Liking as a Result of the Anticipation of Personal Contact," *Human Relations*, 1967, 20, 29–40.

[37] Lewis Carroll, "The Hunting of the Snark," in *The Lewis Carroll Book*, edited by Richard Herrick (New York: Dial Press, 1931). The applicability of these stanzas was suggested to me by Bibb Latané, Judith Eckman, and Virginia Joy, in "Shared Stress and Interpersonal Attraction," *Journal of Experimental Social Psychology*, Supplement 1, 1966, pp. 80–94.

[38] Muzafer Sherif, "Superordinate Goals in the Reduction of Intergroup Conflicts," in Proshansky and Seidenberg (Eds.), *Basic Studies in Social Psychology*.

[39] Pettigrew, *Racially Separate or Together?* pp. 327–328.

Chapter 7

[1] Jimmy Breslin, "Is Lindsay Too Tall To Be Mayor?" *New York* magazine, July 28, 1969.

[2] William R. Berkowitz, Jeffrey C. Nebel, and Jonathan W. Reitman,

"Height and Interpersonal Attraction: The 1969 Mayoral Election in New York City," a paper delivered at the 1971 convention of the American Psychological Association, Washington, D.C.

[3] William R. Berkowitz, "Perceived Height, Personality, and Friendship Choice," *Psychological Reports*, 1969, *24*, 373–374.

[4] Sol Stein, *The Magician*, Dell paperback ed. (New York: Delacorte Press, 1971), pp. 220–221.

[5] Edward O. Laumann, "Friends of Urban Men: An Assessment of Accuracy in Reporting Their Socioeconomic Attributes, Mutual Choice, and Attitude Agreement," *Sociometry*, 1969, *32*, 54–69.

[6] August deB. Hollingshead, *Elmtown's Youth* (New York: Wiley, 1949).

[7] Theodore M. Newcomb, *The Acquaintance Process* (New York: Holt, Rinehart and Winston, 1961).

[8] Donn Byrne, *The Attraction Paradigm* (New York: Academic Press, 1971).

[9] For evidence of husband–wife similarities, see Bruce L. Warren, "A Multiple Variable Approach to the Assortative Mating Phenomenon," *Eugenics Quarterly*, 1966, *13*, 285–290; and J. N. Spuhler, "Empirical Studies in Quantitative Human Genetics," *The Use of Vital and Health Statistics for Genetics and Radiation Studies*, United Nations and World Health Organization, 1962, pp. 241–252.

[10] Charles L. Pratt and Gene P. Sackett, "Selection of Social Partners as a Function of Peer Contact during Rearing," *Science*, 1967, *155*, 1133–1135.

[11] Fritz Heider, *The Psychology of Interpersonal Relations* (New York: Wiley, 1958).

[12] Michael Useem, "Ideological and Interpersonal Change in the Radical Protest Movement," *Social Problems*, 1972, *19*, 451–469.

[13] Herbert J. Gans, *The Levittowners: Ways of Life and Politics in a New Suburban Community* (New York: Vintage Books, 1967), pp. 167–168.

[14] Newcomb, *The Acquaintance Process*. See also his paper, "Stabilities Underlying Changes in Interpersonal Attraction," *Journal of Abnormal and Social Psychology*, 1963, *66*, 376–386.

[15] The Washington study is reported by Timothy J. Curry and Richard M. Emerson, "Balance Theory: A Theory of Interpersonal Attraction?" *Sociometry*, 1970, *33*, 216–238; and further analyzed by Curry and David A. Kenny, "The Effects of Perceived and Actual Similarity in Values and Personality in the Process of Interpersonal Attraction," *Quality & Quantity*, in press.

[16] Gans, p. 155.

[17] Roger Brown, *Social Psychology* (New York: Free Press, 1965), p. 75. For a further discussion of the impact of similarities among "deviant" groups, see Erving Goffman, *Stigma: Notes on the Management of Spoiled Identity* (Englewood Cliffs, N.J.: Prentice-Hall, 1963).

[18] Rokeach's theory is presented in Milton J. Rokeach, Patricia W. Smith, and Richard I. Evans, "Two Kinds of Prejudice or One?" in Rokeach's book, *The Open and Closed Mind* (New York: Basic Books, 1960). Quotes are from pp. 158, 160, and 161.

[19] David D. Stein, Jane Allyn Hardyck, and M. Brewster Smith, "Race and Belief: An Open and Shut Case," *Journal of Personality and Social Psychology*, 1965, *1*, 281–289.

[20] Carole R. Smith, Lev Williams, and Richard H. Willis, "Race, Sex,

and Belief as Determinants of Friendship Acceptance," *Journal of Personality and Social Psychology*, 1967, 5, 127–137.

[21] Chester A. Insko and James E. Robinson, "Belief Similarity versus Race as Determinants of Reactions to Negroes by Southern White Adolescents: A Further Test of Rokeach's Theory," *Journal of Personality and Social Psychology*, 1967, 7, 216–221.

[22] See, for example, Donn Byrne and T. J. Wong, "Racial Prejudice, Interpersonal Attraction, and Assumed Dissimilarity of Attitudes," *Journal of Abnormal and Social Psychology*, 1962, 65, 246–253.

[23] Yochanan Peres, "Ethnic Relations in Israel," *American Journal of Sociology*, 1971, 76, 1021–1047.

[24] Peres, "Ethnic Relations in Israel."

[25] David W. Novak and Melvin J. Lerner, "Rejection as a Consequence of Perceived Similarity," *Journal of Personality and Social Psychology*, 1968, 9, 147–152.

[26] Gans, p. 167.

[27] Frederick Lewis Allen, "The Big Change in Suburbia," *Harper's* magazine, June and July, 1954.

[28] Elaine Walster and Bill Walster, "Effects of Expecting To Be Liked on Choice of Associates," *Journal of Abnormal and Social Psychology*, 1963, 67, 402–404.

[29] Joel W. Goldstein and Howard M. Rosenfeld, "Insecurity and Preference for Persons Similar to Oneself," *Journal of Personality*, 1969, 37, 253–266.

[30] Abraham H. Maslow, *Motivation and Personality*, 2d ed. (New York: Harper & Row, 1970), p. 201.

[31] Howard L. Fromkin, Robert L. Dipboye, and Marilyn Pyle, "Reversal of the Attitude Similarity–Attraction Effect by Uniqueness Deprivation," Institute for Research in the Behavioral, Economic and Management Sciences, Paper No. 344, Purdue University, 1972.

[32] Gans, p. 170.

Chapter 8

[1] Alvin Toffler, *Future Shock*, Bantam Book ed. (New York: Random House, 1970), pp. 105–106.

[2] Leopold Bellak, "Personality Structure in a Changing World," in Philip G. Olson (Ed.), *America as a Mass Society* (New York: Free Press, 1963), p. 417.

[3] Courtney Tall's paper on "Friendships in the Future" is cited by Toffler, p. 108.

[4] Warren Bennis is quoted from his book with Philip E. Slater, *The Temporary Society*, Colophon ed. (New York: Harper & Row, 1968), p. 127.

[5] Bennis, in Bennis and Slater, p. 128.

[6] Nelson Foote's observation is cited by Toffler, p. 250.

[7] Sidney M. Jourard, *The Transparent Self* (Princeton: Van Nostrand, 1964), pp. iii, 46.

[8] Marc Fasteau, "Men: Why Aren't We Talking?" *Ms.*, July 1972, p. 16.

[9] Jourard, p. 48.

[10] Charles F. Halverson, Jr., and Roy E. Shore, "Self-disclosure and Interpersonal Functioning," *Journal of Clinical and Consulting Psychology*, 1969, 33, 213–217.

[11] A brief report of this study is contained in my paper, "Lovers and

Other Strangers: The Development of Intimacy in Encounters and Relationships," presented at the American Psychological Association Convention, Honolulu, 1972. I am indebted to Pierce Barker and Susan Willard for their assistance and to students in Social Relations 830 at Harvard (Spring 1971) for helping to plan and conduct an earlier pilot study.

[12] Laboratory studies of self-disclosure are reviewed by Paul C. Cozby, "Self-Disclosure: A Literature Review," *Psychological Bulletin*, 1973,79,73–91 "Demand characteristics" of experiments are discussed by Martin T. Orne, "Demand Characteristics and the Concept of Quasi-Controls," in Robert Rosenthal and Ralph L. Rosnow (Eds.), *Artifact in Behavioral Research* (New York: Academic Press, 1969).

[13] For a useful discussion of "moves" in relationships, see Suzanne Kurth, "Friendship and Friendly Relations," in George McCall et al., *Social Relationships* (Chicago: Aldine, 1970).

[14] Erving Goffman, "The Nature of Deference and Demeanor," in Goffman, *Interaction Ritual* (Garden City, N.Y.: Anchor, 1967), p. 64. For further evidence on the link between power and self-disclosure, see Dan I. Slobin, Stephen H. Miller, and Lyman W. Porter, "Forms of Address and Social Relations in a Business Organization," *Journal of Personality and Social Psychology*, 1968, 8, 289–293.

[15] Gerald Suttles discusses self-disclosure in "Friendship as a Social Process," in George McCall et al., *Social Relationships*.

[16] Georg Simmel, "The Isolated Individual and the Dyad," in Kurt H. Wolff, *The Sociology of Georg Simmel* (New York: Free Press, 1950), p. 126.

[17] Suttles, in McCall et. al., pp. 115–116.

[18] Suttles, in McCall et al., p. 110.

[19] Joseph Luft, *Of Human Interaction* (Palo Alto, Calif.: National Press, 1970), pp. 57–58.

[20] Simmel, in Wolff, p. 404.

[21] The coed's remark is quoted by Toffler, p. 96.

[22] Rosabeth Moss Kanter, *Commitment and Community: Communes and Utopias in Sociological Perspective* (Cambridge, Mass.: Harvard University Press, 1972), p. 65.

[23] Leon Festinger, *A Theory of Cognitive Dissonance* (Stanford: Stanford University Press, 1957).

[24] Kanter, p. 76.

[25] Elliot Aronson and Judson Mills, "The Effect of Severity of Initiation on Liking for a Group," *Journal of Abnormal and Social Psychology*, 1959, 59, 177–181.

[26] Daryl J. Bem reviews theory and research on self-attribution in "Self-Perception Theory," in Leonard Berkowitz (Ed.), *Advances in Experimental Social Psychology*. Vol. 6 (New York: Academic Press, 1972). My self-attributional analysis of commitment draws upon several additional sources: Charles A. Kiesler, *The Psychology of Commitment* (New York: Academic Press, 1971); Richard E. Nisbett and Stuart Valins, *Perceiving the Causes of One's Own Behavior* (New York: General Learning Press, 1971); and Leonard P. Ullmann, "A Behavioral Approach to the Development of Interests and Commitments," paper delivered at the American Psychological Association convention, Washington, D.C., 1971.

[27] Daryl J. Bem, *Beliefs, Attitudes, and Human Affairs* (Belmont, Calif.: Brooks/Cole, 1970), p. 54.

[28] Jonathan L. Freedman and Scott C. Fraser, "Compliance without

Pressure: The Foot-in-the-Door Technique," *Journal of Personality and Social Psychology*, 1966, *4*, 195–202.

[29] Deborah's quote is from George W. Goethals and Dennis S. Klos (Eds.), *Experiencing Youth: First-person Accounts* (Boston: Little Brown, 1970), p. 214.

[30] Charles Horton Cooley, *Human Nature and the Social Order* (New York: Scribner's, 1902).

[31] Robert G. Ryder, John S. Kafka, and David H. Olson, "Separating and Joining Influence in Courtship and Early Marriage," Section on Family Development, National Institute of Mental Health, 1969.

[32] John Finley Scott, "Sororities and the Husband Game," *Trans-action*, September–October 1965.

[33] Goethals and Klos, p. 203.

[34] Charles D. Bolton, "Mate Selection as the Development of a Relationship," *Marriage and Family Living*, 1961, *23*, 234–240.

[35] The description of "drifting" is from an unpublished research memorandum entitled "The Courtship Phase," Section on Family Development, National Institute of Mental Health, no date.

[36] Kanter, "Commitment and Social Organization: A Study of Commitment Mechanisms in Utopian Communities," *American Sociological Review*, 1968, *33*, 499–517. An analysis of commitment as the "burning of bridges" is also provided by Howard S. Becker, "Notes on the Concept of Commitment," *American Journal of Sociology*, 1960, *66*, 32–40.

[37] Suttles, in McCall et al., p. 132.

Chapter 9

[1] My summary of the Tristan myth follows closely the account provided by Denis de Rougemont in *Love in the Western World* (New York: Harcourt, 1940).

[2] Andreas Capellanus, *The Art of Courtly Love*, written about 1180. The English translation is by John Jay Parry (New York: Columbia University Press, 1941), p. 12.

[3] The story of Ulrich von Lichtenstein is summarized by Morton M. Hunt in *The Natural History of Love* (New York: Knopf, 1959). Hunt's quote is from p. 138. Hunt's book includes an entertaining account of the origins and development of the romantic ideal, including its manifestations in contemporary America.

[4] The saga of Samantha and Sandy is recounted in *Young Romance* comics. It was brought to my attention by Lynn Mary Karjala in an insightful paper on "Love Comics and the Romantic Ideal," Department of Social Relations, Harvard University, 1970.

[5] Andreas Capellanus, pp. 106–107.

[6] John Finley Scott is quoted from "Marriage Is Not a Personal Matter," *New York Times Magazine*, October 30, 1966.

[7] The Kwakiutl and Baiga accounts are cited in William N. Stephens, *The Family in Cross-cultural Perspective* (New York: Holt, Rinehart and Winston, 1963), pp. 190–191. The original source of the Kwakiutl account is Clellan S. Ford, *Smoke from Their Fires* (New Haven: Yale University Press, 1941), p. 149; the original source of the Baiga account is Verrier Elwin, *The Baiga* (London: John Murray, 1939), p. 136. The Japanese account is from Robert O. Blood, Jr., *Love Match and Arranged Marriage* (New York: Free Press, 1967), p. 19.

[8] Ralph Linton, *The Study of Man* (New York: Appleton, 1936), p. 175.

[9] Linton, p. 175.

[10] Isadore Lowenstein, "Les Etats-Unis et La Havane: Souvenirs d'un Voyage, 1842," reprinted in Oscar Handlin (Ed.), *This Was America* (New York: Harper & Row, 1949). This and other travelers' accounts of American courtship are presented in Frank F. Furstenberg, Jr., "Industrialization and the American Family: A Look Backward," *American Sociological Review*, 1966, *31*, 326–337.

[11] Quotes are from the Thirty-one Rules of Courtly Love, Andreas Cappellanus, pp. 184–186.

[12] J. Richard Udry, *The Social Context of Marriage*, 2d ed. (Philadelphia: Lippincott, 1971), p. 163.

[13] Denis de Rougemont, "The Crisis of the Modern Couple," in Ruth Nanda Anshen (Ed.), *The Family: Its Function and Destiny* (New York: Harper & Row, 1949).

[14] Lawrence Kubie, "Psychoanalysis and Marriage: Practical and Theoretical Issues," in Victor Eisenstein (Ed.), *Neurotic Interaction in Marriage* (New York: Basic Books, 1956).

[15] Willard Waller, *The Family: A Dynamic Interpretation* (New York: Dryden, 1938), p. 208.

[16] Cited from the San Francisco *Chronicle* by Ernest W. Burgess and Paul Wallin, *Engagement and Marriage* (Philadelphia: Lippincott, 1953), p. 151.

[17] Richard I. Evans, *Conversations with Carl Jung* (Princeton: Van Nostrand, 1964), p. 51.

[18] The data on "love at first sight" are from Burgess and Wallin, and the interviewee's report is from p. 169.

[19] James H. S. Bossard, "Residential Propinquity as a Factor in Marriage Selection," *American Journal of Sociology*, 1931, *38*, 219–224. Research on residential propinquity was reviewed by Alvin M. Katz and Reuben Hill, "Residential Propinquity and Marital Selection: A Review of Theory, Method, and Fact," *Marriage and Family Living*, 1958, *20*, 27–34, and a recent study of interest is Natalie Rogoff Ramsøy, "Assortative Mating and the Structure of Cities," *American Journal of Sociology*, 1966, *31*, 773–786.

[20] William J. Goode, "The Theoretical Importance of Love," *American Sociological Review*, 1959, 24, 38–47

[21] Marriage statistics are taken from Hugh Carter and Paul C. Glick, *Marriage and Divorce: A Social and Economic Study* (Cambridge: Harvard University Press, 1970).

[22] Zick Rubin, "Do American Women Marry Up?" *American Sociological Review*, 1968, *33*, 750–760.

[23] Burgess and Wallin, p. 176.

[24] Alan C. Kerckhoff and Keith E. Davis, "Value Consensus and Need Complementarity in Mate Selection, *American Sociological Review*, 1962, 27, 295–303.

[25] William C. Schutz, *FIRO: A Three Dimensional Theory of Interpersonal Behavior* (New York: Rinehart, 1958).

[26] The Greek myth is recounted in Plato's *Symposium* and is commented on by Ira L. Reiss, *The Family System in America* (New York: Holt, Rinehart and Winston, 1971), pp. 75–76.

[27] Robert W. White, *The Enterprise of Living: Growth and Organization*

in Personality (New York: Holt, Rinehart and Winston, 1972), pp. 303–304.

[28] Burgess and Wallin, p. 202.

[29] Robert F. Winch's research is reported most fully in *Mate-selection: A Study of Complementary Needs* (New York: Harper & Row, 1958). The literature in this area is reviewed by Roland G. Tharp, "Psychological Patterning in Marriage," *Psychological Bulletin*, 1963, 60, 97–117. Also see George Levinger, David J. Senn, and Bruce W. Jorgensen, "Progress toward Permanence in Courtship: A Test of the Kerckhoff–Davis Hypotheses," *Sociometry*, 1970, 33, 427–443.

[30] John Finley Scott, "Sororities and the Husband Game," *Trans-action*, September–October 1965. Scott provides a more detailed discussion of the functions of the sorority in "The American College Sorority: Its Role in Class and Ethnic Endogamy," *American Sociological Review*, 1965, 30, 514–527.

[31] Robert H. Coombs and William F. Kenkel, "Sex Differences in Dating Aspirations and Satisfaction with Computer-selected Partners," *Journal of Marriage and the Family*, 1966, 28, 62–66.

[32] William Kephart, "Some Correlates of Romantic Love," *Journal of Marriage and the Family*, 1967, 29, 470–479.

[33] Waller, p. 243.

[34] My results are reported in my doctoral thesis, *The Social Psychology of Romantic Love*, University of Michigan, 1969 (University Microfilms, Ann Arbor, Michigan, No. 70–4179).

[35] Margaret Mead, *Male and Female*, Laurel ed. (New York: Dell, 1968), p. 24.

[36] Hugo Beigel, "Romantic Love," *American Sociological Review*, 1951, 16, 326–334.

[37] The interview with the movie star and the director was reported in *Look* in 1968.

Chapter 10

[1] Erich Fromm, *The Art of Loving*, Bantam ed. (New York: Harper & Row, 1956), p. 22.

[2] Harry Stack Sullivan, *Conceptions of Modern Psychiatry*, 2d ed., pp. 42–43.

[3] Abraham H. Maslow, "Deficiency Motivation and Growth Motivation," in Marshall R. Jones (Ed.), *Nebraska Symposium on Motivation, 1955* (Lincoln: University of Nebraska Press, 1955).

[4] David Orlinsky, "Love Relationships in the Life Cycle: A Developmental Interpersonal Perspective," in Herbert A. Otto (Ed.), *Love Today: A New Exploration* (New York: Association Press, 1972).

[5] Paul Tillich, *Dynamics of Faith* (New York: Harper & Row, 1957), pp. 114–115.

[6] Martin Buber, *I and Thou* (New York: Scribner's, 1970), p. 66.

[7] My approach toward conceptualizing and measuring love followed the general strategy outlined by Lee J. Cronbach and Paul E. Meehl in "Construct Validity in Psychological Tests," *Psychological Bulletin*, 1955, 52, 281–302.

[8] Studies comparing women's and men's same-sex friendships include Elizabeth Douvan and Joseph Adelson, *The Adolescent Experience* (New York: Wiley, 1966), chap. 6; and Alan Booth, "Sex and Social Participation," *American Sociological Review*, 1972, 37, 183–192.

9 Erving Goffman, *Behavior in Public Places* (New York: Free Press, 1963), p. 92.

10 Georg Simmel, *Soziologie*, as cited in Robert E. Parke and Ernest W. Burgess, *Introduction to the Science of Sociology*, 2d ed. (Chicago: University of Chicago Press, 1924), p. 358.

11 Harriet L. Rheingold, "The Effect of Environmental Stimulation upon Social and Exploratory Behavior in the Human Infant," in B. M. Foss (Ed.), *Determinants of Infant Behavior*, vol. 1 (New York: Wiley, 1961).

12 Kenneth S. Robson, "The Role of Eye-to-Eye Contact in Maternal–infant Attachment," *Journal of Child Psychology and Psychiatry*, 1967, 8, 13–25.

13 Konrad Lorenz, *King Solomon's Ring* (New York: Crowell, 1952), pp. 156–157.

14 Michael Argyle and Janet Dean, "Eye Contact, Distance, and Affiliation," *Sociometry*, 1965, 28, 289–304.

15 Fromm, pp. 38–39.

16 Andreas Capellanus, *The Art of Courtly Love*, trans. by John Jay Parry (New York: Columbia University Press, 1941).

17 Sigmund Freud, "Group Psychology and the Analysis of the Ego," in *The Standard Edition of the Complete Psychological Works of Sigmund Freud*, vol. 18 (London: Hogarth, 1955), p. 140.

18 See John C. Loehlin, "The Influence of Different Activities on the apparent Length of Time," *Psychological Monographs*, 1959, 73, Whole No. 474; and P. James Geiwitz, "Hypnotically Induced Boredom and Time Estimates," *Psychonomic Science*, 1964, 1, 277–278.

19 Leon Festinger, "Sampling and Related Problems in Research Methodology," *American Journal of Mental Deficiency*, 1959, 64, 358–366. For a further discussion of the problem of "negative results" see Judson Mills, "The Experimental Method" in Mills (Ed.), *Experimental Social Psychology* (New York: Macmillan, 1969).

20 Richard Driscoll, Keith E. Davis, and Milton E. Lipetz, "Parental Interference and Romantic Love: The Romeo and Juliet Effect," *Journal of Personality and Social Psychology*, 1972, 24, 1–10.

21 Edith Hamilton, *Mythology* (New York: New American Library of World Literature, 1942), p. 101.

22 Sigmund Freud, "On the Universal Tendency to Debasement in the Sphere of Love," in *The Standard Edition of the Complete Psychological Works of Sigmund Freud*, vol. 11 (London: Hogarth, 1957), p. 187.

23 The links between external opposition and internal solidarity are discussed in detail in Robert A. LeVine and Donald T. Campbell, *Ethnocentrism: Theories of Conflict, Ethnic Attitudes, and Group Behavior* (New York: Wiley, 1972).

Epilogue

1 See Robert P. Abelson, "Simulation of Social Behavior," in Gardner Lindzey and Elliot Aronson (Eds.), *Handbook of Social Psychology*, 2d ed., vol. 2 (Reading, Mass.: Addison-Wesley, 1968).

2 Rollo May, *Love and Will* (New York: Norton, 1969), pp. 15, 43, 44.

3 Abraham H. Maslow, *Motivation and Personality*, 2d ed. (New York: Harper & Row, 1970), p. 181.

Author Index

Subject Index

A

Address, forms of, 42–44, 129
Aesthetic preferences, among humans, 114–115
 among rats, 115–116
Affection, as dimension of liking, 27–28
 and sex roles, 39–45
Affiliation, 47–64
 among animals, 48–50, 52–55
 and attraction, 65
 and deindividuation, 59–61
 and need for self-evaluation, 55–58, 62
Agape, 213, 214
Age, and attraction, 144
Aggression, and love, 6–7
Altruism, 83–84, 213, 226–228
Animals, affiliation among, 48–50, 52–55
 attraction among, 138
 eye contact among, 223
 musical preferences of, 115–116
Approach-avoidance conflict, 3, 64–65
Approval, and attraction, 75–79
 as element of social exchange, 71
 as generalized reinforcer, 75
 need for, 25–26, 44
 sequences of, 77–79
Archetypes, 193
Archival studies, 19–20
Arranged marriage, 188–189
Attachment, as component of love, 213
Attitudes, definition of, 32

Attitudes (*cont.*)
 interpersonal (*see* Attraction)
 interracial, 33–34
 measurement of (*see* Measurement of attraction)
Attitude similarity, and liking (*see* Similarity of attitudes)
Attraction, measurement of (*see* Measurement of attraction)
 research on, 12
 See also Friendship; Liking; Love
Attractiveness (*see* Physical attractiveness; Popularity)
Attribution, 100–103
 of ability, 105, 108–109
 of personality traits, 101–102
 of self-disclosure, 170
 See also Person perception; Self-attribution
Authoritarianism, 229
Autistic hostility, 92

B

Balance theory, 96, 108, 130, 141
Basic research, 243
Beauty (*see* Physical attractiveness)
Belief similarity, and attraction (*see* Similarity of attitudes)
"Bogus pipeline," 37n
Bystander apathy, 8–9

C

Caring, as component of love, 213, 226–227